AF344843

I love this book—I wish I had written it! There is no greater waste than a product that doesn't sell. This clear, precise, and easy-to-read book is filled with concrete examples. It's the handbook we need to start thinking about designing not just products people like, but products people love.

—**Michael Ballé**, five-time Shingo-prized author, Paris

Flavian and Sandrine introduced me to the lean principles, which have been foundational in how I built ModaResa. *Build to Sell* encapsulates these principles, fostering a culture of problem-solving and continuous improvement. This book is the cornerstone for creating impactful, customer-centric products, and has profoundly influenced my leadership approach.

—**Stéphanie Smith**, Founder & CEO at ModaResa, Oslo, Paris

Build to Sell is exceptionally insightful and perfectly aligned with our product philosophy. The book offers invaluable insights and practical guidance that resonate with our approach to creating compelling digital products. It's a must-read for anyone looking to craft their product strategy.

—**Jonathan Widawski**, Co-Founder & CEO at Maze, San Francisco

As an engineering leader, I aim to build teams where every member understands our customers and how to act in their best interests. *Build to Sell* provides the common language to have engineers and product people work together towards that goal.

—**Najla Elmachtoub**, former Director of Engineering at Etsy, New York City

Build to Sell is a powerful exploration of lean principles applied to product creation. It's filled with practical advice and real-world examples, making it a must-read for anyone dedicated to building products that truly resonate with their audience.

—**Jeff Gothelf**, Author of *Sense and Response* and *Lean UX*, New York City

Lean is brilliant but challenging to grasp in theory until experienced in practice. Collaborating with Sandrine and Flavian as a former CPO, I've witnessed its transformative power in product management. *Build to Sell* offers the practical guidance needed to embark on your own transformative journey and boost your team's energy.

—**Lucia Cinque**, Co-Founder & Chief of Staff at WhiteLab Genomics, Paris

Build to Sell is a masterful and inspiring integration of the most important principles of building great products with a blueprint of the organizational culture and practices that deliver those products to customers. Rather than simply describing what is needed, *Build to Sell* explains all of the critical elements, from the product vision to the emotional appeal to customers, links them and provides a pragmatic framework in which leaders and managers can transform their products, their teams, their company and most importantly their customers' experience.

—**Julie Scherer**, Ph.D., Chief Data Scientist at Motive Medical Intelligence, San Francisco

Build to Sell has profoundly transformed my approach to lean engineering, guiding me to focus on problem-solving rather than mere feature addition. This book is an indispensable resource for creating impactful digital products that truly resonate with customers.

—**Nicolas Silberman**, Director at Bpifrance Digital Factory, Paris

As a CTO, I frequently encounter challenges with product roadmaps. *Build to Sell*'s Chief Product Engineer role revives magic and craftsmanship, moving beyond "feature factory" processes. This organizational change empowers real agility, enabling us to resolve tough engineering trade-offs and create elegant, innovative solutions.

—**Denis Barthélemy**, CTO at EchoAnalytics, Paris

If your work focuses on building and selling products, this is the book for you! I have practiced the concepts and tools presented alongside Sandrine and they have transformed my product management practice forever. A must-read for all professionals in product!

—**Alexis Allen**, Senior Product Manager at SparkPlug, New York City

BUILD TO SELL

BUILD TO SELL

THE LEAN SECRET TO CRAFTING IRRESISTIBLE PRODUCTS

Sandrine Olivencia, Flavian Hautbois and Caroline Besnard

Foreword by **Meredith Bell**

First paperback edition June 2024

Book editing by Benjamin Mathiesen
Book interior hand-drawn illustrations by Diane Rochet
Book cover and interior design by Ian Koviak
Book interior vector illustrations by the authors of this book
Taktique logo by Emma Mathiesen

ISBN 978-2-9594504-0-2 (paperback)
ISBN 978-2-9594504-1-9 (ebook)

To ensure the longevity of hyperlinks mentioned in this book, all URLs have been replaced with redirects using the tktq.link domain (e.g., tktq.link/some-url) and the original URLs have been saved on the Internet Archive. No Personal Identifying Information will be collected as part of the redirection process. For more information, see the privacy policy at https://tktq.link/privacy-policy

You will find all the resources from the book, and more, at
https://www.taktique.com/books/build-to-sell

Taktique
press

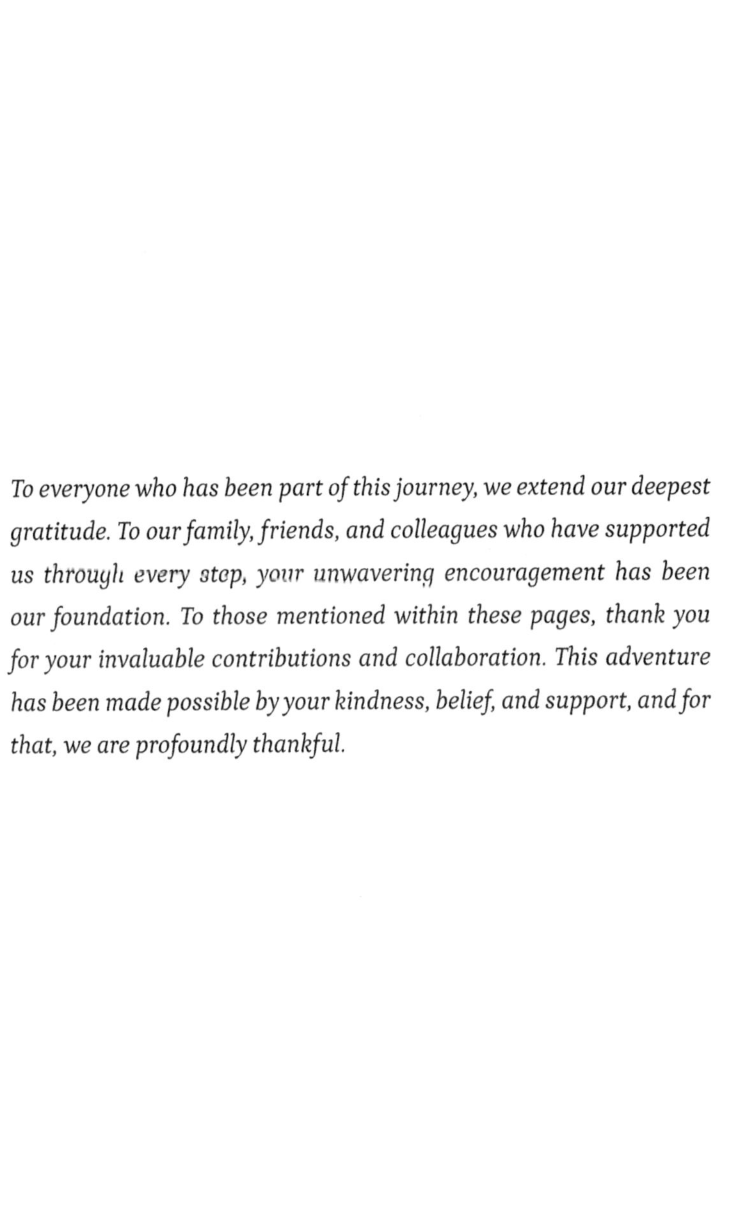

To everyone who has been part of this journey, we extend our deepest gratitude. To our family, friends, and colleagues who have supported us through every step, your unwavering encouragement has been our foundation. To those mentioned within these pages, thank you for your invaluable contributions and collaboration. This adventure has been made possible by your kindness, belief, and support, and for that, we are profoundly thankful.

CONTENTS

FOREWORD

My most precious memories may be of the early days of my children, when they struggled relentlessly, against the odds, to crawl and then walk. There's a teleological drive in all of us to grow into our potential. We imagine what we want to see, to feel, to accomplish. Implicit in that is imagining what we can be. I remember watching my kids on the floor in Montessori school, lost in their work, oblivious to time, struggling to do something they had never done before, to figure it out, and become more than they were the day before. And I remember how proud they were as we drove home, telling me about their struggles and triumphs.

They were in a flow state: self-sustaining creative engagement. They were learning to control themselves. They were learning self-agency.

But I also remember too many times, as we drove home from elementary, junior high, and high school, hearing about the boredom, the anxiety, and the drudgery they felt, imprisoned in the institutional education that too often would close in around them. Certainly, they continued to find great joy in school at times, but things had fundamentally changed.

It seemed that they were falling into the learned helplessness that Martin Seligman identified as a key risk for depression. What, I wondered, would be required in a school environment for that natural intrinsic motivation to continue to drive their growth?

The CEO's letter introducing Gallup's 2023 State of the Global Workplace Report cites the World Bank's chief economist Indermit Gill:

"A lost decade could be in the making for the global economy. The ongoing decline in potential growth has serious implications for the world's ability to tackle the expanding array of challenges unique to our times—stubborn poverty, diverging incomes, and climate change."

Gallup's suggestion? "Change the way your people are managed."

"Poor management leads to lost customers and lost profits, but it also leads to miserable lives. Gallup's research into wellbeing at work finds that having a job you hate is worse than being unemployed—and those negative emotions end up at home, impacting relationships with family. If you're not thriving at work, you're unlikely to be thriving at life."

Deming often said that "work and school are the same institution". School is a twelve-year-long assembly line designed to produce compliant workers. Some "smart kids" may eventually become managers, telling everyone else what to do. Those who don't make the cut will be condemned to roles of limited creativity and autonomy in the industrialized workplace.

In the technology world, the Silicon Valley obsession with finding the "A-players" who can transform a company from the top perpetuates the notion that the C-suite always knows best. This genius culture fits perfectly with the antiquated efficiency models engineered over a hundred years ago by Frederick Winslow Taylor. Taylor, through his influence at General Motors, promoted the idea that workers should simply do as they are told, following patterns of work designed by a few experts.

Born in the age of manufacturing, Taylorism enshrined the assumption that the workplace should be dominated by a few geniuses who tell the rest exactly how to work. These assumptions still haunt us in the era of knowledge work. But by definition knowledge workers produce information faster than their managers can keep up with it.

A genius culture (the "exhibit your greatness" approach) has been scientifically proven to be short-sighted, harmful to the individual, and less effective for the company. Research by Carol Dweck, summarized in her book *Mindset*, demonstrated the superior results that come from promoting a growth mindset that inspires all employees to reach their true potential.

I grew up in the latter part of the twentieth century and was subjected to the well-meaning but disastrous self-esteem movement. The belief was that telling kids they were smart, strong, and good would help them succeed. But this behavior subtly reinforced a belief in fixed traits, and nurtured a craving in children to always be perceived positively. Inadvertently, this encourages kids to avoid learning, so they don't risk being seen as inadequate. The awkward and error-prone process of learning threatens our fragile sense of being perfect. Carol Dweck's research provides compelling evidence that the most effective praise is praise of effort and improvement, rather than praise of fixed traits. Subsequent research has continued to validate her ideas.

The lean principles of TPS, the Thinking Peoples' System, developed at Toyota are a perfect example of the power of a growth mindset as promoted by Dweck. Both ideas focus on continuous improvement through learning in a non-judgmental environment. The lean manager works to create the conditions for a kaizen spirit: taking every challenge as an opportunity to learn and grow.

Teaching children a growth mindset requires tremendous energy. It is easier to separate the "gifted" kids from the rest and call it a day. But science has shown that approach is less effective for everybody. It stunts many and leaves many others behind.

The "genius culture" of modern technology organizations is also an easy approach: Believe that there are A-players; hire them; and let them fix everything. If it doesn't work out, you can always blame the employee for not being an A-player. This appeals to people in power who can hire people similar to themselves, demand compliance, and yell "work harder" when things don't improve. The better way is to model after Toyota, promote a growth mindset, and support every single employee in their own journey of learning. This requires commitment, stamina, and humility.

I met Sandrine two years ago when I was seeking to apply lean methods to the company I work for, AutoRABIT. We knew we needed to dramatically improve our customer experience and the quality of our software. Sandrine became my lean sensei (my coach and teacher). I felt as though I had hired someone to grab me by the neck and force me to look deeply at everything the company needed to do to improve, everything I was doing wrong. As a recovering fixed-mindsetter, I found it brutal.

The early stages of our lean journey were incredibly challenging for the rest of the company as well. It would be wonderful to say things have gotten easy. They haven't. It remains doggedly challenging, but we've gotten better at engaging with the problems and learning to improve. The journey feels hard: the right kind of hard.

Over the last two years, we've seen dramatic improvements in the business. We have reduced our customer churn by two-thirds. And we've doubled the size of the company. But the most rewarding development is the number of employees sharing their stories of personal growth. Again and again, I hear employees express pride in the work they are doing for customers, and express growing confidence in their professional abilities.

Build to Sell takes a dramatically different approach to product development than I had encountered before. I've worked primarily in sales and marketing for the past three decades. Again and again, I've seen innovative products fail to capture the interest of prospective buyers, or fail to convince all of the necessary stakeholders who make up the buying committee in a business.

There are many constraints in product development: technological, financial, schedule, and so forth. Although they may seem inconvenient, such constraints actually enable innovation. They force us to be creative.

My conclusion over many years is that the hardest problem in product development is the "last mile problem". How do you build a product that will actually be adopted by individuals and businesses?

Build to Sell tackles this challenge head on, in a classic lean way. It defines the fundamental creative challenge of product development not as creating an innovative product, but of creating a transformative emotional experience for the buyers. By doing this, it creates a challenge that demands the full intellectual and emotional engagement of the whole company, from engineering and product, to marketing, sales, and customer success.

The authors show us how to build products that satisfy real business needs while also creating strong, lasting emotional effects on users. Sandrine, Flavian, and Caroline's blend their deep knowledge of modern product design methods with decades of lean experience to provide a uniquely effective approach.

> *"Now one plus one equals two, that happens every day, that is not magic. That's the grind. That's when you get up, one. Go to work, one. Go to bed, two...*
>
> *But when one plus one equals three, that's when your life changes, and you see everything new. And these are days when you are visited by visions, when the world around you brings down the spirit, and you feel blessed to be alive."*
>
> —BRUCE SPRINGSTEEN

I worked late into the evening recently. When I left, there was a group of people gathered in the kitchen. Some nights people stay late to have a drink or play a board game. I asked who was winning. But they weren't playing a game, they said. They were figuring out a better way to solve a challenging customer problem. "It's almost midnight. Why can't it wait until tomorrow?" I asked. "Midnight?!" They responded incredulously.

They were so fully engaged in their problem, they had simply lost track of time. Right or wrong, I let myself believe that at least for the night, one plus one had equaled three.

Meredith Bell
CEO, AutoRABIT
May 28, 2024

INTRODUCTION

Launching a startup is much more attainable nowadays than it was in the '90s. Incubators, crowdfunding platforms, business angels, and public aid have multiplied, and are eager to facilitate the launch of any promising venture. If you are a good storyteller, you can attract all kinds of investors. But the vast majority of these startups disappear within three to four years.

Having an idea and attracting investment are not the hardest parts of building a business. The real challenge is knowing how to turn a good idea into a great product, one that will transform the budding business into a stunning success. We all want to build a product that addresses a real need and creates a lasting impression. And we all aspire to build thriving companies that can sustain growth and become desirable workplaces. There are three main schools of thought on how to achieve this:

- It's all about the product... and delivering exceptional value to our customers through innovative solutions and extraordinary experiences.

- It's all about the processes… and establishing efficient workflows, clear communication channels, and continuous improvement practices.
- It's all about the leader… and inspiring teams, fostering a culture of trust and accountability, and driving the organization toward its vision with passion and purpose.

The most successful companies develop all three approaches, but from the outside looking in it is obvious which one they focus on most. Amazon works tirelessly to improve the whole customer experience, delivering a service that modern society can hardly live without. Toyota is widely known as the cradle of lean, and processes that teach every person in the organization to deliver efficiency and quality without compromise. Elon Musk carries his companies forward seemingly on the strength of his personality and vision alone. Again, all three have attained fantastic success and we are not saying their approach to product and business development is unbalanced. But their examples may inspire entrepreneurs and startups to "choose a side" and base their growth strategy around just one, which is a risky prospect at best.

In this book, we argue that it's not a matter of choosing one over the others. A growing company needs a strong product culture, robust processes to deliver value, and visionary leadership to survive. How can we reinforce all three core values from the earliest stages? How can we maximize our chances of transforming initial enthusiasm for our exciting new product into a stable and thriving company? This is what this book is about.

We need leaders who can craft a compelling product vision

that resonates with others, who know how to inspire people and cultivate an "artisan" ethos that encourages innovative thinking. We must cultivate a robust product culture that permeates the entire organization, prioritizing the creation of exceptional customer experiences in a variety of different situations. This means placing the product at the core of all activities, from marketing and finance to operations and technology. Lastly, we must structure the organization to ensure that problems are visible, and that everyone is engaged in collaborative problem-solving. We want to create an organization with unwavering focus on quality, safety, speed and efficiency to foster genuine agility and scalability.

In contrast, many startups spend their time looking for the right market fit, pivoting from one business model to another until they run out of cash. Pushing an already developed product onto a market, then attempting to improve it until it matches the needs and wants of an existing segment, requires much more money and rework than testing and refining a product concept... and a good amount of faith. It is even more difficult if the market is not ready, meaning that our product aims to resolve a problem that does not yet exist, or is not perceived as a priority. We see many new entrepreneurs follow this path, despite the high cost and risk, because they believe so much in their idea that they are convinced investors will leap to finance their venture. And perhaps they believe that their leadership or their product concept is enough to carry them forward. Nowadays, it takes a lot more than a great idea and a great story to convince investors. It takes building a product that people want to buy right now, which implies *finding an innovative way to resolve an existing problem and an organization capable of creating and delivering this value over the long run.*

Among these courageous entrepreneurs, a few lucky ones manage to find a market fit. However, luck is not a repeatable strategy. As soon as the new firm starts to grow, it turns into a rigid structure. Its organization and processes crystallize under the pressures of ambitious growth targets set by investors and a rapidly increasing staff. We've seen this happen time and time again, once a firm reaches about twenty employees. While incessantly chasing Key Performance Indicators, these entrepreneurs gradually lose passion for their product and customers, and spend more time exploiting their initial idea than enriching it. They lose the desire to explore and learn, instead creating (far too soon!) bureaucracies where people no longer know how to think. Too late, they learn that *letting go of the product means letting go of growth*. There are three classic errors that lead to this situation.

The first error is to delegate product conception to teams of developers led by Product Owners or Product Managers. The ultimate responsibility for the product is divided among people with specific and necessary skills but limited influence. Product Owners or Product Managers spend most of their time collecting and prioritizing requests from customers and different departments of the company; their organization becomes a machine for creating roadmaps and sorting large feature backlogs, without cohesion or vision. We call this "feature frenzy". The product grows under their care, but gradually loses its magic while becoming more complex and more difficult to maintain. When the cost of maintenance starts to weigh on income, it's already too late. *Building a successful product is not simply a construction exercise* ("Let's add these features."), *it is a problem-solving exercise* ("What should we do to obtain this result?").

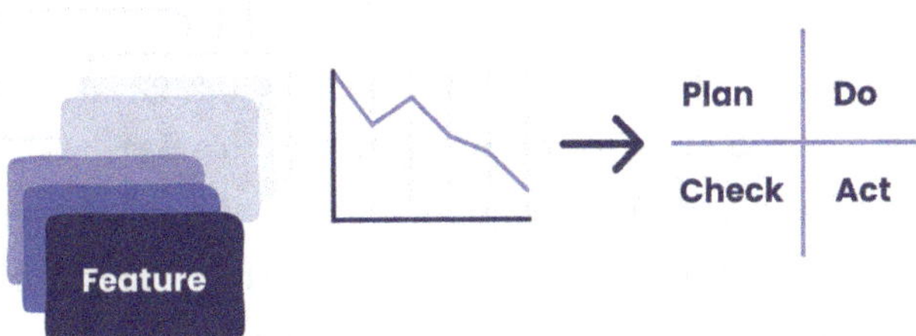

The second error is imagining that the product is only a digital tool or a physical device. Many digital startups base their business model on a mobile app, website, or digital platform, and apply their "product thinking" and creativity only to these elements. Bcyond the tool, *a product is a set of experiences had by its users in different situations.* The tool itself is just one of the enablers that we need to design and build to create the best possible experiences for people. These can be the experiences of using the tool to accomplish different tasks, or the experiences of purchasing the product, sharing it with friends, and customer support.

The third error is to build rigid companies based on fixed processes and a "command and control" mentality. This may arise from outside pressures, such as investors who insist on hiring a C-suite and middle managers, or from a mistaken belief that standards and processes will protect us from making mistakes. But the problem with this approach is that organizations and processes are by nature static, or at least very slow to change, while the needs of the market and the problems faced by our people are changing every day. In order to adapt and survive we need to build an environment that gives people the freedom to solve problems on their own and change processes in the service of value creation and a better customer experience. This is the true agility that organizations need to survive and thrive in a VUCA (volatility, uncertainty, complexity, ambiguity) world.

Now that we've identified some common errors, how can we build an organization that avoids them? In this book we propose several practices to maximize the chances of long-term success, but it all starts with the product. To improve their chances of passing the four-year mark, startup founders must learn to sustain and transmit a passion for the product to everyone in their company, just as when they first started. But for this to work, *they must learn to think more like a designer or an engineer than an administrator*: someone whose vocation is to conceive and make things, not just run things. They must also spread this "artisan" mindset internally, from the very beginning. They cannot just hand over the responsibility of product development over to teams who have little emotional connection with customers. This is a sure-fire way of killing creativity and ingenuity in the organization, yet both qualities are necessary to build fantastic products and scale the business.

Companies like Google, Toyota and LinkedIn, among others, have built whole systems to spread this artisan mindset throughout their organizations. We recently visited the Toyota museum in Nagoya, Japan, and we were struck by the large and lovingly curated displays of machines, products, and technologies. The museum demonstrates how the "artisan" mindset of the original founders was passed down to other leaders over the years: the first thing you see when you get inside the museum is a big loom, one of the original designs before Toyota started making cars, with this inscription:

The circular loom symbolizes the spirit and the theme of this museum: "The Spirit of Being Studious and Creative" and the "Importance of Making Things".

The Google campus in Silicon Valley evokes a similar feeling: everywhere you go you see small teams discussing products and engineering challenges, not just roadmaps and code. LinkedIn is another example among the many high-tech firms applying the concept of "craftsmanship coding[1]."

In lean design and development, instead of Product Managers we have **Chief Engineers**. They act as "super Product Managers" who have this artisan mindset and cultivate it in others. With a team of experts and specialists, they know how to turn concepts into great products that generate emotions and revenue.

A Chief Engineer lives and breathes their product. Steve Jobs (famous for his Apple products), Walt Disney, Linus Torvald (creator of Linux), Coco Chanel, and even Stan Lee (co-creator of Marvel Comics) were all Chief Engineers *par excellence.* They were visionaries who had a visceral obsession with quality and customer satisfaction. They took responsibility not just for creating their product, from A to Z, but also for its evolution over time. Just as importantly, they knew how to get other people to share their vision. With artistry, and a certain eccentricity, they demonstrated relentless dedication to transform their concepts into products that customers can't live without even decades later. At Toyota, the first company to formally create this role, *the Chief*

---

1 See article describing their vision here:
https://tktq.link/build-to-sell/what-is-craftsmanship-and-why-is-it-important

Engineer is considered the CEO of the product, although they have no hierarchical authority over the functional and technical experts who join the product conception team. They do, however, have great influence and are highly respected within the organization.

Behind this image of an ingenious artist and creator of trends, the Chief Engineer has mastered a real product conception practice, which can be learned by anyone with a passion for the customer and the product. The Chief Engineer's practice is built on a key concept of lean design and development: the **gemba**. The gemba is a place where customers buy, use, and consume our products or where people and machines conceive, build, package, store, ship, support, and recycle our products. A Chief Engineer spends a great deal of their time on the gemba looking for opportunities to create value, in order to conceive the best possible products. With the help of a select team of technical and functional experts, and a few key tools, such as the concept paper and the obeya, the Chief Engineer:

- Defines a clear and convincing vision for the next generation of products

- Translates customer preferences into a set of measurable product performances to guide the design and development process

- Makes innovative architecture choices without taking the risk of degrading the product and disappointing customers

- Ensures product consistency by solving systems interface problems

- Uses a pull-flow mechanism to facilitate collaboration between all players of the project

- Respects the product target cost to ensure profitability
- Meets the planned launch date to beat the market
- Learns from all obstacles by applying scientific problem solving

Instead of focusing on growth indicators and delegating their product too quickly to people who do not have the required passion and know-how, startup founders must learn to make the Chief Engineer's practice their own and then pass this mindset on to support business growth. They must always continue to deepen their understanding of:

- their product and the problem it solves,
- their customer preferences and why they decide to buy or not,
- the emotions the product brings to life,
- the effect of this or that technical aspect on customer satisfaction,
- which elements of the product are the most costly and why, and
- what is their vision to make the product even more interesting over the coming months.

All these questions are vital to sustaining growth, because *the business* is *the product.*

In this book, we propose a way to cultivate, develop and sustain a strong Chief Engineer spirit within the organization even as the company scales. We describe the skills and attitude that define these super Product Managers with a strong artisan mind-set. We call these people **Chief Product Engineers**, because they are obsessed with product conception in a true engineering sense, unlike traditional Project Managers, Product Managers or developers who usually focus on one aspect of the project process (discovery, coding, testing, planning, etc.). We describe where to find these Chief Product Engineers and how to train them, but *instilling this mindset in your team always starts with training yourself.*

Therefore, as you read this book, we hope that you will be inspired to try applying these exercises and techniques to your own business. Whether leading a team for a big company or striking out on your own as an entrepreneur, everyone has a product. And when we learn to see our product as a solution for our customers' problems instead of a collection of features, then we take a step into their world. We are building something that they cannot live without—we are *building to sell.*

PART
1

THE MAIN CAUSES
OF PRODUCT FAILURE

90% of startups fail.

This startling figure was calculated over a 10-year period at the time of writing this book[2]. In 2021, the platform *CB Insights* compiled an overview of 111 startups and the reasons why they failed[3]. The top three were "ran out of cash", "got outcompeted", and "wrong business model". But these judgments describe the state of the firm at the end of its run: outcomes, not causes. They do not explain why or how these firms reached the point of no return, usually in five years or less. The "startup

---

2 https://tktq.link/build-to-sell/the-state-of-the-global-startup-economy

3 https://tktq.link/build-to-sell/startup-failure-reasons-top

culture", which for years sold the myth that any good idea could attract funding, is probably partly to blame. It takes more than great storytelling, passionate founders and a first round of investment to build a successful and sustainable business.

In reality, most startups end for the same reason. Simply put, *they did not create great products that people want to buy.* Hence, we should be asking ourselves how to design better products, not how to rescue failing business models. No amount of investment and marketing can rescue a product with lukewarm demand, no matter how innovative the idea. Drawing on our own experiences working with startup founders and CEOs, we have noticed three main reasons why products may not succeed:

1) **The product does not satisfy a real need**: developing our idea without a profound and clear understanding of who our customers are and the problem that we are supposed to resolve is a sure-fire way of building a product that no one will want.

2) **The customer experience is poor**, which degrades the brand. The product fulfills a real need, but it is not doing it well. We must create a great client experience at every stage: purchase, delivery, consumption or use, support, maintenance, and even recycling.

3) **Our processes hinder customer delivery**: customers and employees struggle with quality issues, delivery is slow, and people experience burn out. Internal waste drains the business, preventing it from investing in the product over time.

The last issue is a real challenge, because we often don't notice our bad processes until they start affecting sales, and by then they have become widespread. It becomes easier once we accept that the goal of management is not to build perfect organizations and define quality processes that people must follow, which leads to the trap of adding more and more controls over time. Rather, *the goal is to create a learning environment throughout the company* where each person can easily recognize issues, feel safe sharing them, propose their own solutions to improve quality, and prevent problems from recurring. Wherever this environment exists, processes continuously improve as a result.

In the next chapters, let's look at each cause of product failure more closely and gather some key lessons for startups.

THE PRODUCT DOES NOT SATISFY A REAL NEED

What do the Pet Rocks from the 1970s, Pokémon Go, and Vinted have in common? A great many people wanted to possess or use them. But why would anyone want to buy a rock with plastic eyes? How about Pokémon Go? What need is it really fulfilling? The need for Vinted is somewhat clearer, but why would it generate more enthusiasm than other web services trying to break into the online fashion industry or contribute to the circular economy?

We don't believe that their success was just a question of marketing. People are not stupid: most of us will not acquire something that does not bring some sort of personal satisfaction. In 1943, a psychologist named Maslow identified three main categories of needs: self-fulfillment, psychological, and basic. He organized the spectrum of human needs into a well-known hierarchy:

Maslow's pyramid of needs

What need would you say Pokémon Go satisfies? The need to belong to a community? The need for personal accomplishment? The need to have a "friend"? The people who play the game all have different reasons and circumstances, but the goal of the product engineer behind the game is to find and fulfill the most common needs.

How about Vinted? Is it fulfilling a basic need, like the need for clothes that we could not otherwise afford? Does it improve our self-esteem, because we contribute to preserving the environment? Or both, depending on the situation?

You may feel that we're stating the obvious, so let's look at another example to dive deeper in this quest for our customers' real need.

Starting a product without a profound and clear understanding of the need it is supposed to fulfill is a sure-fire way of creating a product that no one will want.

It is the year 2016. Sophia is a 30-year-old marketing professional and a real fashionista. She and her group of friends are fans of luxury brands, but their budget does not match their expensive tastes. So they have developed a habit of lending each other their nicest fashion items, like Chanel purses and Gucci dresses. They love these moments exploring each other's closets. For them, it is a great way to renew their wardrobe often and cheaply, and they feel good about themselves for not engaging in wasteful consumerism. Sophia is convinced that many other women feel the same way. So she investigates current trends in the fashion industry, and finds out that the re-use market is really taking off: second-hand services like Vinted or ThredUp are multiplying. After quizzing her network of friends and colleagues, she identifies more and more people and potential customers who are interested in lending and borrowing luxury items. So she quits her job and creates a business: we'll call it Lux For Rent. Lux For Rent is an online marketplace for peer-to-peer luxury fashion rental. This model is already taking off in New York City and London via two other startups. Sophia therefore has good reason to believe that the idea will also work in Europe. She creates a pitch and finds a few investors willing to support her venture. She raises enough money to hire a technical consultant who can help her build the first version of her platform. Finally, when the platform goes live, she quickly finds a few clients.

At this point, Sophia is full of optimism and for good reason. But three years later, her business is still not taking off. She has a hard time attracting people to open their personal closets for rental, and revenue is very low. She blames the slow growth on two factors: first, she does not have a permanent programmer on board, so quality issues with the platform and payment system keep accumulating and not getting fixed. Second, she is not doing enough marketing due to lack of cash flow and because she is not able to raise more funds. She is still convinced that her idea is good, but that she just does not have the means to implement it properly.

However, her customer feedback reveals several problems that have nothing to do with technology or marketing. From the renters' point of view, there is not enough variety on the platform in terms of style and sizes. As for the closet owners, they fear theft and degradation of their wardrobe. These are some of the recurring problems that Sophia is facing.

The example below summarizes a real complaint that Sophia received, and what she was able to learn about the problem after calling the customer and digging deeper.

Client: Shelly (renter)

Complaint: Not much choice in my size

What are they trying to do? Looking for a size 12 dress for her sister's wedding. Ideally blue. She can't afford anything above 40 euros for a weekend. We called her to make suggestions, but she didn't like anything we proposed. We offered her a discount for her next visit.

How is their perception different from ours? Shelly expects the items to be available in different sizes, but this is not what we offer. Our model is closer to a closet swap than a shop.

Why is this a surprise? We attracted her to our site via Instagram. Our stories are not clear enough. Need for better positioning: clarify our mission.

As the interaction shows, Sophia and this customer have very different expectations for the product. The mission of Lux For Rent is not so clear after all: the business is closer to a "closet swap" (Sophia's vision) than a "fashion shop" (this customer's vision). The more time Sophia spends understanding her customers' points of view, asking very specific questions with each new complaint, the more obvious it becomes that there is a fundamental problem with her current business model: not enough women are willing to rent their luxury items to total strangers. The few women that Sophia has managed to convince are not motivated by money, because they are already wealthy. They are more interested in doing a good deed and meeting other cool women who share their tastes.

Sophia realizes, a bit too late, that her original idea is not viable. She decides to pivot and explore other options. For example, luxury brands and department stores could use her platform to propose unsold items for rent. But for this idea to work, potential partners tell her that she has to improve the reliability of the platform and accept to become a "white label", which Sophia is not happy about. But even if she accepts these terms, Lux For Rent is running out of cash and Sophia continues to face rejections and empty promises from investors. The COVID-19 crisis is the last straw. In 2021, with a very heavy heart, she liquidates Lux For Rent.

Sophia is a smart and passionate entrepreneur. Her concept made sense, at least on paper. But like many entrepreneurs, she was so attached to her initial idea, so convinced of its potential, that she failed to hear the signals telling her that people were not ready for closet sharing.

Google's former UX researcher, Tomer Sharon, said that "86% of startup founders base their product on personal pain. It's not necessarily a bad thing, but it could be bad if they are convinced that the entire world has this problem, and in many cases, they are convinced that this is so." Sophia's story is not an isolated case. Let's reconsider the fact that 90% of startups fail within 4 to 5 years. When we factor in that 305 million start-ups are created worldwide every year, just imagine the amount of talent and resources going to waste! This is the sad reality reported by several studies. The Silicon Valley startup culture of the '90s sold us a dream, that any good idea could be brought to success with enough funding. Entrepreneurs now realize, but sometimes too late, that it takes much more than passion, great storytelling, and a round or two of funding to build a successful and sustainable business.

Satisfying a real need means first finding an existing *need*, a problem shared and recognized by many people. Let's face it: our best chance of making it big is always to build tomorrow's solution for a problem that people have today. Moonshots require deep pockets and a lot of faith. Sophia found a problem and a solution, but it was not one that people were ready to accept.

Now ask yourself:
- What was the last product you worked on?
- What need did it fulfill for your different clients? In which circumstances did they use it?
- Did your product satisfy an existing need, or did it try to change your customers' behaviors?

CHAPTER 2

THE CUSTOMER EXPERIENCE IS POOR

The second cause of product failure is that while the product addresses a real need, it is not fulfilling it well enough. There can be many reasons for this, ranging from mild annoyances in the product design and unhelpful customer service to major parts of the product that are either missing or even actively working against the user's job. Any bad experience, no matter how small, can become a good enough reason for a customer to "fire" the product.

You can easily find dozens of examples on social networks and forums. Reviews of mobile apps, e-commerce goods, and even whole companies always make for an interesting read, because disappointed users often want to justify giving a low rating by describing their experiences in detail. (Here's a tip: to see the real problems that customers are complaining about, sort the reviews to show the lowest scores or newest posts first). Here are a few examples of bad experiences generated by major products:

- A major internet service provider in France had a service interruption of *9 continuous days*. Customer service was unable to help, give visibility or provide a workaround.

- Atlassian products (e.g., Jira and Confluence) were completely unavailable from April 7 to April 16 in 2022, for a majority of their enterprise customers. They had deleted customer data and the design of their backups meant that they had to manually restore each client.

- A known chain restaurant has delicious food, but the waitstaff asks you if you want something every 5 minutes, interrupting your conversation with your date.

- A smartphone application for mobility started loudly announcing the user's chosen itinerary on the speaker. The bug did not get fixed for at least two weeks.

- A train company redesigned their main web platform, but customers temporarily lost their rail cards and discount programs, among other major bugs.

Several studies indicate that most customers abandon a company when they receive bad customer service. One of them reports that no less than 82% of respondents stopped doing business with a company due to a single bad experience[4]. Exceptional

---

4 2010 Customer Experience Impact Report:
https://tktq.link/build-to-sell/2010-customer-experience-impact

customer experience is crucial for retaining customers and driving growth and profits. A dissatisfied customer typically shares their negative experience with 8 to 16 people, and 20% of them might tell more than 20 people[5]. In contrast, a satisfied customer shares their positive experience with only about 6 people on average. This underscores the need for attention to customer satisfaction throughout the product experience.

The disproportionate impact of dissatisfied customers highlights the need to define our product as an entire experience, rather than just focusing on the core item or service.

To be fair, we have also seen remarkable feats from companies whose products provide a delightful experience:

- Captain Train was a French startup that made it possible to get a train ticket in just a few minutes from your mobile phone. The competing application from public-funded SNCF at that time was clunky, slow, and unreliable. Captain Train was widely praised for their customer service (they even wrote a book about it[6]), which went above and beyond to take care of customers whenever

---

5 The Magazine for Customer Service Managers & Professionals: Customer Service facts—https://tktq.link/build-to-sell/customer-service-facts

6 Jonathan Lefèvre, *L'obsession du service client : Les secrets d'une start-up qui a tout misé sur l'expérience client* (Dunod, 2018). While the book is only available in French, Jonathan translated the original article that inspired the book: https://tktq.link/build-to-sell/captain-train-customer-service

something went wrong. They were acquired by Trainline in 2016 for $189 million.

- Notion offers a single workspace for teams by merging a text editor with a simple database system. Notion is lauded for its simplicity and ease of use. They have an active community that offers tips and templates, and is an excellent source of customer support. Notion is experiencing massive growth and rapid adoption by consumers, startups, and scaleups. It is taking market share from Atlassian and Evernote.

- Stripe is a payment processing platform that allows businesses to accept payments online and manage their financial transactions. At first Stripe was not very well known outside of technology circles, but it gained traction thanks to a superior developer experience. Integrating online payments into websites used to be a painful, error-prone and insecure process, and Stripe mostly solved these problems.

There are three points to keep in mind when growing new products and companies. First, customer service should never be an afterthought. People who adopt a product are also buying customer service and will not hesitate to use it when things go wrong. Second, designing and maintaining a delightful customer experience is an efficient business strategy, because retaining an existing customer costs 5 times less than acquiring a new one[7]. Third, a community of satisfied and engaged customers also enhances the product experience.

---

7 *It Costs Five Times More to Acquire a Customer than to Retain a Customer*, Ipsos Loyalty—
https://tktq.link/build-to-sell/ipsos-loyalty-myth-8

Now ask yourself:

- How many customer complaints has your product generated?

- What are the three most common complaints? How have you tried to address them?

- How many complaints are about the product itself? How many were created by your organization and delivery process instead?

CHAPTER
3

OUR PROCESSES HINDER CUSTOMER DELIVERY

There is a third common cause of product failure: when the company starts getting strangled by its own processes and organization. This usually happens only after the company has found a market and started growing. At this point, its main challenge is to scale fast while maintaining excellence in delivery.

New problems appear as soon as companies start scaling: the leaders build new capabilities as fast as possible to satisfy the growing demand, and in the process they rigidify the organization. As a result the business and the product become less resilient to change. This is what Michael Ballé and co-authors call the "Iron Law" of scaleups in their book *The Lean Strategy*[8].

---

8 Michael Ballé, Daniel Jones, Jacques Chaize, and Orest Fiume, *The Lean Strategy: Using Lean to Create Competitive Advantage, Unleash Innovation, and Deliver Sustainable Growth* (McGraw-Hill Education, 2017).

A major slowdown following rapid growth is inevitable unless a system is established early on to dynamically create value throughout every level of the organization. This life cycle, which every startup hopes to avoid, is illustrated below.

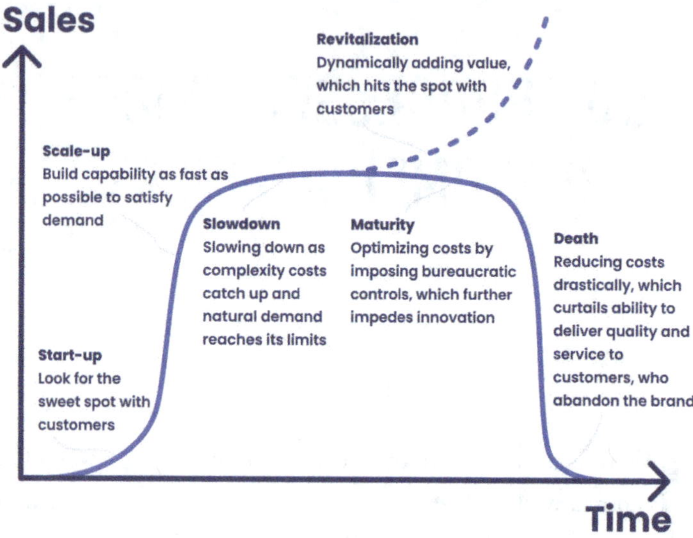

Every company is destined to catch some form of "big company disease" as it scales, a concept introduced in *The Lean Strategy*. As the organization grows alongside demand, complexity sets in and the organization starts to see people more as disposable assets with specialized skills than valued collaborators. Functional silos emerge, everyone has their own agenda, and managers are hired to make people comply with procedures. This is only perceived as a real problem by the business when it starts affecting sales, but by then the damage is done.

In this context, the customer is no longer at the center of the business and team members stop collaborating to improve the customer experience. Costly problems are obscured by bureaucracy and mostly ignored. People fight with all sorts of quality issues, delivery slows down, managers spend their days putting out fires, and any dedicated people who remain are facing burnout. We can cite two examples from our own experience:

1. When his company reached 10 to 15 employees, John, the founder of a successful digital marketing agency called JVWEB, felt like he had to standardize work and create new procedures to reach the ambitious 15% growth target proposed by his partners. But these changes had the opposite effect: operations became rigid, and after 4 years of fast growth, John was becoming overwhelmed with problems coming from clients and employees. In his mind, getting more clients meant having more problems. Since John was experiencing significant stress and was close to burnout, he decided to stop growth. Later on, he started applying lean thinking and got the whole company involved in continuous improvement and problem solving. As a result JVWEB was able to resume growth and even acquired Ocere (see below).

2. Alex is the co-founder of Resi, the UK's leading online service for home extension projects. The London market is huge, and her business grew very fast for a few years. They implemented an innovative digital platform and standardized their processes for interacting with clients and managing projects. But when the company reached about 100 people, Alex realized that she had been battling too

many problems for too long, and the struggle was taking its toll on her and her employees. Most extension projects were not as simple and stress-free as advertised on their website: some customers complained about delays and lower design quality, and these problems were starting to have an impact on the company's growth.

When problems accumulate and execution falters, the most common reactions are to create even stricter procedures, launch a "reorg", or let go of the managers to regain control. However, these knee-jerk responses are counterproductive, because they don't address the real problems the business is facing. The startup is catching "big company diseases" and trying to fix the organization will only make it worse, for several reasons. Firstly, processes and procedures become obsolete almost as soon as they are engineered. Secondly, the more we try to control people through processes and management, the less they are able and prepared to adapt to new problems and come up with creative solutions. Even well-intentioned reorgs that aim to improve communication and collaboration often do not reach that goal, because they can be complicated to implement and distressing for staff.

Like all startups scaling fast, Ocus caught big company diseases as it grew. Their main product, a marketplace that connects businesses with photographers around the world, is very successful. In order to be cost-effective and offer a high-quality service, Ocus created a standard platform to create and manage photoshoot missions. They also hired operators to run quality checks and handle edge cases that the platform could not manage. After completing a series A round of funding, their workforce tripled to over 100 people, and the sales team signed heaps of new deals. As a result, the client base and their needs diversified quickly. They expanded into new sectors, and encountered new types of missions that circumvented the platform. Ocus' leaders were committed to maintaining quality, so growing sales led to hiring more operators and higher operational costs. This dedication to quality was making it more difficult to meet the expected margin, but was it a problem with their business model or a symptom of their growing organizational complexity?

At some point, the founders decided to seek advice from a lean sensei. After the co-founder Julien and the Operations team set up a simple kanban board to visualize the delivery flow, some of their problems became clearer. A kanban board shows the items produced by the company (photography missions, in Ocus's case) from the point of view of the client, and is designed to highlight everything going wrong within the production stream: reworks, stagnation, low quality, and overburden. One of the most striking problems revealed by the kanban was that about 10,000 missions had been stuck for several months or years in the system for various reasons, resulting in substantial lost revenue. Although they were somewhat aware of the stagnating missions, the Operations team hadn't prioritized them because they were overwhelmed with new orders, and the sheer volume was surprising. They deliberately focused on fulfilling newer orders instead of attempting to revive missions that were likely outdated and no longer relevant, a decision that seemed logical.

The Operations team had a tracking system showing which photographer needed to be recontacted for recent missions, but they were missing the bigger picture of the overall mission lead time. Long lead times often indicate of a problem needing urgent attention. In fact, the stuck missions were so numerous that many of them fell under the radar. Furthermore, the team was approaching burnout and didn't have time or energy to address some of the common underlying causes—such as the availability of photographers or the appeal of the mission. Thanks to a transparent kanban system, however, and a good chain of help from the team leader to the co-founder, they detected problems much earlier and dedicated time to finding new ways to engage with the photographers. The hardest part of this process was lifting their gaze from the daily grind, and accepting to invest time in addressing the bigger problems. What made a huge difference was the team leaders' commitment and also the fact that Julien, the co-founder, was personally involved and highly committed in setting up the kanban system and resolving problems with the Operations team.

Yet companies don't need to undergo hypergrowth to have their delivery crumble. Another example from our practice shows this.

Ocere is a 20-person company that does SEO (Search Engine Optimization) outreach. One of the main criteria used by search engines to promote a page is the number of other web pages that link to it. Ocere acts as a broker for paid link placements. Their client asks to place a bundle of links, sometimes with additional content such as graphics or news. An Ocere agent then contacts website owners in their database and sends them the link and content. Selling link placements has been a profitable business for decades, and some website owners in Ocere's network have been active since the start of the internet.

Following Ocere's acquisition by JVWEB, they were given an ambitious goal to double revenue. Tom, the founder and CEO, brought Sandrine in to teach the team how applying lean thinking could support this growth. After implementing kanban to visualize their entire value chain, it was discovered that the drop rate—the percentage of requested links that couldn't be placed compared to the total requested by a client—was much higher than anticipated. Initially assumed to be around 10%, the actual drop rate was observed to be closer to 50% in recent cases. The main challenges were keeping the database of web owners up to date and increasing geographical coverage, since the requested links were often meant for local markets. The high drop rate led to long lead times as the assigned staff searched for replacement links (a kind of rework). Some clients began to notice that Ocere's delivery times were becoming longer compared to those of their competitors. For Ocere, a key challenge in boosting revenue thus involved finding good links on the first try to reduce replacements and minimize lead time. This is just one of the many insights that Ocere teams have uncovered through their daily application of lean thinking to enhance their delivery processes. While the journey has had its share of challenges, it has led to significant improvements in lead time and quality. The results and cultural shift at Ocere are primarily attributed to the dedication to improvement and learning by the company's managers and team leaders.

The real challenge of startups is to scale fast while keeping excellence in delivery. When leaders don't spend as much energy on execution as they do on generating leads, they achieve the opposite effect: quality declines, business slows down, and sales eventually drop. This scenario also hurts the company's ability to reach the break-even point, let alone become profitable, because its operations become saddled with waste. What's more, their capacity to attract further funding for growth is jeopardized, as their results are not sufficiently convincing. Many entrepreneurs hold on to the belief that reengineering their organization and processes is enough to adapt to the new problems that come with rapid growth. But this is a mistake, because the new processes become obsolete as soon as they are created, and the company becomes rigid at the exact moment when they need their agility the most.

Excellence in delivery is about maintaining high quality, while engineering a self-supporting system that allows different people in the company to work seamlessly together.

A better approach to dealing with uncertainty is to promote continuous learning inside the organization. This implies changing the environment to visualize problems as they appear, and providing spaces and support for teams to tackle them creatively and improve processes one problem at a time. Julien and Thibaud at Ocus, John at JVWEB, Tom at Ocere and Alex at Resi all looked for ways to get themselves out of a stressful situation and boost their growth, and they found a solution in lean practice: specifically, the "Thinking People System" (TPS). They learned to visualize the flow of customer requests using **kanban** systems to spot problems early, they implemented chains of help with **andon** to resolve problems faster, and they mentored their people in scientific problem solving to improve quality, value, and speed of delivery. We will learn more about TPS throughout the book.

Now ask yourself:

- If your company is starting to expand quickly, what are the weak points in your capabilities? Is this impacting the quality of your delivery?

- Are your company's internal processes or organization starting to drain energy from your teams and slow down innovation? What activities do your teams see as especially wasteful?

- Do you empower your teams to focus on quality and excellence, trusting them to come up with their own solutions to problems?

THREE HARD-WIRED MISCONCEPTIONS ABOUT PRODUCT MANAGEMENT

Avoiding the common pitfalls of scaleups demands a true product mindset. This whole book is dedicated to developing a product mindset for yourself and your teams, but first we need to overcome three misconceptions that are widespread and deeply rooted among startup founders and tech industry professionals:

1. If we just follow the product roadmap, we will deliver the right product

2. The digital part of the customer experience is the real product

3. An agile team will always build the product fast
    and efficiently

4.1 "If we just follow our roadmap, we will develop the right product"

Elsa, the CPO of a health tech firm, is tasked by top management to build a roadmap for their product suite: a web platform used by medical staff to keep track of patient treatment journeys, and a web app used by the patients. She starts by creating a list of requests based on issues raised by different delivery teams and managers within the company, and on the extensive backlog of bugs and customer feedback. In order to create an 8- to 12-month roadmap, Elsa needs to prioritize the items in this list. This is when difficult negotiations begin, because she knows she is not going to be able to satisfy everyone. After several heated discussions with people inside and outside the firm, Elsa settles on a mixture of urgent bug fixes, features that have been waiting in the backlog for a long time, and some new bells and whistles requested by some of the managers. On the other hand, she faces the tough task of disappointing the tech team, who has been eager to enhance their test coverage for months. She also has to decline several requests from the medical and operational staff who have been seeking improvements for patient follow-up.

Six months later, they are running behind. New requests keep coming in, forcing Elsa to continuously adjust the plan and re-negotiate. Often, the top leaders win: their requests get added regardless of the impact on other priorities. All the while, the bug backlog keeps growing, users of the platform continue struggling, and patients continue to show discontent. Six months later, the roadmap looks pretty different from its initial version: they delivered only half of what was planned, and top management blames the Product and Tech teams for being too slow. During management meetings, executives wonder why patients are choosing competitors, and they brainstorm actions to improve sales and optimize the patient journey. They also question the competence of certain members of the Operations team. At the same time, the Chief Growth Officer, who has not been as involved with the field of customers and teams, advocates for a costly new Customer Relationship Management (CRM) system to support the company's growth and inform future strategies. Believe it or not, her request gets approved! While a CRM system is undoubtedly useful, Elsa believes it's not the most crucial investment at a time when both users and customers are facing challenges, but she is unable to persuade the leadership.

Does this scenario feel familiar? We call it "feature frenzy", and we have lived through it many times. The product roadmap reassures management that their money is well spent. It reassures Product professionals because it gives them an indicator to follow and a plan to engage the whole organization. But the roadmap is a trap. While everyone is busy trying to implement the items in the roadmap, the market and customer experience get a lot less attention.

Are our customers really happy? Are we really creating value for them? Do we understand what is really important to customers? Do we know where they are really struggling and why? Are we addressing their key preferences? What are we learning about how they use our product in different scenarios? What are our competitors up to? Where is our product underperforming relative to alternatives? These are the questions that a product leader and the CEO should be asking themselves continuously.

> **Paradoxically, the more time we spend managing the product roadmap, the less time we spend improving the product, because we forget to see things from the customers' perspective.**

We tend to pack the roadmap full of ideas because we do not know how to make the right choices, then we overcommit to our initial plan. The validated roadmap stretches out for months, so that the plan can contain everything important to the various stakeholders. The traditional roadmap is a compromise based on unclear priorities, but if we are able to answer key questions about our customers' preferences then there would be no need to compromise. A better approach is to introduce just one major change at a time, focus on a high-quality core experience, and deliver in shorter cycles. This way we can see what works and what doesn't, and observe how market tastes are evolving. More importantly, we never stop learning.

Finally, we need to accept that some of our initial ideas might have to be abandoned as we gain new knowledge. Letting go is always difficult, because we get attached to our ideas, but trusting the roadmap to build great products is a costly misconception.

Simply put, *we never know as much as we think we do* while we are designing the roadmap—we are always learning more about our customers, and our circumstances are always changing.

4.2 "The digital part of the customer experience is our real product"

Resi, the UK's home extension leader, is a highly successful scaleup that offers architectural design and coordination services to homeowners via a digital platform. (We met Resi and its founder Alex in Chapter 3.) The market is huge, and by digitizing part of the process, Resi is able to propose competitive pricing and fast services. After registering their renovation project on the platform, a homeowner receives several design proposals from the company's architects, and is put in contact with local builders to carry out the work. As the company expanded, typical of any growing startup, challenges began to accumulate. Understandably, Alex couldn't be everywhere at once, so she recognized the need to build a capable team to support her efforts. Consequently, she shifted her focus towards enhancing the online platform, recognizing significant business growth potential there, and reduced her involvement in day-to-day operations.

After a couple of years, the product management activity within the company was supported by a team made up of a Product Owner, a few developers led by the other co-founder, and a UI specialist who created models of the user interface. The team was receiving many requests for changes and fixes to the platform, and many efforts were made to enhance it. However, discussions with customers and analysis of customer feedback showed that many problems were coming not from the platform itself, but from the plans and designs provided by the architects. This issue became more apparent as sales growth began to decelerate. The founder's initial intuition was correct: from the customer's perspective, Resi's product extended beyond just the platform to include all associated services. Taking care of Resi's product involved enhancing the overall customer experience, even aspects seemingly beyond Resi's control, such as decisions made by the city council.

Resi's example demonstrates that a product is much more than just its digital parts; it encompasses the entire range of experiences that customers encounter in various situations. It is the responsibility of the product team to oversee and enhance all these experiences. When managers structure their product organizations solely around digital and software components, they overlook opportunities to significantly impact their customers' lives.

4.3 "An agile team will always build the product fast and efficiently"

Mike is part of an agile team working on a CRM system. He is the Technical Lead and works with a few other developers, a User Experience (UX) Designer, an Agile Coach and a Product Owner (PO). Mike's team suffers from slowdowns, essentially due to frequent back-and-forth sessions with the PO and rework on past developments. Surely you know these symptoms. In particular, Mike's PO is not happy about one important feature that the team recently delivered: "As a user, when I open the page, I should see a list of customers in alphabetical order." When tested under real conditions, the customer list is displayed higgledy-piggledy: one time the sorting is done on the first name, another time on the last name. The PO understands that when Mike developed the feature, the sorting was correct. But now, looking more closely, they see that the live data are not clean. The PO thinks that the developer should have more carefully tested the feature. Mike thinks that it is the PO's responsibility to provide a realistic dataset. He is just the coder: to each their own job! They keep blaming each other for the problem and leave the meeting frustrated, without reaching an acceptable resolution.

If you have ever worked as part of an agile or Scrum team, you know exactly what we are talking about. We regularly observe this type of conflict between the different roles in the team. In a typical organization, a customer or stakeholder expresses a need, then the PO writes the user story and passes it to the developers through a sprint backlog. A developer codes the user story, then moves it to the "done" column for the PO to test. The PO validates the ticket then leaves it in the backlog for the developers to push into production. If the PO finds problems, they send the ticket back to the developer. All the while, the Agile Coach facilitates daily meetings to check progress against the sprint plan, and is there to remove impediments so that the developers can work without too much distraction.

This team structure is not bad. Agile teams have definite advantages, like increased visibility and better adaptability to change. However, the decentralized nature of the team also leads to fragmentation of responsibilities, especially with regards to the product. The root of the problem is the lack of leadership from both POs and Agile Coaches. We have seen some agile teams with strong POs, Agile Coaches or even Technical Leads who have a real interest in the customer and vision, and who know how to lead the whole team towards building a great product. But there are few such teams, because POs and Agile Coaches are not trained to have this product vision.

Agile development has lost its focus on building great software products, a goal that was at the heart of eXtreme Programming, an earlier flavor of agile. The focus nowadays is on continuous delivery, defined by specific roles, tasks, and responsibilities. The agile workflow increasingly resembles a manufacturing production line rather than an engineering process, ironically mirroring the very scenario software developers have sought to avoid since the late nineties. We are not suggesting that a robust delivery process is not needed, but it is clear that mastering delivery is far from sufficient.

Ultimately, a team that does not know how to collaborate well around a common product vision will always create clunky and savorless products. *A product is always the reflection of the team that designs and builds it*: their skills, their understanding of customer value, and their ability to collaborate effectively. Agile pioneers know this well, and are constantly looking for new ways of building great software products and teams[9]. On the other side, startup founders who adopted Scrum to prepare their business for scaling, often convinced by their CTO, are now

---

9 "We are uncovering better ways of developing software by doing it and helping others do it", an extract from the Manifesto for Agile Software Development which was created in the early 2000s.

backpedaling because they cannot build great products as fast as they grow, which is their number one goal. This limitation is probably why Scrum and its derivatives have lost some appeal lately among enterprise leaders. The big mistake is to believe that scaling simply involves standardizing and replicating agile processes, team structures, and routines across an organization, as seen in SAFe. This approach fails to tackle the real challenge: maintaining a spirit of exploration and innovation as the organization grows into a "big" company. It is central to building irresistible products and long-lasting businesses.

4.4 Why agile is not enough to build great products

Agile alone cannot ensure that our company builds great products that sell, nor can it help a company achieve scale. The three of us have reached this conclusion after years of practicing many different forms of agile in various industry contexts: Scrum, Scrum at scale, eXtreme Programming, DevOps, kanban, etc.

Below each author provides their personal point of view: Sandrine as a lean sensei, Flavian as a CTO and Caroline as a CPO.

SANDRINE

THE LEAN SENSEI POINT OF VIEW

I began my product and tech career in the USA, a few years before the agile movement was born. I discovered agile in 2001 while working on a fantastic project with a biotech firm in San Francisco. I was immediately captivated! For years I practiced agile, because it was a great alternative to waterfall. I became an agile advocate in both the USA and France. I even joined the board of Agile France in 2005 when I moved to Paris with my family, and organized nationwide conferences. Eventually, however, agile methods such as Scrum and eXtreme Programming started showing their limits.

When I led agile delivery teams, I struggled to engage the whole organization and convince managers of the value that agile would generate for the business. This had repercussions on my ability to deliver great products fast and generate results. I soon realized that I was not the only person with this problem in the agile community. To understand why, I had to go beyond the mindset of just building cool software with cool people in our small geeky bubbles. I had to think more strategically. My quest led me to lean. After all, agile principles were mostly built on lean principles, so why not go straight to the source? I am extremely lucky to have learned from the internationally recognized author and lean sensei Michael Ballé. For years now, I have studied and practiced Toyota's original vision of lean: an enterprise strategy for building products with great impact on customer satisfaction and society. The big surprise for me was discovering that this could be achieved by *improving the way people learn.*

While agile and lean share some characteristics, like the drive to better understand customer needs and deliver the product in small increments, lean has three fundamental differences that are at the center of conceiving and building products that sell.

- Lean is not just about developing great software, it is about delivering *irresistible products*, and this goal must involve the whole company, not just the development teams.

- Lean does not separate product design from business results, since the two are intimately linked. By business results, I mean high sales and profit.

- Lean is built on the principle that if we improve how people think and resolve problems together, we can improve the value that our products and services bring to customers.

Throughout the book, we emphasize these key principles. All the tools and practices we present in this book aim to sharpen people's reasoning, so they can face unknown problems autonomously and creatively, and contribute to improving value. This is the true agility that startups need to cultivate if they want to build irresistible products that sell, and grow fast but sustainably.

So the question is not: agile or lean? This is comparing apples and oranges. Agile provides software teams with standards for organizing their activities in a flexible and customer-oriented manner. Lean creates truly agile organizations where people know how to resolve new problems together and are continuously seeking new ways of creating value for customers.

FLAVIAN

THE CTO POINT OF VIEW

Agile frustrates me. At the heart of my frustration is this limitation: *agile is not enough to make good engineers great.* As a CTO, I am obsessed with developing great teams that deliver high-quality software in record time. This is how I understand the agile core value "Individuals and interactions over processes and tools." The problem is that in agile practice I see quite a bit about developing teamwork, but nothing about developing people. Yet there can be no great product without great engineers, however well they get along.

To me, a great engineer not only does the job well but also continuously seeks to improve their skills. Hiring top-notch engineers is important, but we aren't always able to do this, either for lack of budget or because we inherited a team of junior developers and engineers. But even a highly skilled and experienced engineer must continue to learn, because the tech world changes quickly and skills become archaic if not continuously maintained. If I am to build innovative products that align with our evolving society, I need teams of engineers who think innovatively and can challenge their own knowledge.

Developing great teams and fantastic engineers has long been an obsession of mine, and led me to create environments where people can grow and enjoy their job. I have searched for answers in different agile methodologies: Scrum, eXtreme Programming, Domain-Driven Design, and DevOps. None of them provided a satisfactory solution to my problem. They all focus on building processes or tools to deliver more value. While this is surely an important aspect of project delivery, agile tells you nothing about how people learn or how to create environments for developing people's knowledge.

Lean, however, does do this. It offers a system for developing great engineers and great teams that continue to learn over time. I have co-written this book to convince other CTOs and Technical Leads to look at their work with a lean eye, in order to develop great engineering teams.

CAROLINE

THE CPO POINT OF VIEW

After ten years spent building digital products, I am firmly convinced that making a great product involves honing three skills:

- Create value for users by touching the right emotions: the product "concept"

- Figure out what our customers are willing to buy, not what we want to sell them

- Design the intangibles of the product necessary for its success, including production, storage, delivery, distribution, ancillary services and add-ons. Mindfully design everything that contributes to the global customer experience: the "whole product".

Only by keeping an unwavering focus on these three key topics can we build attractive products that people will want to buy and use over the long term. Yet I frequently see something very different happening in product organizations: we spend our time creating feature backlogs, writing and prioritizing user stories, and treating product management as a simple delivery activity rather than a design practice. A "whole product" team needs to:

1. Continuously learn about customers by spending a lot of time with them in their environment. We need to observe their behaviors, deeply understand their problems, clarify their desires, and live their life to get a reliable sense of their reality.

2. Reflect and collaborate closely with tech teams from the beginning because to come up with a great product concept we also need to dive into the technical side of things. A product is not just a set of specifications handed over to the developers, but a collaboration between different types of experts with different points of view on the product.

Agile puts the focus on delivery and reduces the job of product design to the role of Product Owner (PO). The PO acts at such a micro level (the user story) that it is almost impossible for them to take that necessary step back to view the whole product. I often see POs and Agile Coaches act like basic project managers, planning and facilitating daily meetings, demos, and retrospectives, but not engaging the whole team in resolving important customer and product problems. There is a deep chasm between the POs and Agile Coaches on the one side, and development teams on the other, and this is a huge problem. This is also true for UX Designers, where the gap is more widely recognized but who should still be playing a central role.

Then, there is also the *Lean UX* and *Lean Startup* approaches, championed by Jeff Gothelf and Eric Ries, which incorporate elements of lean thinking. They stress the significance of engaging with the gemba, iterating quickly, and embracing the notion of "failing fast" to facilitate rapid learning. They introduce valuable methodological elements to understand customers. In *Build to Sell*, we take it a few steps further and suggest practices to reconcile the client gemba with technology, ensuring an unbiased perspective. Plus, we aim to reduce risks by anticipating better and minimizing uncertainties, understanding that failure is inevitable but can be less severe or even avoided in some cases.

Lean product design and development prioritize developing people before products, which fundamentally alters the approach, and the results. Many methods emphasize creating the "perfect" delivery process and roles without considering the individuals involved and their unique contributions. A successful product is the result of good thinking, so it's essential to invest more time in enhancing mindsets and reasoning skills. This naturally enhances team discussions and fosters stronger collaboration among members from various areas like tech, UX, product, and beyond.

Now ask yourself:

- Looking back at your last product roadmap, how close was the final delivery to the initial plan? Did the final delivery make an impression with customers? Out of all the features or improvements delivered, how many respond directly to known, evidence-based customer needs?

- Analyzing complaints, how often were your customers disappointed by aspects of the customer experience other than the physical product or digital platform, such as sales, third-party services, or customer support?

- If you work with an agile development team, are they mainly churning out features and user stories or also engaged in other activities such as customer research or design impact analysis? Do they consider that everything is known when development starts, or do they leave themselves opportunities to validate hypotheses and pivot if necessary?

**PART
2**

BUILDING THE FOUNDATIONS OF A VISIONARY PRODUCT CULTURE

Overcoming the misconceptions described in the previous part, especially on an organizational level, is not easy. Lean brings us the realization that building great products starts with building great people. In this part, we present a series of practices to fight the three major misconceptions and build the foundations of a product-centric culture in your business.

To build these foundations, we need to change our perspective on three essential aspects of product management. First, we need to switch from building a long-term product roadmap to maintaining a regular product *takt time*; second, we need to shift our focus from the digital product to the *whole* product; and third, we need to evolve our agile team into an interdisciplinary team coordinated by a *Chief Product Engineer*.

CHAPTER 5

FROM THE PRODUCT ROADMAP TO THE PRODUCT TAKT TIME

The most common approach to planning a product team's activity is building a roadmap: first we form a detailed feature backlog, then we sort the top features into a series of development iterations or sprints. As a product team, while building the roadmap we are sure to receive requests from all over: not just from clients and users, but also managers, technology experts, QA, client services, and Ops. We spend a lot of time qualifying and prioritizing these requests, with the intention of satisfying everyone. Under pressure from multiple stakeholders, we end up compromising: we put in a little bit of everything, sacrificing some cohesion, and don't fully satisfy anyone.

The problem with this approach is that by focusing on individual features of the product, we lose sight of the whole. Just like the parable of the blindfolded men and the elephant[10], everyone in the business forms their own ideas about the product related to their specialty, and listening to them all transforms the product into a hodgepodge of features. The major risk is that the product starts losing its appeal, because it lacks coherence and robustness.

Everyone who works in a tech firm, from the employees to the founder, is already familiar with the curse of the product backlog. It's a bottomless well that never runs dry and seems to have a life of its own! New features appear every day, seemingly out of nowhere. The product team has the feeling of never catching up, because neither customers nor stakeholders are ever entirely satisfied. Everyone is working hard, but they know deep down that they should be spending more time with customers and less on internal politics. We call this "feature frenzy".

Having served as the CTO of several tech firms, Flavian knows this problem very well. In one company, the product never seemed to be finished because the roadmap always got delayed. Marketing, customers, the CEO, and even the development team kept asking for more features: fix this, add this, change that. Even worse, no one was willing to compromise. They spent an incredible amount of time and energy negotiating priorities, but in the end the most persistent often won. Unfortunately, this was rarely if ever the clients. The developers never had enough time to refactor the code and redesign parts of the product that they

---

10 https://tktq.link/build-to-sell/blindfolded-men-and-an-elephant

no longer had a handle on, so the technical debt kept increasing. Each new request, complaint or idea was turned into a new feature by the Product Owners, who hoped that by entering them into the product backlog they would get a break from being hassled. But the process to deliver a new feature could take weeks or months from specification to design, code, testing, and deployment, so the backlog was growing faster than what the team was able to deliver. For that reason, the team sometimes chose features from the backlog based on factors that weren't always sensible, hoping these would resonate with customers and become game changers. If not, they could always revert to the previous version or change the product again, right?

Release after release, this product got ever more complex, and eventually adoption and sales went down. When a company reaches this stage, the top leaders often feel like they need to make a radical decision: completely redesign the product, change the business model (pivot), or replace the CPO/CTO. None of these solutions are easy to implement, nor do they guarantee fixing the problem.

Every time we decide to change a product, the risk of disappointing customers is high, and we won't know if it is a good change until the product is in their hands. With each new release, many things can go wrong:

- We break part of the product and degrade the customer experience. A product is a set of intertwined elements, and the bigger and more complex the product gets, the riskier it becomes to change. Like a game of Jenga, we have to be very careful not to remove or change a component that supports the overall cohesion of the product and its ability to meet customers' real needs.

- We modify something that the customer likes very much without realizing it. Remember when Snapchat moved its Discover screen to the forefront and relegated Stories to a secondary screen, confusing many users and leading some to uninstall the app? This resulted in significant losses for them.

- We keep a feature or aspect of the product that we are attached to, but that our customers find old-fashioned or useless. For example, Facebook has become more popular among older generations, losing its appeal to younger users who find Instagram and Discord better suited to hang out and have fun with their friends.

The more changes we make at the same time, the higher the risk of displeasing customers and providing opportunities for competing solutions to surpass our product. By trying to do everything and pleasing everyone, we please no one perfectly.

Therefore, rather than releasing a multitude of features to customers in every update and hoping for a miracle (we call this the Hail Mary approach), which only leads to an ever-expanding backlog since we can't implement everything, we suggest a more strategic method for introducing changes to a product:

- Release a single change at a time

- Innovate vertically AND horizontally

- Establish a flow of value improvements

5.1 Release a single change at a time

The next change to your product can be technical or cosmetic, but it should always strengthen the product's market position as well as the brand. The change needs to be meaningful for the company. Even if it is not a major technological change, it will be announced and promoted as a major innovation. For instance, many of us upgrade our mobile phones every two to three years to get the latest innovations, even though the models remain much the same. We might get a camera with slightly higher resolution, a marginally larger screen or reduced weight, or some other incremental improvement. The regular introduction of changes allows a product to keep its appeal to existing customers and attract new ones, thereby maintaining leadership in its market.

Releasing a single change at a time may seem counterintuitive to high-tech startups, whose main goal is to beat the market and scale fast. A product with lots of features is more powerful for its users and harder for competitors to copy, right? This is a misconception: addressing many different kinds of problems and customer segments by releasing multiple features at once is much riskier for the reasons described above, and this strategy inevitably slows us down. Many startups break their teeth on this hard-wired belief and end up providing half-baked solutions and features that are not useful in their customers' real context. In doing so, they disperse their efforts and resources, trying to please too many people with a product that is unable to do any one thing well enough to build loyalty. Targeting the right audience is akin to bowling: everyone wants to roll a strike, but attempting to knock down all the pins at once also disperses the force. Most of us hit the middle of the grouping and leave some pins standing. But when we hit a single pin with a well-aimed ball, it always goes flying.

Releasing a single change at a time actually *speeds up delivery*, and gives us a better chance of hitting the mark without losing customers' trust. It provides the firm with a quicker, surer way of validating a new hypothesis on the market. We release one feature, then another, then another and with each incremental change we keep a close eye on customer satisfaction and the market fit. We call this regular release pace the **product takt**. (Takt is a German word that means the beat or pulse in music.)

New startups developing their Minimum Viable Product should focus on a single "Job To Be Done"[11] or customer segment at a time, hence a single major product "change". For the first version, we consider this a change relative to existing solutions that the product is supposed to replace. At the end of the chapter, we will propose a method for setting different takt times for your products.

---

11 See Chapter 10 for a more in-depth description of Jobs To Be Done.

5.2 Innovate vertically *and* horizontally

A product takt is a cadence of new product releases within the same product family. A new release might aim to resolve a different problem for another customer segment, or it might be an upgraded version of an existing product to keep customers interested in the brand. We call these approaches **horizontal innovation** and **vertical innovation** respectively.

As an example of the first approach, consider that Apple regularly releases new phones within the iPhone family, as illustrated in Fig 1. Within a generation, each new version of the base model addresses a specific Job To Be Done or customer need: the Plus takes better photos for those who prefer it, the Pro takes professional-quality photos, and the Pro Max takes professional photos for longer periods of time.

To illustrate the second approach, Fig 1 also shows two generations of the same product (iPhone Pro 13 and iPhone Pro 14). Apple releases a new generation of iPhones every year, but not all at once. The iPhone Pro 14 might come out months before the iPhone Pro Max 14. This ambitious and regular schedule of new releases keeps current customers interested in the brand, so they are not tempted to look elsewhere, as well as attracting new customers who need the latest technology. For example, a few key performance metrics were enhanced in the iPhone Pro 14, but it largely retains the same technologies and features as its predecessor.

FIGURE 1. Horizontal and vertical innovation in the iPhone series. Different models in the same generation target different customer segments, who need professional-quality photos and/or longer battery life. Upgrading a model to the next generation, on the other hand, grants an incremental improvement to essentially the same user experience.

Vertical innovation is a good way to develop customer loyalty. It gets our customers excited about something new without asking them to change their behavior too much. Most customers want to upgrade their iPhone from time to time, to benefit from better performance like more memory, a larger screen, or a new software feature as illustrated in Fig. 1. But the most important and overlooked feature of each release is its stability: Apple's customers are keeping *essentially the same phone.* This is reassuring (people may feel anxiety when it comes to changing products) and can be seen as a reward for loyalty (the brand keeps supporting me).

Horizontal innovation means adding new products to a product family, in order to touch new segments with different Jobs To Be Done. In horizontal innovation, we aim to reuse our technologies and know-how from previous products to speed up delivery and keep costs down. Extending a product range in this way can significantly increase market share because customers are able to use a brand they already trust to resolve different types of jobs, either for themselves or for their friends and relatives. In short, horizontal innovation is a great cross-selling technique.

In order to strengthen the brand and scale a product, we need to work on both vertical and horizontal product innovations, each with its own takt time. In the example of Apple iPhones, each new generation (13, 14, 15...) is a vertical innovation aiming to please its existing users, while different versions of the iPhone in the same generation are horizontal innovations targeting different customers with a different problem (mini, plus, Pro, Pro Max). Of course, Apple manages other major product families, such as tablets and laptops, with their own innovation strategies and schedules.

Sometimes, scaling also means removing a product from a product family if it becomes less relevant to the market. For instance, between generations 13 and 14 Apple decided to drop the "mini" version of the iPhone. The mini surely resolved a real problem when it came out, targeting people who used their phone mainly for calls rather than as a tablet or media screen all day long. We can easily imagine that this segment has been rapidly shrinking, making the iPhone 13 a less attractive option for Apple to invest in. The model was officially discontinued in September 2023; Apple will know soon enough whether they made the right call.

Changing the size of the basic version of their phone between generations 13 and 14, allowed Apple to test a hypothesis about the market. There is always a risk of error even when we make an educated guess, so it is better to avoid making too many changes or too big a change at the same time. The product *takt* forces us to check our product bets on a regular basis and minimize the risk of disappointing customers. It also prevents us from burning our cash on several wrong ideas at once.

The concepts of vertical and horizontal innovation are similar for digital products. Software versioning is not new. It corresponds to vertical innovation if it is done intelligently; that is, as an upgrade of quality characteristics and not an opportunity to stuff the product with new features, bells and whistles. There is a widespread misconception that changing software is easy and cheap, so we can afford to build features fast and fix them later. But customers get lost when there are too many changes at once. And as we'll see later in the book, this strategy is not so cheap after all because of the high cost of rework and technical debt.

The meaning of horizontal innovation in software is not as clear-cut, because digital products do not have as many physical limitations. For instance, we can design a software product or platform with different modules to satisfy different "jobs". Uber Rides and Uber Eats are an example of this approach: the two services can be seen as separate product families even though they share many functions and technologies and are distributed via the same channel (Uber's phone app). Uber benefits by sharing resources, speeding up turnaround and reducing maintenance costs. But introducing additional complexity into a product can also have the opposite effect.

Another common example of horizontal innovation in software is creating different "tiers of service". Antivirus software commonly takes this approach, with the free or lowest-cost tier providing basic protection and higher tiers providing additional functionality such as analytics, real-time protection while browsing the web, and so on. More recently, OpenAI also offers multiple tiers ranging from free to use to "Plus", "Team", and "Enterprise".[12] Each tier opens up new advantages such as a higher data limit and access to new kinds of models.

5.3 Establish a flow of value improvements

Expertise comes from repeating a skill over and over, in many different contexts. In the realm of product conception, this means seeing each product not as a one-off event, but as a regular series of improvements and innovations paced according to the market, the product takt. Each product cycle is an opportunity to analyze the value we created or destroyed with our

---

12 https://tktq.link/build-to-sell/openai-pricing

previous releases, so we can more easily decide what new change will improve value. We call this cycle **value analysis / value engineering** or VA/VE (Figure 2).

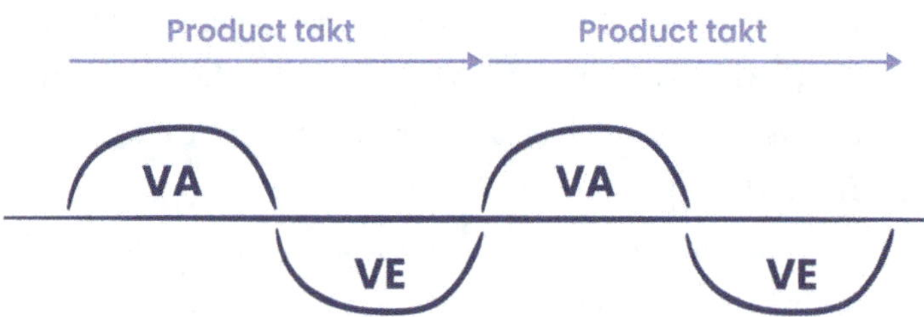

FIGURE 2. Each product takt consists of two phases. First, value analysis revisits the client gemba[13] and looks at lessons learned from the previous release, to make a hypothesis about what change to the product will bring the most value. Second, value engineering proposes a new product design that implements the change without degrading the customer experience or product identity.

Value Analysis is about solving quality issues in existing products, with the aim of understanding:

1. what customers are trying to do with our products, and situations in which they are not succeeding;

2. where are the flaws in our products and what waste do they reveal in our own processes and working methods;

3. how rival products are better, and what design choices they made to better meet customer preferences or become more cost-effective.

---

13 We first defined gemba in the Introduction. The client gemba refers specifically to the places where our customers find, buy, use, consume, and recycle different products and services.

Value Engineering is about improving the function performance of future products based on findings from the value analysis activities, and deciding the next innovation that will convince customers to remain loyal to the brand in the near future. We want to keep the desire and excitement for the product alive, but we don't want to change customers' habits too much either. In product takt mode, we are not aiming for a sudden, groundbreaking innovation that shocks the market. Instead, we prefer a steady pace of incremental changes, allowing us to test the market quickly and often, minimizing the risk of alienating customers and avoiding significant financial exposure.

> **Maintaining a product takt over time can eventually disrupt the entire industry: when each micro-innovation pleases its target segment, competitors are compelled to follow.**

After being burned by her roadmap experience, Elsa, the CPO of the health tech firm, experimented with VA/VE. Together with the mobile app lead, they chose a one-month takt time based on their understanding of how often users were willing to receive a new version and on the speed of evolution of competing solutions. Every month, they analyzed value by conducting some of the field activities described in Part 3 (see Chapter 11, "Step into your customer's shoes"). Then, based on their analysis, they picked a single important change to improve the customer experience.

In their first VA/VE cycle, by carefully analyzing customer feedback and conducting interviews with the nurses, they learned that patients needed to feel reassured about their treatment, so they were contacting company nurses and medical assistants at all hours. As a result, these medical professionals were swamped with requests and didn't always respond to messages in a timely manner. Plus, they were not working at night. The mobile app was evidently not doing a good enough job at answering patients' questions, let alone reassuring them. Therefore, the first major change that Elsa and the head of product decided to implement was to humanize the mobile app: they changed the look and feel to create a more relaxing environment, added reassuring words at each step of the treatment process, welcomed patients every day by asking them how they were feeling, and provided useful advice. This single change had an immediate and very positive effect in lowering the volume of patient requests. This success comforted the team that VA/VE was leading them in the right direction.

A product is part of a value stream. It has a history and a trajectory. The product history is represented by all the key value improvements that have been made to follow new trends and market constraints. For example, a (highly simplified) history of the telephone[14] could be summarized as follows:

- Late 19th century: a disruptive technology emerges addressing the need to connect people who are geographically distant. The ability to hold real-time conversations was a major improvement compared to the telegraph.

---

14 https://tktq.link/build-to-sell/timeline-of-the-telephone

- **1910–30s:** Long-distance communication becomes possible thanks to rapid expansion of the infrastructure, widespread adoption, and business consolidation. Major improvements in the quality of communication.
- **1940–50s:** Direct dialing and intercontinental cables make the telephone network more accessible.
- **1960–70s:** Aesthetics take the forefront as the telephone becomes a major household appliance.
- **1980–90s:** Maneuverability improvements both within the household (wireless handsets) and outside (commercialization of satellite and cellular networks).
- **2000s:** Mobile phones gain internet access and a host of utility functions.
- **2010s:** Smartphones emerge with social network connectivity, multimedia support, and installable software to support almost any service.
- **2020s:** Most phones are fully functional handheld computers and personal assistants.
- **2030s:** What will come next?

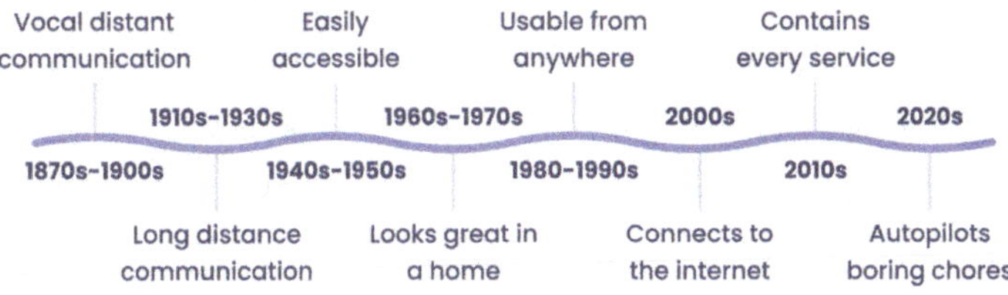

FIGURE 3. The history of the telephone, represented as a value stream of major improvements to the basic product.

Understanding a product's history is key to imagining its trajectory. We move in the direction that the market pushes us to take, but keep the product's history in mind to ensure that we do not eliminate anything essential to its experience, its "DNA". Your product probably has less history than the telephone, but it is still helpful to imagine its timeline and understand how its past versions delighted customers in different ways. This analysis is also useful for setting the product takt, as we will see in the next section. Your product history can give you insight into the pace of innovation that the market will bear.

A striking example is the keyboard: it has been around for almost two hundred years, from the simple typewriter to the electronic memory machine, from the modern computer keyboard to fully digital, touchscreen versions. Many improvements have been made over the years, *but the layout of the letters has hardly changed* even though the problem of keys getting tangled has long since passed. Several companies have tried to innovate with the key layout but they are no longer here to testify. Some power users train themselves to use alternative layouts, but overall the market has not been clamoring for a change. Who knows what the trajectory of the keyboard will be? When will the market be ready to accept a completely different concept? The product takt requires us to ask these questions regularly, even if the answer appears evident. One day, customers probably will turn away from the traditional keyboard, perhaps when speech to text technology becomes cheaper and more reliable than entering text by hand, or after the skill of touch typing dies out over a few generations.

Adopting the product takt and performing VA/VE in every cycle yields very different results compared to the product roadmap approach. Companies spend a lot of time designing road-maps that become obsolete almost as soon as they are validated, then creating and prioritizing feature backlogs without delivering the required value to customers. We have an unfortunate tendency to stuff as many features as we can into a single release because we are scared of leaving problems unaddressed or scared of losing customers. This leads us to create generalized products that fail to solve any one problem really well for the users.

When designing a new product, it is useful to retrace the key stages of its history to understand the innovation choices that were made (with each new takt). This product change timeline brings out the heritage aspects of the product, i.e. those aspects that constitute its DNA and should not be changed. We will dive deeper into identifying and protecting the heritage aspects of your product in Chapter 14.

5.4 Set product takt times

Product takt times are different for each industry, and are often set by major events. For instance, fashion designers launch new collections twice a year, typically in spring and fall, in order to join special fashion events where customers can learn about the next trends. At least, this is the traditional pacing! Recently, fast fashion companies have turned the industry on its head by reducing their takt to one week. The mobile phone industry has a product takt of 6 months to one year. Mobile phone companies often create buzz with major announcements about their upcoming products. In the digital sphere, takt times are comparable and can sometimes be even shorter. Here are some examples:

- Airbnb and Salesforce follow a quarterly *takt*; they even call their new product versions the winter, spring, summer, and fall editions.

- Google follows a yearly *takt*: they usually announce new products at their annual IO conference.

- Node.js typically releases new products on a semi-annual basis or *takt*, with announcements usually made on their website.

- Toyota has released new car models within its Prius family every year, following a yearly *takt* for that product range.

In the digital world, we must clarify the difference between continuous integration and product takt. Continuous integration is a software development practice that focuses on consistently delivering new code whose quality is guaranteed through automated testing and early issue detection. On the other hand, the product takt is about regularly introducing new products to the market, maintaining customer engagement, and attracting new customer segments. Both practices are important, but they address different needs.

Let's imagine that we are leading a digital startup, without a major public event driving our schedule. How can we choose the right takt time for our product?

The first consideration is our competition. The takt time we choose should drive us to keep a healthy pace of innovation and stay in the race. Setting a takt time also forces us to think about how to promote our new product. We need to let our customers know that the new product is coming, that it will be even better, or that we are expanding the product range to satisfy new needs. We need to do this *before* customers start losing interest in our brand and looking at emerging solutions.

When we consider our market position in this way, we see that we can actually define two takt times: one for vertical innovation (new product generations) and one for horizontal innovation (product family extension). In both cases we need to choose a takt time that we can sustain in terms of both technology innovation and promotion. In the digital world, we can also define a more frequent takt time for maintenance, equivalent to minor releases. For example, high-budget video games often release new content every few months (innovation takt) and frequent "hotfixes" consisting mainly of bug fixes and minor gameplay adjustments (maintenance takt).

The second major consideration is our company's organization and capacity. The takt time we choose will create a series of firm milestones that drive all our internal activities, from sales and marketing to operations and delivery. The product takt becomes the heartbeat of the organization. We create a plan with firm release dates of all our products, and display it prominently so that everyone can consult it easily and make decisions together. Similar to a flight control tower, this plan gives leadership and everyone else a central location to find the "arrival times" of all major releases, anticipate conflicts or delays, and adjust the company's investment to maintain the takt. Of course, the company must have enough resources (financial and human) in the first place to keep this promise! If risks and delays start piling up, it might indicate that the company is attempting to handle too many product families simultaneously.

Figure 4 shows an example of a **product takt plan**:

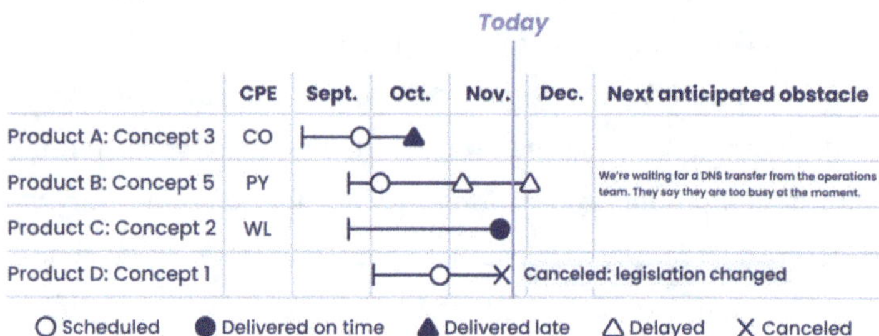

FIGURE 4. Example of a product takt plan showing the release dates of the next concepts of the company's four products (A, B, C, D), the Chief Product Engineer (CPE) responsible for the product, and the next major risk or obstacle to overcome which pushes us to be proactive rather than merely reactive. Each product has a different takt time (the length of the bar from its start to the circle) and promised release date (the circle). The four projects demonstrate different outcomes and ways of using the symbols to indicate problems. If this were a real situation, the many delays for project B clearly show the leadership team that they need to go to the gemba to understand the problem at its source and help the team fix it.

The product takt plan shows just a few vital pieces of information for each upcoming product release: the name of the product (this can include a short statement on the core concept of the release), the Chief Product Engineer (CPE), the promised release date (takt), and the most important anticipated obstacle. In lean companies, the product takt plan also initiates a **kanban**[15] system for each project, which allows different teams to coordinate their design, development, release, and post-release activities.

---

15 Kanban systems will be covered by the next book in this series, *Build to Scale*.

The product takt plan supports weekly discussions among the company's leadership team to anticipate and resolve potential issues that might disrupt the smooth progress of various projects. Naturally, as with all lean tools, this should be used not as a command and control instrument, but as a means to guide and support the entire organization.

In the next chapter, you will see that the first and arguably most important decision for each product is to appoint its "Chief Product Engineer": the person who will take responsibility for its delivery and profitability, attract and inspire the right team of experts, and lead the product concept to success. Startup founders are usually the first Chief Product Engineer of their company.

Now ask yourself:

- What does your next product release look like? How many changes are you planning on making to the product? Which change do you expect to have the biggest impact on your customers?

- In which specific situations are your customers not able to do what they want to do with your product? Are your planned changes addressing this problem?

- Consider your flagship product. What were its most important innovations over time? Were these innovations vertical or horizontal? How often are your customers ready to accept a major change?

- What are your different products and product families? What would be a meaningful takt time for each product? Is it driven mainly by your company's capacity, or by external events?

FROM THE DIGITAL PRODUCT TO THE WHOLE PRODUCT

With Resi's example, we learned that a product is not just the physical object we sell or the digital platform we create to aid the purchasing process; it is really the sum of customer experiences in different situations.

SaaS products are the same, at least in name: they do not sell software as a product that the customer "owns", they sell a complete service. In practice the support is not always complete. Even when the digital tool *is* the product, such as Microsoft Office or certain mobile apps, the software is only part of the customers' global experience. Our clients pass through a whole set of significant experiences from the very first touchpoint: how they find the product, how they purchase it, how they install it, how they learn to use it, how they maintain it, how they fix it, how they get support, and even how they stop using it. The digital product is only one of the assets we must work on to make all these experiences live up to customer standards.

In Resi's case, the digital platform manages several steps of the home extension project life cycle, from obtaining the online quote to reviewing and approving the architects' and builders' recommendations. The platform sets Resi apart from the competition by facilitating low prices, quick quotes, project transparency, and easier communication. However, Resi went through a phase where improving this platform was not where the biggest efforts were needed. The company was facing challenges in retaining customer trust, and this was mainly due to the quality of the renovation designs. In fact, Resi's core product *was never the platform*. It was a new, innovative way of managing home extension projects from A to Z. This service must involve several enablers and actors in addition to the customer and the platform: architects, planners, builders, city councils, and so on. Alex understood that narrowing the focus on the digital platform could lead to shortcomings in other areas. To gain deeper insights into customer issues, she dedicated extensive time to the gemba. Additionally, she led weekly problem-solving sessions with operational teams and revamped the company's key performance objectives to prioritize the overall customer experience. Gradually but steadily, her results started to improve.

Amazon is a great example of a digital startup that understood the nature of its whole product very early in its development. Although it is usually considered a tech company, Amazon is not just an online shopping platform: efficient logistics, guaranteed on-time delivery, and excellent after-sales services are also big parts of the global experience. Amazon has put a lot of work into designing and improving these non-digital features as part of their value proposition.

6.1 Design the whole product

As product conceptors we need to consider the **whole product** in our design and development approach, not just the tech part. We base our concept of the whole product on an interesting model invented by Harvard professor Theodore Levitt called the "total product". It states that people do not purchase the basic or core product; they purchase the service they expect the product will provide. Theodore Levitt popularized the well known saying, "people don't want to buy a quarter-inch drill, they want a quarter-inch hole!" Yet we continue making and marketing our "quarter-inch drills" and wonder why they don't sell. Some contend that consumers also desire the drill itself, beyond the need to make a hole, because people enjoy acquiring new items even if they do not end up using them. Although there may be truth to this, designing products solely on the premise that people like to buy new things is risky and, from an ethical standpoint, questionable.

The total product includes all the complementary attributes of the product, often intangible services or other benefits, that are needed to make their experience a good one. The following wheel, adapted from a concept introduced in *Crossing the Chasm* by Geoffrey Moore, offers examples of complementary attributes to help describe your own product.

FIGURE 5. A product consists of the physical or digital core product (center) and all complementary attributes and services that make the customer experience great.

For example, Uber's product includes a website dedicated to its drivers, which offers services related to the "standards & procedures" and "training & support" spokes of the wheel. The website:

- facilitates the onboarding of a new driver through partnerships with training providers; and

- provides tutorials and help on using the Uber app, and understanding Uber's service values, notably with a complete guide for drivers.

Without this onboarding website and the large community of well-trained drivers, Uber couldn't function. Any problem with a rude or unsafe driver degrades the brand and gives newly arrived, more flexible and hungry competitors an advantage. Yet when we think about Uber's product, we tend to see only the mobile app and the rides.

We propose to take the total product model a step further. We consider that the constellation of attributes and services supporting the core product are not just complementary but *integral* elements of the product and its entire life cycle, from the moment the customer places an order to construction, storage, delivery, consumption and even recycling. We call this viewpoint the **whole product**. We need to put these elements on equal footing with the technology of the core product if we are to create great experiences for customers.

As product engineers, we don't just conceive technological solutions; we conceive entire product flows that create customer experiences across many different situations.

With Resi, it became evident that reducing the product to the digital platform created opportunities for degraded service in other areas. However, by refocusing on their whole product, and working with people on resolving problems, they managed to restore their top-notch customer experience.

Remember Sophia, the founder of Lux For Rent? Here is what her whole product looked like:

FIGURE 6. Example of a whole product: a peer-to-peer rental service for luxury clothing brands.

The core product is the mobile app and digital platform for connecting renters with owners and managing transactions. On the other hand, the whole experience includes many different moments in the customer's life, such as creating their own "closet" as an owner, browsing closets as a renter, contacting owners, interacting with the community, wearing and enjoying the rented outfit, and finally returning it.

We need to design the whole product *simultaneously* if we want to ensure that all these experiences are great from the user's point of view. For instance, some of Sophia's clients encountered annoying delays in receiving the rented article, and reached out to Sophia's team to get help. At first, Sophia considered the article's owner fully responsible for delivery, as is the case with most peer-to-peer marketplaces. But renters kept contacting her when they could not reach the owners, and she personally spent hours following up delayed requests. At times, she had to pay for a priority delivery service or even perform the delivery herself! Clearly her customers considered timely delivery an essential part of her product, so she had to figure out a way to improve that part of the experience even though she had not originally planned for it. In other cases, the owners experienced theft or degradation of their items. In addition to creating disappointment in Lux For Rent, they also went through a cumbersome reimbursement process. Sophia had to seriously think about which capabilities to put in place to better protect the owners.

Kard, a neobank serving the 12 to 25 demographic, has done particularly well working on their whole product. Scott Gordon, their CEO, had the ambition of becoming the new banking standard and, in his own words, "a super cool, nice and fun product". They have succeeded in conquering the younger population. Scott shared how they did it at the MobileOne conference in 2019[16]: "Rather than creating a bank, we tried to create a brand. We talk very little about tech or our features, we talk more about a lifestyle, an experience, and belonging to a community."

If we apply the whole product concept to Kard, this is what it might look like:

---

16 Batch x Kard.eu - Conference @ MobileOne 2019:
https://tktq.link/build-to-sell/batch-kard-mobileone-2019

FIGURE 7. Example of a whole product: the Kard online bank targeting minors and young adults.

All the attributes of the product appearing in Fig. 7, which we also call experience enablers, are the result of strong and conscious choices that Scott and the Kard team have made over the years. They have designed a remarkable and consistent set of experiences for their customers and today are considered a leader in their market.

6.2 Understand the whole customer experience

The most important result of applying whole product logic is discovering which elements are necessary to build the best possible set of experiences for customers. To achieve this, we first need to understand the whole customer journey in a variety of different situations. With this information, we can build a product model that will help us improve the product globally in each takt cycle, one change at a time.

There are a number of techniques to perform this client discovery work: client gemba walks, Jobs To Be Done interviews, customer journey mapping, Live My Life, Consumption and Provision mapping, customer complaints analysis, and user behavior analytics, to name a few. We will present several of these techniques in Part 3.

Returning to the example of Kard, we can study the conversations between young clients and its customer service, as well as interview these clients directly. By doing so we can learn about and zoom in on their unique experience and problems linked to the generation gap. Going to the gemba taught the Kard team that some young people have difficulty convincing their parents to create a Kard account, which gave them the idea of creating a homepage and blog dedicated to parents.

Here are four practices to integrate into our everyday routines if we want to design great customer experiences:

1. Go regularly to the gemba to better understand the experiences our customers have in different real-life situations, instead of just relying on usage analytics.

2. Design the whole product, not just the core product or what we believe to be the core product.

3. Continuously analyze value throughout the customer journeys, through their different experiences. Do not just settle for adding new features to the product.

4. Set up a space for people to collect and analyze customer feedback every day as a team, to better understand what is really important to customers, instead of just following a roadmap.

Now ask yourself:
- What are the different experiences your customers go through with your product and your company?
- How would you describe your product using the "whole product" model?
- What elements of your whole product are not meeting customer expectations? How do you know? Where are you creating real value and where are you not?

FROM THE AGILE TEAM TO THE CHIEF PRODUCT ENGINEER'S TEAM

The world of high tech tends to disperse the responsibility of product design and development among several different people with specific skills and limited influence, an approach that creates insipid products. For instance, a typical agile team includes a Product Owner (PO), an Agile Coach, a Software Architect, a Technical Lead, developers, and sometimes an analyst when the PO is not familiar enough with the technology or the business domain. The myth is that by having all these roles in the team, and by following a structured delivery process, the final product will fulfill all requirements. If only everyone just did their job exactly as managers planned, everything would run smoothly, right? Clearly, it's not so simple. There is no guarantee that even an agile team will build products that please clients and help the company scale. As illustrated by our story about Mike the tech lead in Section 4.3, as soon as people start thinking about their job as just a role with specific responsibilities and boundaries, it encourages siloed thinking and creates conflicts. Even in agile teams or organizations that actively try to dismantle silos, similar challenges can emerge due to the division of labor or shortcomings in leadership and teamwork. This is the same kind of division that causes companies to negotiate and compromise on their product roadmap, to the detriment of customers.

To break this mindset, the most important thing is to make the customer the center of everyone's preoccupation throughout the design and development process. This customer-centric approach is personified by the **Chief Product Engineer**[17]. The Chief Product Engineer is not a role with limited responsibilities. They harmonize everyone's ideas, efforts and activities to create a cohesive whole product. They ensure that the different elements of the product and the project work together seamlessly, aligning them with overarching goals and customer needs. The Chief Product Engineer is pivotal in merging technical aspects, design elements, user experience and people's knowledge and ideas, to deliver a product that meets or exceeds expectations.

Assigning a Chief Product Engineer to lead the successful design and development of a great product has been a growing

---

17 We first described the Chief Product Engineer in the Introduction.

and effective practice in several industries, including high-tech firms. We can think of these people as "super Product Managers", with strong customer focus, vision and leadership. Unlike a traditional Product Manager or Project Manager, a Chief Product Engineer is not a delimited role. They take full responsibility for the product and will cross boundaries to make it succeed. They are not UX Designers, Product Owners, Product Managers, Agile Coaches, Technical Leads or Project Managers, although they will collaborate with all these experts and may contribute to their areas as needed. Three characteristics set them apart from the traditional leaders of an agile team: 1) Their passion for the client and the product is so profound that they consistently prioritize the customer's experience above all else, 2) they are responsible for the profit and loss of the product, and 3) they have no hierarchical authority over the product design and development teams.

7.1 What is a Chief Product Engineer?

The Chief Product Engineer is the one individual truly responsible for the product and its success. They know the product inside out and have a strong product vision. Just as importantly, they know how to surround themselves with experts who can turn the product vision into reality. They know how to select team members with the right mindset and build an effective, collaborative team to carry out the vision. They understand how to leverage technology for valuable outcomes, even if they don't have the deep technical expertise of the team's specialists. They don't have to be marketing and sales wizards, but they should understand the nuances of these fields and be adept at working with experts in these domains to guarantee their product's success. Primarily, they are *product crafters* with an engineering ethos: their mission is to conceive and construct a compelling product, harnessing the precision, expertise, and ingenuity of their entire team.

The dream of a Chief Product Engineer is to conceive products that people want to own and become attached to. They will put immense care into the finest detail, as long as they are convinced it will matter to the customer. For instance, we know the Chief Product Engineer of a highly successful banking app who spent a lot of effort on making the retrieval of the IBAN from a PDF file a no-brainer for users. Chief Product Engineers have such a deep understanding of customers' reality and of their product that they are able to sense what will trigger the right emotions.

The late Steve Jobs embodied the spirit of a Chief Product Engineer. Jobs was involved with most of the design of the first iPhone, and Tony Fadell, who inherited this mindset, relates the story of why they chose glass for the iPhone's screen[18] against all odds. During design reviews, Steve Jobs relentlessly pushed the engineering team: "We need glass instead of plastic for the iPhone screen!" he would say. Over and over, the engineers would explain that plastic was stronger than glass. If you dropped your phone, a glass screen would shatter. Jobs kept advocating for his point, but the team would not budge. Then, when they demoed

---

18 See Tony Fadell: iPhone, iPod, Nest, Steve Jobs, Design, and Engineering | Lex Fridman Podcast #294— https://tktq.link/build-to-sell/tony-fadell-steve-jobs

the iPhones at Macworld 2007, the team started to notice fine scratches on the plastic screens even though they were protected. Further, the reviewers were unpleasantly surprised by the choice of plastic. These clues reassured Jobs in his conviction that glass was the better choice.

But how to convince his engineers? In the end, Jobs decided to frame the question differently: "If we design it with plastic and it's in their pocket all the time and gets scratched by coins... that is a *design* problem. We need to *fix* it. That is our bad." Fadell quotes Jobs, "If they go off and drop it, or even slightly drop it, and it cracks, it's the customer's fault. And they'll have less likelihood to complain. Yes, they'll complain but they are part of that failure." The phone in their pocket is normal use; the phone dropping is abnormal use.

This explanation clicked with the engineers. The team understood that Job's request was coming from a deep understanding of the customer's point of view, and everyone pulled together to build a glass screen. Was it the right decision? This is still not clear, as from an engineering perspective there are clearly important trade-offs between glass and plastic: price, durability, weight, and so on. All we can say is that this design choice didn't stop people from buying iPhones! The point of this story, however, is to illustrate what being a Chief Product Engineer is all about: to be a visionary designer, to frame technical challenges in the customer's best interest, and to get the team of experts to work together in resolving tough product trade-offs.

Even though Steve Jobs is often thought of as the stereotype of a lone genius, he is just one of many Chief Product Engineers thriving outside of Toyota. In his book *Creativity, Inc.*[19], Ed Catmull explains how he built a team of passionate film directors, and how he was inspired by Toyota's lean approach. His product management philosophy seems to be similar to that of Sakichi Toyoda, the forefather of Toyota and inventor of the first intelligent loom in the late 1900s[20]. Catmull's retelling of the Pixar directors' desire to touch emotions, and how the story and technology of the film emerge from that fundamental concept, strongly evoke the stories of Toyota's Chief Engineers[21].

Aside from their vision and passion, Chief Product Engineers have two defining characteristics that make their contribution to the business very different from other product leads.

Firstly, they have full responsibility for the product's profit and loss. In other words, they have to meet sales expectations as well as the overall target margin and cost. This explains why we often say that they are the "CEO" of the product. Because they own the financial aspect of the product, the Chief Product Engineer prioritizes two critical elements in every design and development choice: customer satisfaction and profitability.

Herein lies the difference between a Chief Product Engineer and a typical head of product or Project Manager. The latter primarily seek customer satisfaction and/or timely delivery, while the global profit and loss (P&L) is managed by Finance or

---

19 Ed Catmull, Amy Wallace, Creativity, Inc. (The Expanded Edition): *Overcoming the Unseen Forces That Stand in the Way of True Inspiration* (Random House, 2023).

20 James P. Womack, Daniel T. Jones, Daniel Roos, *The Machine That Changed the World: The Story of Lean Production* (Free Press, 2007).

21 You may read more about the story of Toyota and their Chief Engineers in this article: https://tktq.link/build-to-sell/the-story-of-toyota-chief-engineers

Marketing independently of product activities. Because costs are generally not controlled during design and development, Finance may declare haphazard cost-cutting measures when P&L targets are not met. In short, separating the quality of the product from its profitability is not just illogical, it is a recipe for disaster.

Customer satisfaction and profitability form the cornerstone of successful and scalable products, with continuous learning serving as the secret, yet essential, ingredient.

Secondly, Chief Product Engineers usually have no formal authority over their product design and development team. Their experts usually come from different business and technical functions, and sometimes from external consulting firms. The Chief Product Engineer is the link between all of them. They cross all silos to form a cohesive team for the lifespan of a conception project. Given their lack of a hierarchical relationship with team members, the Chief Product Engineer must be persuasive. At Toyota, Chief Engineers are highly respected for their track record of success, collaborative abilities, and determination, which grants them significant influence. Ultimately, Chief Product Engineers cannot enforce their ideas on the team as a manager could. Some of their ideas are bound to be unreasonable, and the design and development team needs to feel free to push back. This is more difficult to do if the product lead is also the boss. On the other hand, a product created by a team that isn't fully invested in both the product and the Chief Engineer's vision (because they have a hierarchical relationship or other reason), will not achieve the same level of success. A strong product is the reflection of a strong Chief Product Engineer, one who has influence without hierarchical control.

While they are all innovators together, the team of experts tends to be more conservative than the Chief Product Engineer, sometimes with good reason. This is the yin and yang of product design. By removing any hierarchical connection between the Chief Product Engineer and the teams, we are able to keep a healthy balance between innovation and stability. In Chapter 15, we discuss this concept further.

It would seem that the Chief Product Engineer is given an impossible task. How can you build a product and motivate people to follow you without having authority? According to Jeff Liker and Jim Morgan in their fantastic book *Designing the Future*[22], a Chief Engineer at Toyota is considered a type of System Integrator: a person whose job it is to bring both people and technologies together to build a coherent and successful product. To achieve this level of collaboration and engagement, they need to develop exceptional leadership and communication skills. By leadership, we mean knowing how to get people to work and resolve problems together to achieve a shared result. By communication skills, we mean knowing how to do this in a way that is engaging and respectful. All the techniques presented in this book contribute to developing Chief Product

---

22 James M. Morgan, Jeffrey K. Liker, *Designing the Future: How Ford, Toyota, and Other World-Class Organizations Use Lean Product Development to Drive Innovation and Transform Their Business* (McGraw-Hill Education, 2018)

Engineers and improving their leadership skills. They must also learn to listen, seek win-win solutions, and make decisions when necessary without dampening people's motivation. In this footnote[23], we suggest two of our favorite books on these essential managerial skills.

7.2 Find and develop Chief Product Engineers

The people who make good Chief Product Engineers are often non-conformists and entrepreneurs by nature. They may be hard to spot within traditional organizations designed around delimited roles and processes, but they do exist. They are the ones who have a passion for the client, the product and the technologies, all at the same time. Even when their job is confined to just one area, they are unafraid to venture beyond these boundaries. They are the ones who spend a lot of their time looking for value creation opportunities and helping people resolve problems. They are curious people and innovators at heart.

They are not always where we expect to find them: their title may be Product Owner, Product Manager, Head of Product, CPO or Product Marketing specialist, but Technical Lead, Software Developer, and CTO should be considered just as likely. Startup founders are usually the first Chief Product Engineer in their company, despite having an organizational title such as CEO and authoritative power. After all, they conceived the company's first

---

23 Mark Goulston, *Just Listen: Discover the Secret to Getting Through to Absolutely Anyone* (AMACOM, 2015); and L. David Marquet, *Leadership Is Language: The Hidden Power of What You Say and What You Don't* (Portfolio Penguin, 2020)

products and services, and built a team with all the capabilities to deliver them. But when the company starts to grow, they will need to find and train new Chief Product Engineers to help grow the product line. This step is critical for the future of the business.

Whatever their official title, Chief Product Engineers are comfortable with both the client side and the technology side of a product. Because they have grown used to a delimited role, some candidates might not display these characteristics at first glance, but they will quickly reveal themselves when given the opportunity to expand their activity. The problem is that we often focus more on getting people to comply with their roles than on helping them grow! All we need to do to recognize them is start paying closer attention. For instance, consider a UX Designer or an Agile Coach who naturally gets involved in the team's technical discussions, provides useful insights, and seeks to understand the product technologies. Similarly, a good candidate could be a tech lead or developer who is empathetic to users, likes to resolve their problems, and cares about their feedback. In addition, these people usually have a growth mindset, meaning that they are eager to explore different solutions and challenge the status quo. These are the types of people whom we can train as Chief Product Engineers. You are probably already thinking about who in your organization fits the profile. This is a very good start.

As a CTO, Flavian introduced the tools presented in this book to the software engineering team. One person picked up the customer analysis board[24] and ran with it, conducting mul-

---

24 See Chapter 11 for an example of this technique.

tiple client observation sessions that brought a brand-new perspective on the company's main product. Seeing that leadership, the CEO proposed that she take the lead on a small product as a way to test her ability. Before long, this software engineer emerged as a promising Chief Product Engineer in training.

To find the next Chief Product Engineer, we need to seek the qualities of a Toyota-like Chief Engineer among existing teams without being influenced by their current role in the organization. We can put them to the test gradually, by introducing them to the practices and tools in this book. Junior product engineers can be developed into Chief Product Engineers by tackling simple projects under the guidance of a mentor, much like in an apprenticeship. Establishing a product takt also introduces a natural rhythm for identifying and nurturing new Chief Product Engineers, since each cycle offers a new chance for junior product engineers to show their mettle. They get to practice going to the client gemba, coming up with a new concept, building a convincing business case, collaborating with all the functional and technical experts to build a quality product, and so on.

To summarize, when looking for our Chief Product Engineers, we need to be open to candidates who display the right qualities without being influenced by their current title or role in the organization. Ultimately, finding and developing Chief Product Engineers is more art than science. Any member of an agile team could become one. It is about giving the chance to everyone with the right mindset and passion, and then developing the most promising candidates.

7.3 The Chief Product Engineer's main tools

The Chief Product Engineer's primary challenges include 1) crafting a compelling vision and business case for their next product that garners widespread support and 2) assembling a team of experts to transform that vision into a successful product, while ensuring effective collaboration among them. Lean proposes two key tools to help in this endeavor: the concept paper and the obeya.

The **concept paper** is a concise two- to six-page document, rich in insights and visuals, that outlines the next breakthrough product idea. It is written during the discovery phase of the product innovation cycle. As opposed to creating a laundry list of features to develop then push onto the market, the concept paper forces the Chief Product Engineer and the design team to describe an innovative *solution* to an existing problem faced by customers, and make a convincing business case for developing, marketing and selling this solution. The concept paper is a great way to engage people around a product vision and make better product bets as a company. We describe it at length in Chapter 15.

The **obeya** is a dedicated physical or virtual space designed to intensify collaboration among individuals and systems. It's where the product team congregates to identify and address potential challenges arising from conflicting or high-risk product changes. Typically used during the design and development stages—after the Chief Product Engineer has received endorsement on their concept and strategy from essential stakeholders—obeyas are instrumental in establishing a conducive environment for successful outcomes. Rooted in visual management principles, an obeya highlights the most important problems needing attention and enhances teamwork to speed up decision-making. An obeya has no fixed design, no prescription for success. Any restriction on its structure or content would defeat the purpose. Each Chief Product Engineer builds an obeya according to their needs and the circumstances of the moment, starting from a few basic principles. Nonetheless, there are three key characteristics that every obeya should have:

- At a glance, we can determine if we are fulfilling our promise to customers by examining the key quality characteristics of the product, not just through adherence to a plan

- The product is the focal point, occupying a substantial area of the room and showcasing the conflicts and design trade-offs between various components, as well as how the team is addressing them

- The obeya is a dynamic space, not pristine and pretty. It is a space for the team to reflect and resolve technical trade-offs to meet the next challenge.

Our next book in this series, *Build To Scale*, will delve deeply into obeyas and how Chief Product Engineers use them to involve all experts in building scalable products from their concept papers. In the current book, our focus is on the discovery phase and conceiving a viable product strategy, as summarized in the concept paper.

Now ask yourself:

- Who in your organization embodies some of the characteristics of a Chief Product Engineer, including yourself?

- What issues or problems are your product and tech teams struggling with most?

- What is the next problem you need to resolve for your customer? How do you know that this is the most important one to solve now?

CHAPTER
8

DEVELOP PEOPLE BEFORE MAKING PRODUCTS

So you've made it! You have conceived a superb product that is getting some traction. To handle the increasing demand, you start to build new capabilities: recruiting fast, defining procedures and roles, building new processes, and maybe also looking for funding because sales are too low to pay for all this growth. But after the honeymoon period is over (usually just one to three years), waste starts creeping in and people can no longer keep up with the demanding pace. Compared to the heady early years, it takes twice as long to deliver anything, people burn out and leave, quality becomes optional, and sales are slowing as customer interest turns toward the new kids on the block. At this point, the knee-jerk reaction of management (often under investor pressure) is predictable: add even more controls, define more processes, fire and hire, and replace the leaders. By "fire and hire" we mean cutting costs by letting go of more experienced employees and bringing in less experienced employees with specific skills. Such corrective measures are very traumatic for a business, yet we have seen them implemented over and over.

The key to building irresistible products that sell and support company growth is not to be found in cost-cutting or designing perfect processes and organizations. The life of a company is not so straightforward: the market changes faster than we think, disruptive technologies can appear overnight, and processes start to become obsolete almost as soon as they are written down. Plus, people are not machines: you can't just plug them into a matrix and expect everything to work smoothly if they follow the process as designed. As counterintuitive as it may sound, *the key to building great products and companies is to develop people's knowledge and sharpen their thinking, starting with ourselves.* Only then can we build an organization that is ready to meet all the challenges a startup will face.

8.1 Good products come from good thinking

Lean is based on a simple yet powerful idea: good products come from good thinking. The problems we described in the previous chapters are very common among new firms trying to find a market fit and scale. An early-stage company goes through two phases. The first is to conceive and build a product that gets traction: the startup stage. The second is to scale the product and organization into a thriving and sustainable company: the scaleup phase. Scaling means increasing revenues exponentially without incurring significant costs.

Conceiving a great product that gets traction is always somewhat of a gamble. But we believe that startup founders can improve their odds substantially if they start by finding a real problem to resolve and then come up with an innovative solution—*in that order.* This book provides tips and tools that can help new entrepreneurs and intrapreneurs find the right client problem more efficiently, conceive an attractive and cost-effective solution, validate their idea before putting all their money on the line, and better prepare themselves to scale later on. The price of admission to the scaleup world is high, and few startups make it that far. This book goes beyond merely finding a market fit; it concentrates on preparing for and successfully navigating the scaleup phase.

We want to keep the initial enthusiasm going for as long as possible. Jeff Bezos refers to this enduring mindset as "Day One". When we start a business, creative ideas are popping up everywhere, and we spend all our energy thinking about how to test them and resolve problems. As sales begin to surge, the informal and flexible approaches often used in early stages no longer suffice. This growth requires a more structured approach to manage the increasing demand and complexity, ensuring that the business can sustain and build upon its success. This is where we start making mistakes.

In response to growing demand, new processes and rules are implemented, compelling team members to adapt. This shift, perceived as necessary to maintain order, can lead to discomfort among early employees. Often, those who were part of the initial journey depart, feeling constrained by the new rigidity. So we bring in people who prefer structure and follow rules. This is when we start to feel like a "big company", where there is less creativity and innovation. The focus shifts from innovation to compliance, leading to a gradual slowing of the company's momentum, although this effect might not be immediately apparent.

The problem with processes is that the environment is always changing too fast for them to create value on their own. Almost as soon as a process is created, it no longer reflects reality and grows more and more difficult to apply in the field. This is a catch-22. Processes are designed to face known problems and situations, but every day people face a myriad of unplanned problems and situations. Staff are expected to comply with existing processes and follow the rules, not to improvise, so they are not armed to resolve new problems. In fact, they forget how to think for themselves when confronted with a new problem. To break this cycle, we need to teach people to make better decisions on their own as they run into new problems every day, and give them the tools and power to *change processes as they see fit.* This is the true agility companies need to grow and stay healthy.

Building great products means teaching everyone in the company to build great products, not just a few specialized people.

Everyone in a company works to build and service the products. Can you imagine a company where everyone is engaged in finding innovative ways to do their own job, every day? We need to provide the framework and capabilities for everyone to think and be creative, as we were during the startup phase, if we want to create a solid foundation for scaling.

Let's consider a real-life example: JB is the former founder and CEO of a highly successful insurtech. He proudly designed his company's organization and processes with the help of his initial team, and was adamant about people complying. For instance, he wanted to reduce direct contact with customers, as he believed that a high-quality, fully digital service should not need to provide too much human-based assistance. Therefore, he set a goal to reduce the number of direct interactions with customers to a minimum. What he didn't expect were the strange behaviors this rule would create in the organization as demand for their products increased.

Challenged by Sandrine, his lean *sensei*[25], JB agreed to start a routine of reviewing several customer support tickets to better understand their customers' needs and the value they created for them. One customer had sent an email to complain that she couldn't complete her online transaction. She provided all of the necessary information in her email, hoping that someone would call to help her complete the purchase, or even do it for her. When JB and his Customer Support Manager read the email history together, they realized that her request had not been handled in an ideal way by the agent in charge. The problem is that the customer never followed through with her purchase. This single lost

---

25 "Sensei is not a title you can take for yourself. It is given to you as a sign of respect from the people who want to learn from you because they recognize your mastery, such as it is." Learn more in the book "The Lean Sensei" co-authored by Michael Ballé, et al.

sale amounted to several hundred pounds. This may seem like a drop in the bucket for a business generating millions in sales, but the impact is much bigger than one might think. Where one customer speaks up, dozens of others remain silent and simply walk away in frustration. The Customer Support Manager tried to contact this customer by phone to apologize for the trouble, but she never responded. He realized that not only would this customer never come back, but she might also have become an active detractor of the brand.

To evaluate the extent of the problem, they looked for similar support tickets. JB was surprised to find out that five more customers had experienced a similar problem that same morning. JB's frustration stemmed from the fact that each complaint had been handled differently, yet none had resulted in any purchases. So, within just one day, they estimated a potential loss of several thousand pounds in sales, probably leaving numerous dissatisfied customers who chose not to voice their complaints.

These findings led JB to conduct experiments with the customer support team, to ensure that every sale was closed and every customer was fully happy. For example, one Customer Support Agent decided to ask a customer who couldn't complete their transaction if they would like to be called back and if so to provide their phone number in an email. Within a couple of minutes, the customer responded accepting the help. The agent called them immediately and took it upon himself to offer them a discount as he helped them complete the transaction. In the end, the customer decided to purchase more services and showed their gratitude by sending a thank you message to the agent. Based on Brian Chesky's theory[26], this happy customer will bring in ten new customers.

The agent who closed the sale so brilliantly over the phone had never before felt empowered to take this type of initiative because they were encouraged to limit direct interactions with customers. When he set this goal, JB's assumption was that more phone calls was evidence that the digital application was not providing customers with the expected value and autonomy, which defeated the purpose of having a digital business in the first place. Although it is true that support calls are often an indicator of non-quality in the digital product, the rule created unexpected behaviors from employees—such as avoiding calling a customer who runs into problems. The way the team interpreted JB's goal was to hold conversations mainly over email until some countermeasure was found or until the customer stopped responding. After an agreed upon number of email interactions, the ticket would be closed even if no solution had been found to help the customer. In the end, JB changed the team's orientation by framing the goal in more customer-oriented terms: every customer who comes to the site to purchase their services must succeed and be fully satisfied. This new orientation gave Customer Support Agents the authority and space to propose innovative ideas to serve each customer and improve underlying processes with every new problem they had to face. JB also made repairing bugs on the application the number one priority of the Product and Tech teams, which gave the Customer Support

---

26 Listen to Brian Chesky's interview by Roxanne Varza at Station F incubator:
https://tktq.link/build-to-sell/station-featuring-brian-chesky-cofounder-airbnb

Team a new voice in the company. They had been frustrated in the past because the customer issues they highlighted weren't sufficiently addressed by the product/development team. As a result of these and other improvement actions, sales increased by 40% over the following seven months[27].

From a lean perspective, a product mirrors the skills and thought processes of those who design, construct, and maintain it, as well as their capacity to make the right decisions at the right moment. We develop our own skills by sharpening our thinking, and we sharpen our thinking by resolving difficult problems with other people. *Make people before you make products*, the lean mantra goes.

The goal of lean is to empower everyone to solve problems constantly and everywhere, but guided by a unified purpose: to make better and more profitable products. Because in the end, the enterprise exists with the same intention: to build and sell marvelous products and services that change people's lives.

When everyone in the organization learns to spot and face problems that impact customers, in a creative manner, it achieves two benefits:

1. It develops their skills so they become better and better at their job and at "making things:" it teaches them to think independently, identify flawed processes, and make appropriate adjustments as needed.

2. It makes tough production and delivery problems more obvious, which in turn helps product engineers be more

27 Read JB's article on Planet Lean where he tells his story:
https://tktq.link/build-to-sell/lean-quality-improvement

confident about the issues they need to tackle first. The host of local problems and waste they would otherwise be submerged in are now mostly taken care of by other workers in the company, all along the product value flow. This is why a Chief Product Engineer is not only responsible for conceiving the end product for customers but also how it is going to be built, maintained, delivered, and serviced.

To develop people's thinking, we must shape the whole organization for learning about value.

The main job of someone conceiving a product is to:

- understand clearly and deeply what value means for *each* customer,

- learn how to improve value and keep products and services interesting before they are surpassed by the competition, and

- actively seek places where the enterprise is not creating value anywhere along the product flow, encompassing all forms of waste like defects, rework, redundant tasks, and so forth.

This continuous and thorough value analysis and engineering effort is needed in order to make informed decisions about what to change next in the products and services.

8.2 The Thinking People System

Lean proposes a concrete model for shaping an organization where value and waste are readily visible, creating an environment where people are constantly resolving problems together and learning together. This organizational blueprint helps Chief Product Engineers access crucial information to address the previously mentioned three activities, rather than relying on guesswork. Fundamentally, a business revolves around its products and services, and its success depends on how much people want to buy them. So it makes perfect sense that the whole company be "engineered" for the sole purpose of making its products and services better and better.

A lean organization is one in which every person is constantly looking for smart ways to create value by removing waste in the way they do things. The waste we generate inevitably affects the customer, influencing their experience and the price of the product. This happens everywhere in the company, not just in the Quality or Support departments. The business model used to shape an organization that fully supports Chief Product Engineers in the hard task of conceiving valuable and profitable products is called TPS, the **Thinking People System**[28].

---

28 We suggest the following articles to learn more about TPS:
https://tktq.link/build-to-sell/now-is-the-time-for-resilience-and-adaptability
https://tktq.link/build-to-sell/tps-the-thinking-people-system

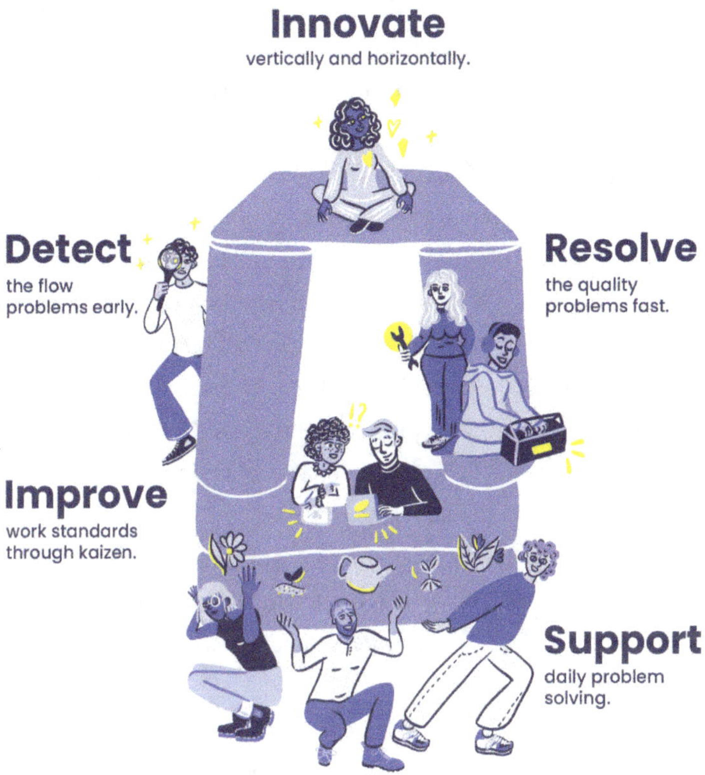

FIGURE 8. TPS, the Thinking People System.

Each part of this model offers techniques and tools to help spot problems and improve people's thinking and skills. The detailed description of this model is beyond the scope of this book, although we are applying several of its key ideas here. If you would like to learn more about TPS, a great starting point is *The Lean Strategy* by Michael Ballé et al.

TPS is highly strategic for a company, because Operations (where we build, package, ship, maintain, sell, and service our products) always reflect the poor product decisions we make, day in and day out. The areas where customers and people involved in Operations run into difficulties show us where we have introduced waste in the product and service designs. It is only fair that we, as product artisans, should spend a lot of our time on the gemba in our own company looking for these problems and using this information to improve products and services. Think about it for a moment: how many times in the last month have you personally gone to visit the help desk, or other services involved in building, stocking, delivering, maintaining, selling, or servicing your product? Have you discussed the concrete problems people in these departments and customers are facing? When was the last time you observed your own customers as they tried to resolve their problems using your products? *Our job is to learn from the visible (and invisible) problems at the gemba and eliminate waste in both the product and its design and development processes.*

The biggest sources of waste are introduced during conception, but they become most visible once the product is in production or in the customer's hands. This is true whether teams follow one-week sprints or 3-month release cycles, but identifying (and fixing) problems is simpler with smaller work segments. However, we often neglect to invest sufficient upfront effort in improving value throughout the entire product flow, leading to a myriad of issues down the line.

By making waste visible along the product flow with TPS, we can quickly identify the impact of our poor design decisions. Chief Product Engineers are tasked with creating exceptional client experiences from start to finish, all while minimizing costs. This means ensuring that the product not only meets customer needs but also can be efficiently produced, supported, maintained, and modified by company staff and partners. To make a real difference, we must seek opportunities for value improvement throughout the entire design, production, delivery, and consumption flows. The operational and design/engineering processes are interconnected and should be viewed as two sides of the same coin. The Thinking People System, applied in operations and production, and lean engineering, practiced in product design and development (the focus of this book), work hand in hand to enhance value across the organization, all the way to the customer. To fully harness the benefits of lean, we must utilize both systems simultaneously.

There are three main types of waste that we introduce in design and development:

- The first, worst of all, is a product that doesn't satisfy customers.

- The second is a product that is too expensive to build and maintain, and therefore less profitable.

- The third is that development doesn't go well, mainly due to quality issues and a lack of collaboration between the various contributors along the product flow.

FIGURE 9. Three types of waste in product design and development.

In order to avoid the first form of waste, we must learn to deeply understand the real customer problem or need, and the technical trade-offs to resolve in the product, before we start talking about which features to develop or technologies to change.

In order to avoid the second form of waste, we must adopt a radical quality approach and learn to continuously improve value along the product flow.

In order to avoid the third form of waste, we must appoint a Chief Product Engineer who will rally people around their concept, and create an environment where they can collaborate and build knowledge in a safe way.

The goal from the outset is to avoid introducing these wastes in our products and services, and as product designers we need to learn to do this better. Lean product design and development practices and tools teach us to continuously improve value to reduce waste. This means:

- **Improving the value that our products bring to the customer.** Does the customer think that the product is solving the right problem? Is it easy to use or cumbersome? Is it a good deal? Does it make customers want to use it over and over? Is it in line with current trends?

- **Improving the value created throughout the process of product design, development, and distribution.** Is it easy to recognize and reduce waste at every stage? Where are we creating value? Where are we destroying value? What can we do to improve value without increasing costs? Waste is often created involuntarily, due to our own misconceptions or lack of understanding about how things and people work.

- **Improving value for employees.** Is the product beneficial to everyone? In other words, do people feel concerned about the value they create and the company's objectives, and do they actively participate in the project?

- **Improving the value created for society.** Do the product, its manufacturing, and its distribution effectively address current and future challenges of society, such as the environment, equal opportunities at work, employment, safety, and security?

Now ask yourself:

- Do all your customers say that your product is solving the right problem for them?
- Is your product in line with current trends?
- Do you know where your processes generate waste?
- How do you involve people in your organization in improving value along the product value flow?

**PART
3**

TRAVELING INTO YOUR CUSTOMERS' MINDS

art 2 gave the keys to building the foundations of a lasting product mindset within the business: set product *takt* times, design the *whole* product, and develop *Chief Product Engineers*. Now let's dive into several of the specific practices that a Chief Product Engineer uses to *build great products that sell*. Building a convincing case for a new product concept starts with the following activities:

- **"Start with why."** What problem are we solving for our customers? What superpower will we provide them with? While it is tempting to start with an idea, a sales goal, or a desire to try out new technologies, coming back to the "why" always reconnects us with our customers. It is crucial to do so, because their needs and wants are changing all the time as new players join the market and set new trends.

- **Experience your customers' world.** It is not enough to look at what the competition is doing, analyze data (however complex), or imagine in isolation what the product will look like. Instead, let's immerse ourselves in the customer's world. We need to gather deep insights into their life habits, their environment, their emotions, how they are really using our products, and what makes them *not* use our products.

- **Build a client model** that will guide our design decisions over the next change cycles. The client model identifies and evaluates the key customer preferences: i.e., their main criteria for choosing our product. The client model is our north star for balancing technology trade-offs in the design to ensure that all key preferences are respected and we find opportunities to surpass expectations. The client model also allows us to compare our product to competing solutions so that we can more easily spot where we need to improve.

In Part 3, we delve into various activities central to lean product design and development. We introduce tools that enable you to deeply immerse yourself in the world and mindset of your customers (and non-customers), empowering you to uncover your next big idea.

PICK THE *RIGHT* CUSTOMER PROBLEM

Let's dive into a story to understand what we're talking about. This story is inspired by actual events, but names and identifying details have been changed to protect the privacy of those involved.

A few years ago, Lila's design team started working on an app to help nurses treat and follow up patients with wounds. She knew that to build a great product, it was important to meet with nurses to understand their needs and problems. The product's sponsor, Product Owner, Product Manager and Lead Designer spent months interviewing nurses to understand what was important when treating a wound, and showing them different prototypes. These learnings allowed them to create the first version of the app. This minimal viable product (MVP) allowed nurses to take pictures of the wound and guided them through a series of questions to evaluate its severity.

The MVP was well received by the first population of nurses to learn about it. However, even with time, the user population did not grow, and some of the early adopters even stopped using the app. Lila decided to conduct another discovery phase with the team. This time, she decided to go to the client gemba instead of just conducting interviews.

Going to the gemba means going to see clients (here nurses and patients) in their own environment: wherever they use our product or try to resolve the problem our product is supposed to address. What is tricky with gemba walks (the act of going to the gemba) is to see through the noise of day-to-day activity and spot what is really important. This requires knowing how to listen and see—and sometimes smell, feel or taste—without judgment. It also requires having a model for recognizing wasteful and tedious tasks and movements that customers do when resolving their problem, with or without our products.

Over the course of a month, the Product Manager, Product Owner, and sponsor spent several days accompanying nurses on their rounds. The first difficulty that Lila ran into was convincing some nurses to let her accompany them on patient visits. Contacting the nurses directly met with no success. But the Product Owner had a good relationship with some customer success representatives who were very close to the nurses. He managed to convince them to put in a good word. Finally, five nurses agreed to let a team member come with them. As it turned out, that was more than enough to get a good idea of the nurses' day-to-day life and constraints. Knowing how to find the right people to talk to is key, especially when clients are not easily reachable or observable.

What Lila observed was intriguing. Observing the nurses on their rounds highlighted how the product struggled to fit into their everyday routines. They discovered needs and opportunities that they had not envisioned, and that never came up during interviews. To give just one example, one of the nurses was constantly using her phone. She would ask the phone's voice assistant to bring up a patient's profile several times: once to confirm the address, again to retrieve the apartment building code, and so on. She also asked Lila more than once "How many patients have we seen already?" You cannot find this type of precious information about user behaviors and circumstances in surveys or interviews.

Here are some other important discoveries that Lila and the team made during the gemba walks.

Generally speaking, nurses have a strong oral culture: few of them take notes in the patient's home, as they prefer to spend their time caring for the patient. They prefer not to spend much time on their phones while at the patient's bedside, only taking them out briefly to capture a picture of the wound. To expedite this process, they utilize the quickest method available: without unlocking their phone, they swipe, take a picture, and promptly return the phone to their pocket.

Also, they like to talk with other nurses and medical professionals, to share information and advice. But more importantly, because their job is tough and lonely, they need to interact with their peers. These nurses care for people who are elderly and unwell, or who have serious wounds that sometimes lead to severe outcomes such as amputation or death. They need to alleviate their stress with human interactions. Having an oral culture also means that nurses need to remember things. They hold an impressive amount of information in their head, and are quite capable of recalling specific medical information whenever needed. One of the nurses whom Lila accompanied looked at her notebook *only once* in a seven-hour round (roughly twenty patients)! When she met with her colleague in the middle of the day, they were able to share medical information without even mentioning their patients' names or looking up their profiles.

This oral tradition, coupled with their remarkable ability to recall patient details, is very effective when an independent nurse works with patients whom they see regularly. However, challenges arise when the same patient is attended to by multiple caregivers, such as nurses rotating shifts at a hospital. This situation creates a new need for seamless communication among the nursing staff, despite their busy schedules. For instance, during Lila's tour, she observed her nurse attempting to schedule a coffee meeting with a colleague, which took them over three hours to coordinate due to conflicting schedules. Hence, there exists a tangible dilemma between the imperative for efficient and precise sharing of medical data, and the nurses' reliance on oral communication. This presents a significant challenge to the proposed product: how to align a phone app with these conflicting needs?

Upon returning from the gemba, Lila resumed work on her product. One thing that immediately caught her attention was the number of steps needed to add a photo to the application. It involved unlocking the phone, opening the app, logging in, searching for the patient, clicking on "add photo", capturing the image, and finally saving it—seven steps in total. In contrast, nurses in the field accomplished this task in just two steps: a swipe and a click. It's hard to compete with that!

Reflecting on our observations from the gemba, it becomes apparent how this could pose a significant obstacle for many nurses, disrupting patient care with numerous steps and clicks. To extend their assistance to more nurses, Lila and the team realized that they needed to understand and address a different problem. They thought that the major purpose of the app was to record wound treatments: first, so that nurses would not have to hold all this information in their head; and second, so they could easily share it with other medical staff and Social Security. Don't misunderstand; nurses do genuinely need to document wound assessments for regulatory purposes. Through fieldwork, they realized that nurses are adept at retaining information mentally. But in order to facilitate sharing their assessments and treatment with their peers and other medical staff, the design team needed to find a way for nurses to input data into the app without disrupting the care provided by the nurse to their patient.

It took walking the client gemba with a strong sense of cognitive empathy and a deliberate quest for the unknown to uncover the real problem to resolve. Section 11.4 discusses gemba walks and cognitive empathy in more detail.

Now ask yourself:

- What problem does your product or service aim to solve?

- Based on the lifestyles and habits of your customers that you have observed, why do you believe this is the right problem to address?

- When was the last time you discovered something new and unexpected about your users or customers? How was it different from your preconception?

CHAPTER 10

IMPROVE THE "JOB TO BE DONE"

product is a solution to a problem encountered by many people. In the lean sense, a problem is a gap between what someone tries to achieve and how they manage to do it now, using existing solutions.

In his book *Competing Against Luck*, Clayton Christensen uses the term **Job To Be Done** to describe what people try to achieve with specific solutions. A person "hires" a solution or service to accomplish a "job" in specific circumstances. In doing so, they are facing specific social, emotional and functional complexities that influence their choice of solution. Christensen gives the enlightening example of a fast-food chain hoping to sell more milkshakes. After asking customers about their favorite flavors and what types of improvements or new products they'd like to have, they released new flavors that were a total flop. To understand why, they went to the gemba asking different types of questions, ones that probed into the circumstances and complexities influencing people's decision to buy a milkshake. Surprisingly, they discovered that the "job" that pushed people to "hire" their milkshakes had nothing to do with variety of choice. Rather, it was to stay awake during their long morning commute and remain satiated to avoid the mid-morning craving. The types of products they conceived after this study were markedly different.

The theory of Jobs To Be Done highlights the need to understand what progress a consumer is trying to make in specific circumstances, if we want to truly grasp the problem they aim to solve. A Job To Be Done comprises three elements:

- **Progress.** The goal or aspiration the customer aims to achieve, framed as an action.

- **Circumstance.** The specific context or situation in which the customer seeks progress. Useful questions include: Where and when is this taking place? Who is present? What activities are being done concurrently? What preceded and will follow this activity? What are their life, family, and financial statuses?

- **Functional, Social, and Emotional Complexity.** The challenges and considerations the customer must navigate to make progress.

Addressing these questions allows companies to pinpoint their customers' Jobs to Be Done and develop more effective products and services. This approach offers a deeper and more nuanced view than traditional approaches such as market segmentation.

Companies will have a better chance of hitting the target if they conceive products around Jobs To Be Done, framed by the specific circumstances of real customers, rather than the "preferences" of hypothetical or abstracted personae. In the milkshake example, it is practically impossible to condense the market into a single representative persona. The Job To Be Done, however, is very concrete and useful for defining the product concept. The job is to keep a customer entertained and satiated during a lengthy commute. We can say that one job corresponds to one customer segment.

It is also much easier to identify and understand competing solutions if we look at the Job To Be Done rather than personae, features or technologies. In fact, it completely redefines the competitive landscape. For example, Facebook competes with calling a friend or relative on the phone for one obvious job (staying in touch), but also competes with cigarettes for another job (short and rewarding breaks from work). Netflix competes with any extended activity that we do to relax after work, like playing a video game or enjoying a drink with friends. The commuters' milkshake competes with eating a muffin, but also with non-food options such as listening to an audiobook.

Once we understand the Job To Be Done that people want to achieve, the next task is to see if existing solutions already do the job well. This is not a one-time activity. Teresa Torres, in her book *Continuous Discovery Habits*, emphasizes that the success of a product rests on continuous customer research to better understand their changing desires and needs. New products emerge every day, and often they address some problems that current solutions have not yet been able to resolve.

> ## We need to be constantly aware of what customers like and dislike about today's solutions, and also the reasons for their preferences.

In the case of the milkshake, in addition to obvious criteria like flavor and price, the *consistency* of the beverage also contributes to the job fulfillment. If the milkshake is too liquid, the customer swallows it more quickly, so the experience doesn't last through the whole commute and they are less satiated when they arrive. Understanding this preference, a new milkshake concept might include chocolate chips or fruit pieces to make the activity longer and more entertaining, as well as adding a more filling ingredient to prevent mid-morning snacking. Without clearly defining the purpose of the product, we take the risk of resolving the wrong problem or introducing innovations that fall flat. Our goal, as product conceptors, is to find innovative ways of solving the current customer's problems better. This is what we mean by improving the Job to Be Done.

Turn back the clock to 2010: you are dining out with friends in an isolated neighborhood, and you don't have your own car. How will you get home? Your choices are: (1) call a taxi and wait a long time for it to arrive, (2) ask one of your friends to go far out of their way to give you a ride home, or (3) walk to a busier neighborhood with more traffic and public transportation options. All three are time-consuming and inconvenient. This Job To Be Done—getting a convenient ride from almost anywhere—is the need that Uber chose to fill. The bigger the need, and the more widespread the problem, the more likely it is that people will adopt a new solution.

Building a great product consists first and foremost of resolving an *existing* problem. However exciting it may be, imagining solutions for tomorrow's problems is quite risky and many startups break their teeth on solving a "problem" that only they can see. This is because people naturally resist change unless they see an immediate benefit. *The trick is to find innovative ways to resolve today's problems, but better than everyone else.*

Sometimes we are confident that we are resolving a known problem, but our product does not generate the expected level of enthusiasm and adoption is low. When this happens, the problem may be real but not as widespread or painful as we thought in terms of our customers' Jobs to be Done. However, it is not enough to rely on our own assumptions about what constitutes a good problem to address and on market analysis data. In the next sections, we make the case that choosing a valuable problem to solve requires knowing where and how to look for it effectively.

Now ask yourself:
- What existing problem is your product aiming to resolve?
- How is your product resolving this problem better than existing solutions in an innovative way?
- How would you formulate the Job To Be Done of your customers? Do you have more than one?

STAY ROOTED IN YOUR CUSTOMER'S REALITY

In this section, we propose several techniques for immersing yourselves in the customers' world and finding good problems to solve. All of them will force you to think outside the box and not to let your own cognitive biases influence you. This is a very important aspect of customer research, because we all find it much easier to recognize what we already know (or are already convinced of) than to perceive the unexpected or experience reality from someone else's perspective. Generally, humans are just not very good at spotting realities different from our own. We tend to rationalize and find justifications for our own beliefs. Under these conditions, how can we conduct objective and realistic customer discovery? We will answer this question by providing several real-life examples and practical tools to understand and evaluate problems from your customers' point of view. We will:

- Learn to bypass our own misconceptions

- See how to earn clients' trust and loyalty

- Analyze customer complaints

- Go to the client gemba

- Practice "live my life"

- Conduct regular "Jobs To Be Done" interviews

- Map out the customer experience

11.1 Bypass your own misconceptions

The client gemba seems an obvious place to start, and visiting your customers is just common sense. Ask any product team what techniques they use to understand the customer, and they will surely have plenty of data at their fingertips from survey forms, interviews, or customer journey maps. But it is uncommon for them to spend time observing customers at their place of work, or trying to reproduce the circumstances where customers will buy and use the product.

Of course, going to the gemba is more difficult than conducting surveys and interviews, and for some types of products the gemba might be hard to access. Another reason that product specialists might avoid going to the gemba is that they do not know how to behave, or are unsure that they can see what is really important. Going to the gemba is a skill to be learned like any other. Knowing how to use all our senses to pick up on our customers' feelings, both negative and positive, takes practice. But it is the only surefire way to identify problems that are real game-changers.

Whatever techniques we use to understand our customers, jumping to conclusions is a universal tendency that we all need to overcome. We cannot allow ourselves to change the product based on the first data to come in, or on the data that is easiest to obtain. The risk of falling prey to our own preconceptions and biases is too great. We *must* always ask ourselves if our understanding of the problem to be solved is really the same as our customers'. Skipping this step results in half-baked product concepts that either 1) don't hit the "sweet spot" or 2) are too expensive to build and scale.

This is exactly what happened with Lila and the team, who developed the mobile app for nurses described in Chapter 9. The design team did six months of customer discovery using popular UX tools. Then developers worked for two years on the mobile application. They applied agile methods and regularly tested features with a few client representatives and users. The app worked as advertised, but it did not generate enough retention to make the investment worthwhile. They had to start the discovery process all over again, and learn to see, listen and care about the customers in their real circumstances in order to figure out ways to touch their emotions.

During their first discovery phase, Lila's designers experienced a common cognitive bias called **confirmation bias**, which influences how human beings process information. Peter

Cathcart Wason, a cognitive psychologist, described this bias as "people's tendency to favor information that validates their preconceptions or hypotheses and personal beliefs, regardless of whether they are true or not." Fig 12 illustrates this problem—unless we are aware of this bias and actively resist it, we are perfectly capable of ignoring a vast amount of information that contradicts our preconceptions!

FIGURE 10. Confirmation bias prevents us from noticing evidence that contradicts our own preconceptions, and from recognizing that our customer's perspective is as valid as our own.

Once we are on the gemba, confirmation bias narrows our focus, prevents us from asking the right questions, and seeing real behaviors. Going to the gemba will not be productive if we already know what we want to see and hear. There are several theories on how to minimize the effects of confirmation bias, starting with developing our critical thinking skills. However, critical thinking is something we usually apply after the fact, when we need to analyze or interpret data. On the gemba, the goal is to be receptive and observant, without interpretation. First and foremost, we need to learn to see and listen as objectively as possible. In some cases, we also need to learn to smell, touch and taste to get a real feel for a situation. This is not an easy task but with continuous practice, we get better. When we really focus on the customer, see what they are doing, listen to what they are saying and tune into their emotions, their pain points and frustrations become obvious. This is what gives us insight into the real problems that a new product could solve.

> **Resisting confirmation bias requires forgetting yourself entirely and considering the person you are interacting with as the most important person in the world.**

There are several other types of biases that cloud our judgment and lead to inaccurate observations:

- The **halo effect**, where our overall impression of a situation or person influences our judgment. For example, we more often accept unsupported statements from people whom we admire and respect.

- The **contrast effect**, where our perception is distorted based on recent similar observations. For example, a three-day resolution window for customer complaints might seem short if the team regularly talks about their planning and indicators over much longer periods.

- The **anchoring bias**, where we are overly influenced by the first piece of information we encounter in a new context, such as the original price of a product compared to its discounted price during a sale.

- The **recency bias**, where our judgment is swayed by the most recent information we encountered.

- The **sampling bias**, when we assume that a sample accurately represents the population being studied. For example, we might interview a few users near at hand, then decide that we have collected enough information.

There are many, many more. If you are interested in exploring this subject further, Daniel Kahneman's book *Thinking Fast and Slow* is an approachable and fascinating introduction to cognitive biases through the lens of behavioral economics. However, in our experience confirmation bias tends to obscure our perceptions more than any other, and overcoming it is a lifelong challenge.

So as you read about the gemba activities below, don't let your own confirmation bias fool you into believing you are already performing them or something very similar. Each exercise is meant to teach us to see, listen and think differently about our current customers and potential future ones. Keep an open mind, try them out in different situations, and see what you learn. Approach each situation with the intention of discovering something new, rather than seeking confirmation of what you already believe. If you adopt this mindset of active and curious exploration, you're more likely to uncover insights that challenge your existing assumptions.

11.2 Earn customer loyalty

The number one factor of sustainable growth is to develop customer loyalty early on. And the simplest way to become more customer-centric is to start treating every single complaint very seriously, and build knowledge from this analysis to improve our products and services.

Customer complaints are often handled as an after-sales activity rather than a learning activity: a customer calls or makes a request, a customer support or service team creates a ticket, and the ticket travels throughout the organization to be resolved. Sometimes requests end up as a bug fix or enhancement request in the product backlog (which is probably already full to the brim). Many companies don't even bother with customer complaints, delegating this activity to third-party service providers who have no incentive to reduce the volume. One source of this attitude can be company culture: supporting customers may be seen as "degrading" or at best a poor use of their engineers' time.

It can be difficult to hear customer complaints, because our pride gets in the way. But when a customer actually makes the effort to complain, it is not a judgment on our competence or personal worth; it is a call for help. Our product or service did not solve their problem, and they are telling us that *they really need us to come through for them.* If our product were not important to them, they would not bother to complain. They would simply choose another option. It is gratifying to know that we are valued and needed. Customers are taking time out of their busy day to tell us what really matters to them.

Each complaint represents a golden opportunity not just to keep a customer who wants our product, but potentially to gain several new ones.

To develop loyalty, we need to earn trust. Customers need to trust that our product will always help them do their job exactly when they need it. They need to trust that we will take care of problems quickly, respectfully and definitively. A fully satisfied customer is more likely to talk to their friends, colleagues and family about our brand and products. A customer who does not trust us will at best silently depart, and at worst become an active detractor. This phenomenon is well known, but can grow out of all proportion in the digital world. A single mistake can have a huge impact on a brand's reputation, as each unhappy customer shares their opinion instantly with dozens, hundreds, or thousands of people online. Hence, keeping our current customers interested and happy is not only key to increasing revenue rapidly and over time, it is our best and cheapest way of attracting new customers. When customers are happy, they come back for more. When they are not, we have to work twice as hard to grow sales.

Many startups ignore this fact and spend their cash developing many new features and an array of products as quickly as possible, often under pressure from investors. They also place a lot of faith in marketing and sales. Although both are strongly needed, without a clear strategy to build and maintain customer loyalty from the start, we will sooner or later start losing them.

The theory behind their approach is to find a market fit as soon as possible by "failing fast". This typically means launching an MVP, introducing lots of new features, learning from what works, and adjusting the product frequently. Many startups succeed in rolling out features that gain traction, but don't invest sufficient time in understanding their customers (why they bought, why they didn't, what works, what doesn't work, and so on). As a result, they end up wasting effort on reworking the product and convincing customers to buy rather than letting the product sell itself on its own merit. Also, they are so preoccupied with delivering fast and testing the market with the product that they don't pay attention to quality. Even the startups who make it through this stage run into problems later. Bogged down by quality issues, lack of product flexibility, and lower than expected adoption, most of them end up having to downsize because sales are disappointing and they cannot attract additional funding to continue the spree.

Our customers complain all the time, but we may not realize it (or we may simply be choosing to ignore them). Whenever they write or call, whenever they leave an online review or speak to a customer representative, they are talking to us. The trick is knowing how to collect and exploit this information so that it makes a real difference, both for them and for the company. If it is done well, the regular analysis of customer complaints by the product and top management teams is chock-full of learnings, for example:

- Who are our customers, really? (We often discover that they are nothing like the abstract personae we came up with during the discovery phase.)
- What aspects of our product are most important to them, that we should continuously improve and nurture?
- What good or bad design choices did we make, because we didn't understand their emotional complexity?
- Is our product still in tune with the times, or are we hanging on to things that don't matter anymore?
- How is the market changing? What new products and needs are emerging?

Through their complaints, our customers are educating us and showing us the way forward. This learning simply does not happen the other way around. Both startups and established companies keep repeating the same old refrain: "We have to teach people how to use our product," or "We need to educate our customers." This attitude is ridiculous. People are not being stupid or demanding because they do not understand how to use our products, or because they do not follow our rules and procedures. But when we try to "educate" our customers, this is how we are making them feel. No one can inspire loyalty by associating their product with emotions like this.

In his letter to Amazon shareholders[29], Jeff Bezos said that "customers are always beautifully, wonderfully dissatisfied, even when they report being happy and business is great." Like Jeff, we need to become obsessed with understanding all the ways that we are failing to fully satisfy customers. We can usually find actionable cases easily in the form of support tickets and online reviews, not just formal complaints. For each customer who complains, we take the time to understand the following:

- **Where did our internal processes fail to deliver the expected value?** In other words, where is there a source of waste or non-quality that we must get rid of? For instance, the existence of a software bug is a signal that something is not functioning well inside the organization. After fixing the bug, what is our next step? We should certainly not just move on, and adding another quality gate will only help prevent that specific problem from recurring. Instead, we must find and eliminate the root cause that explains *how the bug reached the customer in the first place.*

- **How did we handle the complaint?** Did we bend over backwards to help the customer complete their task quickly and easily? Did we show respect and empathy? Did we provide compensation for their troubles? Each time a customer reaches out to complain, we also have a great opportunity to train people throughout the company

---

29 https://tktq.link/build-to-sell/amazon-letter-to-shareholders

to become more customer-centric and continuously seek out new ways to create value for customers.

- **How was the customer trying to use your product, and how did their experience differ from what we expected?** If a customer is trying to use our product in new ways but not succeeding, we have a perfect opportunity to observe use cases and circumstances that we never anticipated. A complaint about the product may also be a sign that the market is shifting due to new trends set by competitors, especially if similar reactions continue to pop up. Here we have an early warning to continue innovating, to keep our product interesting so that our customers remain loyal.

11.3 Take customer complaints seriously

When analyzing customer complaints, it is important to look at each complaint individually, in order to really dissect what people are saying. Our goal is to avoid the trap of proposing a generic solution that misses the mark. This happens when we start abstracting our customers, for example by sorting complaints into fixed categories and looking for a Pareto distribution to guide our strategy. Instead, we strive to enter our customers' minds and circumstances. Try asking yourself the following questions for *each* complaining customer:

- In what specific context and situation do they encounter the problem?
- What are they trying to achieve, to accomplish?

- Why is it important to them, given their circumstances?
- What is the difference of perspective that separates how they use the product, how they would like to use it, and what we have designed?
- What is surprising about this discrepancy?
- What did we, the product conceptors, have in mind when we designed that part of the product? Why did we think it was smart at the time?
- What information was missing when we made that decision? What has changed?

Asking ourselves and the customer these questions is more than common sense advice. It is a methodical way of thinking that forces us to confront our own cognitive biases and analyze the situation from their perspective.

Let's look at a real-life example.

Sandrine is the Chief Product Engineer of the "Build To Sell" training program[30]. She solicits feedback from students at the end of each training program via a Google form, but she also collects any comments or complaints she hears throughout the training. Every new complaint is dealt with immediately. Sandrine's first goal is to give something to the person with the complaint, show them she is listening, and to find a way to keep their trust, even with a temporary countermeasure. She doesn't always agree with their requests, but it is her responsibility to ensure the students can effectively use the product. After addressing the complaint, Sandrine inserts it

---

30 See https://tktq.link/program

into the following table to understand their perspective and the reason behind it:

Date	Client name (a real person)	Client complaint (their own words)	What is the client trying to do? In what circumstances?	Where is the perception gap about what should happen?	What is surprising about this difference of perception?

TABLE 1. Example template for a customer complaint analysis board.

This table is called a **customer complaint analysis board**. Every column is meant to teach Sandrine something very specific about her students:

Date. When did we first hear from the student? Did we react immediately or did we let the problem drag on? We want to take each complaint very seriously and react immediately. If we don't, the client leaves and gives us a bad review. We must address their complaint as soon as possible, while it is still "warm".

Client name. What is the name of the person who complained? It shows that we are interested in the real person, not the organization or the brand. A person has emotions and specific circumstances, and these are what we want to better understand.

Client complaint. What exact words and images did the student use? We want the complaint verbatim, not our interpretation which is full of biases. Every word and punctuation mark contains vital details about our customer's context and emotions, which we need to thoroughly comprehend.

What is the client trying to do? What Job To Be Done was the participant trying to achieve? What about their specific circumstances (time, place, environment, who they are with, what they did just before, what they're about to do next...) prevented them from achieving the job? We cannot fill in this column simply by imagining what is not working with our product and the customer's process. To answer this question, we have no choice but to step into the client's shoes. Often, we need to call the client back or return to their "gemba". But this is also an opportunity to *rebuild trust* by showing empathy and providing an alternate or temporary solution. Even if we lose them as a customer in the end, at least they will leave with a good impression. We can try to win them back later with different, better offers, if we have not lost their trust.

Where is the perception gap? What was the customer's perception of how the product should be used to achieve their goal? What is the product conceptor's perception of how the product should be used or behave in this situation? Either the client is using the product in a different way, or their circumstances have changed or are unexpected. The difference between the two perspectives reveals our own misconceptions about how the product should behave. This is true even when the complaint is due to a bug: Any defect remaining in the product that raises a complaint, even if left unintentionally, suggests that the designer and team lack understanding of what truly matters to customers in their environment.

Where does the element of surprise come from? Why is it surprising that we have such different perceptions about how the product should behave, in this specific situation? What did we have in mind when designing the product? Why is that point of view irrelevant to the customer in this case? Was it ever relevant? Here, we must be careful not to rationalize our design decisions. Rather, the goal of this exercise is to pinpoint our misconceptions. Rationalizing leads to rushed decisions and knee-jerk reactions, such as "We just need to change this UX element in the product", "We need to better explain to customers how to do this", "This is a special case that we don't need to do anything about", or even "This is not what we want our product to do, so this is not the type of customer we want." We hear these excuses all the time. Of course, we do not have to perfectly fulfill every new customer request. But we *do* have to take the time to really understand where each customer is coming from, and then decide what to do with that information, so customers remain happy with our brand.

A few years ago, one of Sandrine's students, the CEO of a scaleup, complained that she did not have enough time to do the exercises on her own during the week between sessions. She expressed that the exercises took her much longer than anticipated and she would have appreciated knowing this beforehand to better prepare or seek assistance. Here is how Sandrine filled out the first part of the table:

Date	Client name (a real person)	Client complaint (their own words)
01/12	Laura, founder and CEO of scaleup *Alpha*	The customer complaint analysis exercise takes too much time for me, more than the 2 hours that were announced. I cannot do this exercise in just a week especially since I have a 9 to 7 job.

Table 2. Example of a customer complaint.

An obvious solution might be to increase the time requirement announced in the course's advertising and curriculum, in order to avoid receiving future complaints. This action would make sense if Sandrine decided that the time investment is necessary for learning, so it is better to filter out people not interested in doing the exercises. However, this train of thought is not in the service of the customer. *It is a rationalization of the original course design.* Leaving the situation unchanged could prevent Sandrine from getting other startup leaders into future "Build To Sell" training programs.

Instead, Sandrine's immediate decision was to grant Laura a time extension for completing the exercises and allocate some of her own time to assist her if needed. The other students agreed to postpone the group session by one week. Some were happy for the opportunity, while others were disappointed by the delay. Sandrine preferred this situation to the alternative of Laura not completing the exercises or feeling dissatisfied with the course. However, on the day of the group session, Laura still had done very little work. While the time extension and additional help did not significantly impact exercise completion, they did greatly contribute to maintaining a positive relationship with the student. Sandrine's prompt response to her complaint and offer of assistance were appreciated.

This anecdote shows how a customer complaint can be an opportunity to build loyalty. But what does this complaint tell us about the design of the training? Sandrine took the time to analyze Laura's complaint further. Here is what she came up with:

What is the client trying to do? In what circumstances?	Where is the perception gap about what should happen?	What is surprising in this difference of perception?
Laura has very few open slots in her agenda: she runs from meeting to meeting, and from crisis to crisis. So she asked her COO to fetch the customer complaints for her, which he did, but it took a few days because he had to extract them from the ticketing database that he doesn't know very well. When Laura tried to do the analysis, she realized she didn't have enough background info. She asked one PO for help, but the PO had to ask Customer Success because they were not in direct contact with the customers. In the end, nothing got done in time.	Laura is under the impression that collecting and analyzing customer complaints is a time-consuming activity that distracts her from running the day-to-day business. She expects her customer team to provide her with numbers and pie charts in a quarterly report to help her make decisions. For this exercise, I want Laura to go to Customer Success herself and discuss two to three tickets with them, which in my mind should not take more than 2h. I see this as a key learning step for her as a leader. I have designed this exercise for leaders to get closer to their customers because it is the foundation for building customer-focused companies. Laura has built walls between her and her customers and this is already hurting her business. My intention with this course is to get Laura to bring down these walls (process and mental walls).	Laura wants to learn new ways of growing her product and company, but she's swamped with putting out fires every day and she seeks quick solutions that resolve her immediate problems. I was surprised that she delegated the exercise and expected to get second-hand information. What Laura is not seeing is that the root of most of her current problems is a lack of customer focus in her organization. I have to make the link between the two clearer so that she sees the value in this exercise before starting. Also, I should explicitly ask Laura and the other students to go to the source (in her case Customer Success) to discuss just the last 2 to 3 tickets in person, so that they do not waste time. I also have to warn them ahead of time so they can be better prepared.

TABLE 3. Analysis of the customer complaint in Table 2.

In this example, Sandrine's initial misconception was that startup CEOs and founders will want to take the time out of their busy schedules to learn more about their customers as individuals. She also assumed that a startup leader would already have a certain attitude toward learning about their organization. While Laura had good intentions, Sandrine did not take into account the slowing effect of the habits and barriers that typically form around startup leaders. This does not mean that no one will take the time to do the exercise. But Laura was looking for a quick solution and was used to having other people do the legwork.

This realization encouraged Sandrine to redesign this specific exercise and other aspects of her course in a few ways:

- She gave students the option to go directly to customer service agents rather than looking up recent tickets in a database.

- She revised the course curriculum to provide clearer instructions for all exercises, allowing participants to better prepare in advance.

- She simplified some exercises significantly to ensure that they could be completed in a shorter time frame.

- She offered additional coaching as an optional supplement for students who wanted more in-depth guidance on the exercises.

After more discussions with Laura, and other students with similar profiles, Sandrine also discovered that many CEOs and founders like to learn by reading, listening to podcasts, and discussing with their peers. These are fun, relaxing activities that they can do on their own time or fit into the short gaps between meetings. Importantly, many of her students said that learning this way doesn't feel like work. Balancing this learning mode with the need for practical exercises to reinforce the concepts presents a challenging trade-off, which Sandrine has partially addressed by introducing the concept of "learning bites":

5-minute videos that students can access at their convenience, at any time and from any location.

Analyzing customer complaints *every day* with the team teaches us not to interpret, judge or decide too hastily. It teaches us to challenge our own beliefs about the product and uncover our misconceptions about what is most important to customers and why. Laura's company is one example of a widespread pattern: most startups establish big-company structures with silos very early in their development, and quickly lose their customer focus as a consequence. As soon as these barriers fall into place, it becomes very difficult for CEOs and founders to remain knowledgeable about their customers and the market. Sandrine wants to reach founders and CEOs, so she has been using this information to find ways to improve her training program.

In order to get the most out of customer complaint analysis, here are three things to keep in mind:

- **Show empathy** for our customers' problems. This way it is easier to perceive their frustrations and set aside our own biases.

- When a customer takes the time to tell us what's wrong, **they expect us to improve their experience** fast.

- Complaints are sometimes hard to hear, but we have to try to **get past our own ego**. Otherwise, our customer will look elsewhere.

11.4 Go to the client gemba

The second practice we propose is going to the client gemba, sometimes called a "gemba walk". Going to the client gemba means observing customers perform their tasks in their own environment, both with and without our products and in a variety of specific situations. It involves understanding the alternative solutions that the customer can use to perform their tasks, and which ones work better in what circumstances. We seek to fully understand their experience in real time, to gain a first-hand intuition for their values and challenges.

If the customer uses digital tools, going to the gemba means sitting next to them at their desk and watching them perform their tasks. Most of the time, their Job To Be Done involves a number of manual tasks and a variety of tools. Our goal is to immerse ourselves in their world, grasp their motivations, pick up on their emotions, and capture the complexity of their environment, not just see how they are using our own product.

Going to the gemba is the only way to clearly see the sources of frustration that customers do not talk about on their own. Maybe they no longer think of this difficulty as a problem because they are used to it, or maybe they assume that they don't have a choice. They may even consider a problematic, wasteful task to be part of their expertise! This tendency to silently accept problems explains why data and interviews are far from sufficient to conceive a great product. We also need to go to the client gemba, and do so regularly.

The client gemba is also a good place to confirm that we are working on resolving the *right* problem. Sandrine once worked with an international engineering firm that was building a ticketing system for a train station. These systems included physical gates, sensors, and software. They were designed to recognize real people, objects and pets going through the gate and check for fraud. The engineering team was behind schedule, and an important deadline was coming up that they couldn't miss without incurring significant penalties. The team was feeling a mix of nervous anticipation and dread as their contractor maintained a relentless sense of urgency. Sandrine asked two questions to gauge the engineers' understanding of the situation:

- What is the most important problem we need to solve for the client? Why do you think this is the most important problem to solve now?

- When was the last time you walked into a train station to see how it works? What did you learn?

The vague and conflicting responses provided by the team confirmed Sandrine's fears: they did not really understand what was going on in the client's world, and they had no clear plan to address the client's concerns. The first thing she recommended to the Project Manager was to take a couple of developers and go to the train station where their solution would be deployed. They spent several hours there, just observing who was passing through the gates. Sandrine gave them a template and guidelines to record their observations. They had never done this before, and came back transformed! They did several more gemba visits to observe different times of the day and week. Here is what they learned:

Most people passing through the station were workers. There

were very few families, elderly individuals, or wheelchair users. No large bikes either. That could be explained by the fact that the station was located near a business district. This information was a revelation to the team, because they had been fighting with bugs linked to the recognition of large objects like bikes, wheelchairs and strollers. The machine would interpret this situation as multiple people passing the gate at once, triggering an alarm. Other features of the passenger detection system were also not working properly, for instance alarms not triggering when they should, or small animals going unrecognized.

Armed with this new knowledge about their future users in that station, they reviewed their priorities and proposed a new plan to the client focused on the majority of passengers, while reassuring them that they would resolve the problems with large objects and pets at a later time. The client approved the emergency plan (it was crucial for them to open the new station at the date announced to the press). Working together, the engineering team and the client designed a temporary, human-based process to address non-standard situations that the system was not yet able to handle systematically. The team delivered the system on time for the station opening and their client was satisfied with the result.

Let's take another example. Here is a picture taken by Caroline during one of her gemba walks to improve a ski resort mobile app. Caroline worked on this exciting project while serving as Chief Product Officer at BAM, a digital development firm whose founders have long been committed to integrating lean principles into their approach to product development. What do you see? Are you able to spot problems or intriguing behaviors?

FIGURE 11. Some potential users of the mobile app for a ski resort. Do you notice anything about their circumstances and behaviors that changes the way you think about the app?

Here are some of the questions Caroline asked herself at the gemba to collect useful information:

- What are these people doing?

- Are the people alone or in groups?

- Why are they waiting?

- How long have they been waiting?

- What are they looking at?

- Are they talking to each other?

- Do they seem at ease? Angry? Happy? Tired? Other?

Now, here are some of the things that Caroline saw and heard:

FIGURE 12. Visitors at the ski resort with some of Caroline's observations.

These observations helped Caroline and the team better understand the Jobs To Be Done of skiers and the specific problems they were having in performing them. Would a remote design team hired to develop the resort's web app realize how often skiers are encumbered by their equipment and gloves while using their phones? How does knowing this change your concept for the app's main interface?

We have seen three gemba examples so far: the nurses on their rounds, the gateway for train passengers, and the ski resort. In all three, the duration of observation is critical. Five minutes or even one hour was not enough to understand the difficulties faced by users. Typically, it takes at least a couple of hours to start noticing interesting details. The longer we observe, the more problems and incoherencies we see, and the easier it becomes to look beyond first impressions. We have to keep all five senses wide open to catch the details that are going to make a real difference for the users. Another key point is to observe many different scenarios, to avoid jumping to conclusions too soon. As humans we have a tendency to extrapolate single observations into general rules. The more gemba observations we do in different situations, the sharper our senses get and the more we are able to grasp what is really going on.

People often ask us: "How many observations should I do and for how long before I have enough information to identify the right problem to solve?" The answer is that it depends! The more, the better. When your observations start converging and patterns start emerging, it is probably a good stopping point... for the current product iteration. Going to the client gemba should be a recurring activity. It helps us stay in tune with our customers and refine our client model over time. We need to keep going back to the client gemba because customer preferences change. Finally, it is better to do a few thorough observations than many superficial ones. Lila's deep dive into two nurses' daily routines was enough to understand the gap between their habits and the product. However, to ensure they addressed the right problem, observing just two nurses would have been insufficient. It was necessary to see several more—five to ten—to avoid being misled by outliers. In Lila's case, each team member joined the effort, and they shadowed a total of five nurses. To avoid sample bias, it is also crucial to include all different types of customers, even those who were difficult to reach.

Attention to detail is crucial. It is not enough to know if people performed their task successfully. We must observe each step of their experience, the actions they take to make progress, as well as the objects they manipulate and the information they use. During our observations, we also seek to understand how people feel as they perform their tasks: their positive and negative emotions. These minute details are essential to learn which parts of the experience require human intelligence and intervention, and which parts can be automated by our solution.

We often think that automation is the answer while lacking sufficient information to make this judgment. We might end up introducing new, meaningless tasks. For instance, the automatic cash registers in supermarkets require frequent human intervention to reset the scale, to handle unregistered products and so on. Another example: a robot vacuum cleaner does not work well in a cluttered apartment, so the user spends as much time rearranging furniture and unblocking the robot as they would have spent using a manual vacuum cleaner. Automating without a full understanding of the customer experience defeats the purpose of creating a new tool: to ease the human burden so that people can put their energy and brain power into more meaningful tasks.

Here are a few tips for rich and unbiased client gemba observations:

1. Observe customers interacting with their environment and the product **in all types of situations**. The same person might use the product in different ways depending on their immediate need. For instance, using Zoom for training as opposed to a team meeting.

2. Observe **different types of customers and users** interacting with the product. People will have different preferences depending on their relationship with the product. Users and sponsors have different relationships with a software product, just as a parent and their child have different relationships with a box of cereal.

3. Do not ask the user what they think of the product or what they want, **ask them to show you real life cases**. We have all heard the saying commonly attributed to Henry Ford: "If I had asked people what they wanted, they would have said faster horses." This is not an argument to ignore the customer, but to look below the surface in finding a solution to their problems.

4. Observation must be active. We have the right to **ask questions** to better understand what we see, hear, smell, feel and possibly taste. Why is it happening this way? Why this effect? What possible causes can we establish here? The more cases we observe, the sharper our senses get and the more relevant our questions. With practice, it will become easier to spot the real problems.

5. **Find out what alternatives to your product** customers use or would like to use, and when they are relevant. This is a way to compare your concept to competing products and services.

6. **Understand what customers are looking to improve** in their daily lives and the solution they currently have in mind. This is an opportunity to offer our help, even if our current concept or product does not solve their

problem directly. Going to the client gemba is not just an exercise to validate your own idea—it is an opportunity to discover their world.

7. **Pick up on their emotions** as they perform specific tasks: when are they excited, annoyed, content, or angry? A product must touch the right emotions if it is to make a real difference to the user or consumer.

8. **Do not try to analyze while you're on the client gemba.** Analysis comes after observation. While on the gemba, just write down what you see and hear, without any judgment, interpretation or analysis.

You can use a template to help you record what you see. This will make it easier to analyze the data later on. Here is one you may use:

Observation topic	Observation location	Observation date	Who are we observing

Time	Action/step	Duration	Observation details

TABLE 4. Example template to record observations on the gemba.

To help you recognize problems while on the gemba and during the analysis, it can be useful to use the 7 wastes model:

Waste	Definition	Example
Overproducing	Producing more or earlier than the next process needs	Batching, unsynchronized concurrent tasks
Waiting	People waiting for materials, information, or decisions	Waiting for decisions, information distribution
Conveyance	Moving material or information from place to place	Hand-offs, excessive information distribution
Processing	Doing unnecessary processing on a task, or an unnecessary task	Stop-and-go tasks, redundant tasks, re-invention, process variation—lack of standardization
Inventory	A build-up of material or information that is not being used	Batching, system overutilization, arrival variation
Motion	Excess motion or activity during task execution	Long travel distances, redundant meetings, superficial reviews
Correction	Inspection to catch quality problems or fixing an error already made	External quality enforcement, correction, and rework

TABLE 5. The seven-waste model.[31]

Last but not least, for successful gemba walks we must cultivate cognitive empathy and a thirst for discovering the unknown.

Cognitive empathy involves understanding how people feel and think independently of our own emotions and thoughts. This form of empathy enables us to interpret others' emotions and perspectives accurately. While there are numerous books on the subject, here are some tips to help you cultivate your cognitive empathy:

---

31 James M. Morgan, Jeffrey K. Liker, *The Toyota Product Development System: Integrating People, Process And Technology*, (Productivity Press 2006)

- **Practice active listening.** Listen without judgment or interruption, paying attention to both what the person says, and their body language and tone of voice to grasp their perspective fully.

- **Ask questions.** Clarify the other person's statements by asking for further explanation, encouraging them to express how a situation makes them feel. This demonstrates genuine interest in understanding their perspective and encourages open communication.

- **Put yourself in their shoes.** Try to see the situation from their perspective and understand why their viewpoint is valid, regardless of whether you agree with it.

- **Be fully present in the moment.** Give your undivided attention to the person you're engaging with, listening attentively.

- **Show compassion.** Seek to understand their challenges and emotions, demonstrating empathy and kindness.

Success means actively seeking out what we do not know, rather than awaiting confirmation of what we already believe. If you feel comfortable with what you're seeing and hearing, you're probably not exploring beyond familiar territory. When you encounter something unfamiliar, it's an opportunity for discovery. Dive deeper, ask for examples, and seek clarification to better understand what's happening.

What happens when we cannot easily go to the client gemba?

Sometimes, it is difficult or even impossible to observe customers in their environment. For instance, if we are working on a product to be used by doctors, it can be complicated to observe them as they examine a patient. The next best thing is to go through the same user journey ourselves, a well-known practice called "live my life". Like going to the gemba, the goal of this exercise is to put ourselves in our customers' shoes and avoid being tricked by our confirmation bias.

For example, when working on an e-commerce site we can't sit down with actual customers due to data privacy issues, but we can place several orders ourselves and evaluate the different phases of the customer experience: search, navigation, purchase, delivery, customer service, and merchandise returns. Jeff Bezos is recognized for his hands-on approach to understanding customer experience at Amazon. He is known to regularly use Amazon's services himself and contact customer support incognito to assess the quality of service. Brian Chesky of Airbnb has reportedly stayed in his company's apartments to experience firsthand what the customer experience is like. A startup PM we worked with, who conceived an inventory management system for supermarkets, took a job as a shelf stocking clerk for several months. When going through a "live my life" experiment, it is even more important to use a model like the 7 wastes to analyze our observations. This will help us recognize real problems, not just rely on our own perceptions.

What about data?

Some teams collect extensive usage and consumption data, and base their decisions more on "customer analytics" than field observations. This strategy may be a response to the difficulty of observing customers directly, as in the e-commerce example. However, the kind of learning we described in the previous examples can only be discovered in the field. Data is useful, but trends and models always need to be backed up by real observations. Data can tell you that users are engaging less with a feature, but not why the feature is failing to meet their needs. Where do you think people die most often? Statistically speaking, it is in their beds. If we followed Pareto logic, we would try to find a solution for dying in bed, but of course this conclusion is ridiculous. Data is always collected and viewed through a specific lens based on human choices, so our interpretation of data is never fully objective.

Data can orient us, it can tell us where to go and see, but it will never tell us the human reasoning and emotions underlying a problem. Also, the goal of data analytics is to detect trends in the population of customers based on a few criteria. This viewpoint necessarily hides the unique characteristics of each individual. However, we can only differentiate our products from alternatives by solving the real problems of individual users.

Going back to Lila's example, she noticed that nurses who created three or more patients in the app had lower turnover. The team's initial reaction was that they could improve adoption by finding ways to encourage nurses to create at least three patients in the app. They made the assumption that it took at least three uses of the application to feel comfortable with it. However, when Lila went to the gemba, she discovered that the nurses who adopted the app often first used it to record a complicated case that required exact transmission to her peers or consulting with different medical experts. In this situation, they found the application very useful for sharing data and treatment advice with multiple people. Then they continued using the app, even for simpler cases, because they had seen the value. In light of this new information, the team reconsidered their plans for the next version.

11.5 Interview customers to discover their "Job To Be Done"

Lila's designers devoted a year to releasing the initial version of the app for nurses, doing everything from design and UX workshops to Agile development "by the book". However, it did not retain users as much as anticipated. As described previously, Lila resolved to visit the client's gemba with a fresh, unbiased eye, in an attempt to uncover what they had overlooked.

Her first course of action involved conducting interviews to delve deeper into the nurses' Job To Be Done. Lila was convinced that in wanting to address a real problem, they had overlooked the true challenges that needed to be addressed to achieve their goal. Dismissing the app, she broadened her focus to understand the nurses' profession, their daily lives, and their significant memories. By eliciting their emotions she hoped to grasp what problems truly mattered to them and what they were truly struggling with. She intentionally remained receptive to subtle cues, striving to generate novel ideas. She wanted to see the gap between her discoveries about the nurses' world and the product they had developed. The gap proved substantial: they had designed a tool whose interface was tailored for tech-savvy users, overlooking the nurses' strong oral culture.

The design team had also conducted interviews during their initial analysis. The pivotal difference lay in the types of questions they asked and their manner of inquiry. One year ago, their focus was on comprehending the workflow for a particular use case and the pain points within that process. They meticulously mapped out the stages of wound care, homing in on the questions nurses asked themselves during an initial wound assessment. Their objective was to align *the app they already envisioned* with the information flows of the profession. Their intent was to digitize a segment of the nurses' journey. They did not ask any questions to uncover their routines, to understand their values and thought processes, or to appreciate their unique life stories. They had already decided to build a digital tool for a specific medical workflow, so they didn't approach the situation with the mindset necessary to uncover the underlying challenges.

This is why it is imperative to conduct exploratory investigations—gemba walks and interviews—to understand the problems faced by our customers without the development mission in mind but to be ready to discover new insights.

When we already have a solution in mind, a substantial portion of our effort during design interviews is often spent persuading individuals (and ourselves) of the soundness of our idea.

This is another form of confirmation bias, and we might turn the interview to these ends unconsciously. However, it is hard to stop ourselves from imagining a product. After all, this is also what gets us excited about a project.

We can avoid biasing the interview by steering clear of questions that inadvertently cast the client in the role of a designer, by suggesting or seeking their opinion on specific solutions or use cases. Two examples of common but leading questions are "Would it work for you if we did this?" and "Do you prefer this solution or that one?" Likewise, customers sometimes strongly advocate for their own specific solutions rather than explaining their preferences: "I want a big red button here," or "I need to export the data in XLSX format." Such requests conceal genuine problems but cannot be taken at face value. We need to find out why they want the feature, and reformulate it as a Job To Be Done: for example, "I want [a big red button] to alert my colleagues and supervisor when I notice something wrong." As product creators, it is our responsibility to look beneath the surface and comprehend the underlying problem. Perhaps they do not need an alerting system at all, but rather a solution to prevent critical issues from arising in the first place. There is an ever-present risk that we are designing a product that customers have requested but won't ultimately use. We can all stumble into this pitfall during the discovery phase, if we have overlooked the fundamental Job To Be Done.

Figure 13 reproduces one segment of an interview with a shopper interested in activewear. The interview was conducted by one of Caroline's designers who was spearheading a new e-commerce product.

PERSONAL QUESTIONS

How old are you?
I'm 31.

Do you buy activewear?
I buy pants and technique sweatshirts.

Where do you buy your activewear?
T.J.Maxx

Which brands do you buy?
I don't pick a brand, I'm not really sure. The pants have to be long enough because I'm tall. And comfortable. I have to try them on. At T.J.Maxx you have to return often to find something interesting because their stock changes all the time. I buy activewear a couple times a month. I could get them online, but I don't because I need to try them on. I own about 15 pairs of pants.

Do you care about your impact on the planet?
Sure. I don't think about this every day, but I suppose I care.

PRODUCT QUESTIONS
We're launching a new activewear brand that will be chemical free and sustainable.

What do you think about this idea?
I don't really know. Maybe for toilet paper I might be interested. I had no idea my yoga pants had so many chemicals in them. But sure, I guess I would be interested.

How do you find out about sustainable and chemical-free clothing?
I don't really do any research on that. I sometimes check the labels when I buy a new piece of clothing but I don't necessarily look at what chemicals it contains.

...

FIGURE 13. A customer interview conducted by designers for a new e-commerce website.

Does this interview yield sufficient information to understand the Job To Be Done? Do we gain insights into the shopper's lifestyle, emotions, and true priorities? Do we grasp the shopper's context and the emotional intricacies they experience? The answer is no. The questions are mainly about the product, not about the shopper. The shopper's responses are relatively brief. This is because most of the interviewer's questions are directive in nature and do not pertain to them. There is a lack of probing follow-up questions. The designer appears to have preconceived notions, and is guiding the shopper in a particular direction rather than trying to empathize and understand their perspective.

In Figure 14 below, we provide some suggestions for improving the interview with open-ended questions. Of course, the follow-up questions you ask could take many different forms, depending on the customer. The important thing is to show interest in their lives and experiences, not just focus on the product you have in mind.

PERSONAL QUESTIONS

How old are you?
I'm 31.

Missing follow-up questions: "What do you wear these clothes for? In what circumstances? Tell us a bit more."

Do you buy activewear?
I buy pants and technique sweatshirts. 

Where do you buy your activewear?
T.J.Maxx

 **Missing follow-up questions such as: "When was the last time you bought something at T.J.Maxx? What did you buy? Can you tell me about your experience? Who were you with? Did you go to other places before or after T.J.Maxx? Why did you buy those items?"**

Which brands do you buy?
I don't pick a brand, I'm not really sure. ==The pants have to be long enough because I'm tall. And comfortable.==

 **Interesting information about the shopper's preferences.**

 **But they needed to be explored further. The interviewer could have found out more about his disinterest for brands.**

I have to try them on. At T.J.Maxx you have to return often to find something interesting because their stock changes all the time. I buy activewear a couple times a month. I could get them online, but I don't because I need to try them on. I own about 15 pairs of pants.

 **Missing follow-up questions: "Do you wear them all? On what occasions? Which ones are your favorites? Why?"**

Do you care about your impact on the planet?
Sure. I don't think about this every day, but I suppose I care.

 **This is a loaded question, which has nothing to do with the previous one. The questions are no longer about the shopper. There is no logic in the flow of questions. Hence the detached and vague response.**

FIGURE 14. Suggestions to replace or extend the e-commerce interview topics with open-ended questions.

PRODUCT QUESTIONS

We're launching a new activewear brand that will be chemical free and sustainable.

This is closer to a sales pitch than an interview to learn about the shopper's Job To Be Done.

What do you think about this idea?

I don't really know. Maybe for toilet paper I might be interested. I had no idea my yoga pants had so many chemicals in them. But sure, I guess I would be interested.

This question is about a product that the shopper doesn't know so naturally their answer is vague. The fact that the shopper is not particularly interested in chemical-free clothing is useful to test our product idea, but it is not useful to understand the Job To Be Done.

How do you find out about sustainable and chemical-free clothing?

I don't really do any research on that. I sometimes check the labels when I buy a new piece of clothing but I don't necessarily look at what chemicals it contains.

The designer keeps insisting on a topic that is of no interest to the shopper.

FIGURE 14. Continued.

As you can see, the original interview did not provide substantial insights into the shopper's Job To Be Done. The designer had a promising opportunity to explore the customer's needs and preferences (specifically tall, comfortable clothing that requires trying on, shopping twice a month), but didn't fully take advantage of the window because they changed the subject too quickly to their own idea for a new product. Such interviews are more prevalent than we realize. It is quite common to spend the entire conversation discussing our own product, ideas, and perspective, rather than genuinely understanding the person's underlying problem.

Let's look at another example. Caroline conducted this interview with a vacationer at a ski resort:

How long have you been going to the resort?
Yeah, I often go to the resort, in the summer and the winter, more in the summer lately.

Really? Where did you go?
I went to several resorts growing up. My parents love the mountains, so we have been going to resorts for years. For a very long time we went to a small resort near Alpe d'Huez, in a small Swiss village. We did all sorts of activities together.
Since they've recently bought an apartment in Chamonix, I have been going to Chamonix with them in the winter mainly.

silence
I also go there a lot in the summer. I've lived in Lyon for 4 years so I enjoy going to the Alps on weekends.

What do you like about your stay in the resorts?
The sporty aspect for me is really important. I like to ski. I once went skiing with some school friends and they partied every night. I didn't enjoy that. I told myself ok I will never do that again!
It's really not my way of enjoying the mountains.
What I love is to get up at 4 a.m., climb to the top of a mountain, breathe the fresh air, and enjoy the view.

Can you tell me what is your fondest memory?
I have lots of great memories hiking for instance. At some point, I was a member of a hiking association and one year we organized a big race with 250 students. We did a lot of hiking, running and rafting. It was awesome!
We slept in tents on football pitches, it was super fun. Everyone was really into it. It was so intense that we all went to sleep at 8 p.m.! We got up at 5 a.m. every day and spent the day running.

silence
After three days hiking and running in the mountains, crossing paths with wild horses and enjoying shady fir forests, we reached the beach! The race itself was somewhat stressful but it was amazing to go for a swim and relax after such an intense effort. Quite high in emotions.

...

FIGURE 15. A customer interview conducted by designers for a new ski resort.

Compared to the first interview about activewear, the second interview got the person to open up and candidly share their emotions. This enabled Caroline to gain valuable insights into the person's Job To Be Done: Enjoying stunning landscapes while achieving peak athletic performance. Now, let's see what we learned in this interview and what could be improved:

How long have you been going to the resort?
Yeah, I often go to the resort, in the summer and the winter, more in the summer lately.

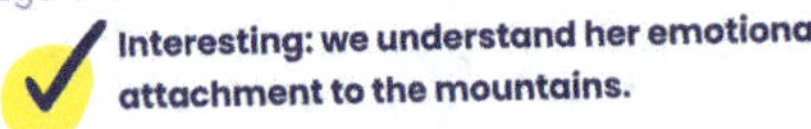

Really? Where did you go?

Show interest, invite the person to say more.

I went to several resorts growing up. My parents love the mountains, so we have been going to resorts for years. For a very long time we went to a small resort near Alpe d'Huez, in a small Swiss village. We did all sorts of activities together.

Interesting: we understand her emotional attachment to the mountains.

Since they've recently bought an apartment in Chamonix, I have been going to Chamonix with them in the winter mainly.

silence

Active silence to encourage the person to continue speaking.

I also go there a lot in the summer. I've lived in Lyon for 4 years so I enjoy going to the Alps on weekends.

Interesting information: she goes to the resort year-round, she mostly takes short trips, and she goes there whenever she has an opportunity on weekends.

What do you like about your stay in the resorts?

Follow-up question to encourage the interviewee to dig deeper into her emotions, and also to try and understand her key preferences.

The sporty aspect for me is really important. I like to ski. I once went skiing with some school friends and they partied every night. I didn't enjoy that. I told myself ok I will never do that again!
It's really not my way of enjoying the mountains.

Interesting information: we are starting to understand her Job To Be Done. It is about fulfilling her need and desire to exercise often in a natural environment. Even though she is young, she hates the typical spring break college get-togethers with noise, alcohol and late nights. She is sharing strong emotions.

FIGURE 16. Suggestions to replace or extend the ski resort interview topics with open-ended questions.

What I love is to get up at 4 a.m., climb to the top of a mountain, breathe the fresh air, and enjoy the view.

 **Interesting information: it reinforces the Job To Be Done.**

 **But Caroline missed an opportunity to understand the emotional implication behind. She could have asked a follow up question such as: "Wow really? How courageous! What do you love about this? Or how do you feel when you do this? Or what do you do once up there? Are you going alone?" And so on.**

Can you tell me what is your fondest memory?

 **This question encourages the interviewee to continue sharing her emotions**

I have lots of great memories hiking for instance. At some point, I was a member of a hiking association and one year we organized a big race with 250 students. We did a lot of hiking, running and rafting. It was awesome!
We slept in tents on football pitches, it was super fun. Everyone was really into it. It was so intense that we all went to sleep at 8 p.m.! We got up at 5 a.m. every day and spent the day running.

 **Interesting information: it reinforces the job to be done. We really hear a positive emotion: doing athletic activities with a group in a natural and beautiful environment makes her feel good in her body and mind. It takes her back to her childhood.**

silence

After three days hiking and running in the mountains, crossing paths with wild horses and enjoying shady fir forests, we reached the beach! The race itself was somewhat stressful but it was amazing to go for a swim and relax after such an intense effort. Quite high in emotions.

 **Interesting information: she likes the mental rush of competition followed by the relaxation at the end. It's something that she will look for in her future trips.**

FIGURE 16. Continued.

Notice that throughout the conversation, Caroline refrained from discussing her own product concept—a high-tech solution designed to enhance the skiing experience by reducing waiting times. At this point, Caroline's focus lay in comprehending vacationers' priorities and identifying their most impactful emotional triggers.

We recommend preparing your questions in advance and subsequently refining them after each interview. As illustrated in the ski resort interview, it is easy to overlook critical points and questions without this systematic review process. It is essential to start with a strong foundation of open questions that elicit personal experiences, and to avoid leading and closed questions where the expected answer is obvious. For further information, we suggest two books that offer excellent and insightful tips on interview preparation: *Competing Against Luck* by Clayton M. Christensen can assist you in uncovering the customers' essential Jobs To Be Done, and *The Mom Test* by Rob Fitzpatrick provides a wide variety of interview questions and gives insights into their formulation.

Additionally, developing strong listening skills is crucial. Listening means giving your complete attention to the person, setting aside your own thoughts and desires. It is a skill that requires consistent practice, since it is not inherently easy. We highly recommend the book *Just Listen* by Mark Goulston as an excellent resource to improve your listening skills.

11.6 Map out the customer consumption process

A **consumption process** consists of a sequence of actions performed by the customer to obtain the desired value. It can be viewed as a way of breaking down the Job To Be Done, with the details depending on what solution the customer adopts.

A consumption process, or for that matter every process, is composed of three types of actions:

- **Value-added** actions have a real positive impact on the customer experience, and customers are willing to pay for them directly or indirectly.

- **Waste** includes all actions that add no value to the customer experience, and result from dysfunctions within the company and our misconceptions. Customers do not want the added cost of waste passed on to them

- **Ancillary** actions are those that need to be performed to keep the company and its processes running, such as reporting or time management, but which add no value to customers either.

Actions or tasks that create value typically generate positive emotions among customers when they use or interact with our product. It is our duty to enhance these moments within their experience. It starts with identifying value-added activities and separating them from wasteful steps, and then aiming to reduce wasteful steps from their process.

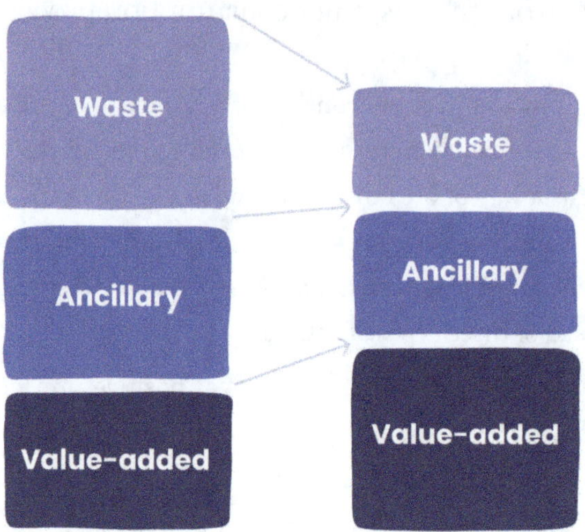

FIGURE 17. Our objective in mapping out a customer's consumption process is to increase the proportion of value-adding activity, while decreasing the proportion of waste.

To achieve this, we propose another tool to investigate the customer's world: the **client consumption map**. In their insightful book *Lean Solutions*, Dan Jones and Jim Womack suggest using a similar tool, the "provision map", to identify gaps between the customer's consumption experience and how that experience is provided. The provision map describes all the actions required for a company to deliver value to the customer. In contrast, the consumption map focuses on actions the customer takes to create value once they have the product. A client consumption map is also akin to a "customer journey map", a tool often used by Product Managers, but describing this journey from a lean perspective. Here we use the consumption map merely as a tool for immersing ourselves in the client's world, but it can provide many more insights. We encourage you to explore this topic and related concepts further.

The customer consumption map illustrates the detailed process of how a product is consumed or utilized, while highlighting the customer's emotions and frustrations as well as which steps create value and which do not. This approach readily identifies potential improvements in the process flow. The consumption map must be based on actual observations of the product in use, to ensure that it accurately reflects the customer's experience as they navigate a real-life problem-solving process. Below we illustrate a customer consumption map for a robot vacuum cleaner.

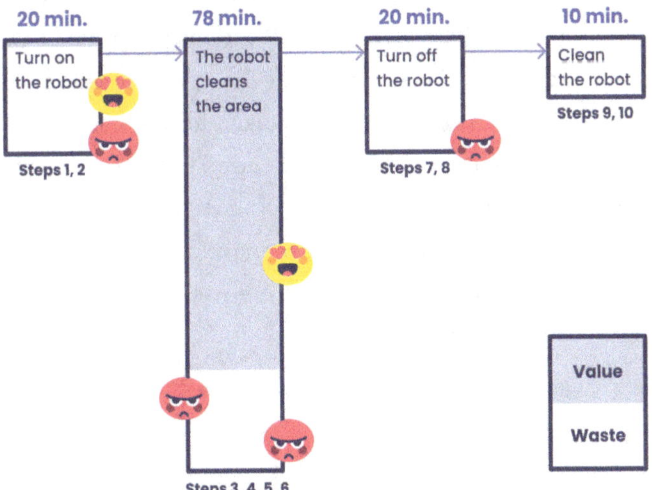

FIGURE 18. A customer consumption map illustrating Sandrine's experience using a robotic vacuum cleaner.

This map illustrates Sandrine's experience using a robot vacuum to clean her living room floor. The process includes 10 steps condensed into four main experience phases, each identifying both wasteful and value-adding steps. The filled areas indicate the time Sandrine considers valuable, while the empty areas are the wasteful, irritating actions she must perform. This representation helps identify waste in a customer's experience and challenges the assumption that all steps are necessary parts of the process. The efficiency of this cleaning process is only about 60%: it takes over 2 hours to clean the living room floor, with only 1 hour of true added value while the robot operates independently. Sandrine could sweep the floor herself in less time, although that would require more physical effort.

To create a consumption map, we start by listing the steps of the process in a table. We include all actions performed by the customer to accomplish the Job To Be Done, with or without our product. We try to record the time taken for each action, or at least the total time for the entire journey. These time estimates are crucial for assessing the impact of wasteful activities on the overall experience. Additionally, we make annotations regarding any aspects of the process that are particularly delightful, irritating, useful, or wasteful.

Step	Action	Time (s)	Observation (positive)	Observation (negative)
1	Clear the floor of anything that could get in the way of the robot or block its path or be sucked up by the robot – 20 min	1,200		Tough to move heavy furniture with bad back, time-consuming to put little things away.
2	Start the robot – 3s	3	Easy with the remote	
3	The robot sweeps the floor on its own – 1h	3,600		Robot is not very silent.
4	Intervene when the robot sounds an alarm because it's stuck – 3 x 2 min on average	360		The beeping sound is annoying. Hard to reach the robot, sometimes stuck under the coach, must bend over. Gets tangled in strings and fabric, can rip it.
5	Empty the robot's container because it was full – 7 min	420		Hard to put the dustbin back in the robot.
6	Guide the robot back to its charging base because it gets lost – 5 min	300		Not possible with the remote?
7	Turn off the robot – 2 sec	2	Easy with the remote	Can it turn itself off once it reaches the base?
8	Put furniture back where it was – 20 min	1,200		This is really annoying!
9	Empty the robot and throw the trash out – 5 min	300	Easier the second time	But it was not even that full.
10	Clean the robot because it is full of dust – 5 min	300		Can't use water so difficult to clean really well.
	Total time	7,685		
	Efficiency (robot autonomous)	47%		

TABLE 6. Step-by-step process of using a robot vacuum to clean Sandrine's living room.

Next, we differentiate between value-added and wasteful actions, leveraging the seven-waste model introduced in Section 11.4 "Walk the client gemba".

Step	Action (abbreviated)	Time (s)	Observation (positive)	Observation (negative)	Waste/Value
1	Clear the floor	1,200		Tough to move heavy furniture with bad back, time-consuming to put little things away. 😎	Excessive motion
2	Start the robot	3	Easy with the remote 😍		Value
3	Robot sweeps the floor	3,600		Robot is not very silent. 😎	Value
4	Intervene when stuck	360		The beeping sound is annoying. Hard to reach the robot, sometimes stuck under the coach, must bend over. Gets entangled in strings and fabric, can rip it.	Rework
5	Empty the container	420		Hard to put the dustbin back in the robot.	Overprocessing
6	Guide the robot back	300		Not possible with the remote?	Overprocessing
7	Turn off the robot	2	Easy with the remote	Can it turn itself off once it reaches the base?	Value
8	Put furniture back	1,200		This is really annoying! 😎	Excessive motion
9	Empty the robot	300	Easier the second time	But it was not even that full.	Overprocessing
10	Clean the robot	300		Can't use water, so it is difficult to clean really well.	Excessive motion
	Total time	7,685			
	Efficiency	47%			

From this table, we can create a consumption map like the one in Figure 18 to visualize the customer experience and identify the gaps between their expectations and the real experience delivered by our service. Sandrine devoted two-thirds of the overall time to preparing the room and attending to the robot. From Sandrine's perspective, some tasks are more wasteful than others, and some are particularly irritating. She is used to a manual vacuum cleaner, so she is already used to performing some of the less value-added tasks like emptying the robot. What she is less willing to accept is the new waste the robot is creating for her. For instance, she finds that it takes longer to prepare the room for the robot than for a traditional vacuum cleaner, because the robot can get stuck in narrow spaces.

We can also clearly see where the added value lies. The true value-added time for her was when the robot operated autonomously—this is the primary reason she bought the robot. In the best-case scenario, after preparing the room and switching on the robot, it would do its work for one hour without needing intervention. But that is not the case. Sandrine says that she is no longer using her robot cleaner because she has to do more prep work and she is interrupted too often. She didn't see the added value, so she reverted to using a broom. As an added bonus, she enjoys the workout.

As the Chief Product Engineer of the robot vacuum cleaner, we want to maximize the performance of step 3 ("The robot sweeps the floor on its own"), while reducing or even eliminating some wasteful parts of the process, like steps 4 and 6. For instance, we could find software innovations to prevent the robot from getting stuck in narrow spaces, or hardware innovations that give the robot new abilities, like climbing small obstacles or pushing small floor clutter such as cat toys out of the way.

Another example for a digital product

Flavian documented his experience utilizing a 2022 Smart TV to look for a science fiction movie. He spent 2 minutes and 58 seconds just to find a movie he likes—a seemingly short time that actually involves numerous steps. In the digital world, where seconds can feel like hours, such durations are far from trivial. Companies can achieve significant increases in adoption rates simply by enhancing speed. While it may be tempting to dismiss this analysis because the whole process is quick, a closer examination of Flavian's experience reveals several underlying issues. He devoted 85% of the overall time to waiting, clicking, and typing. His journey looked like this:

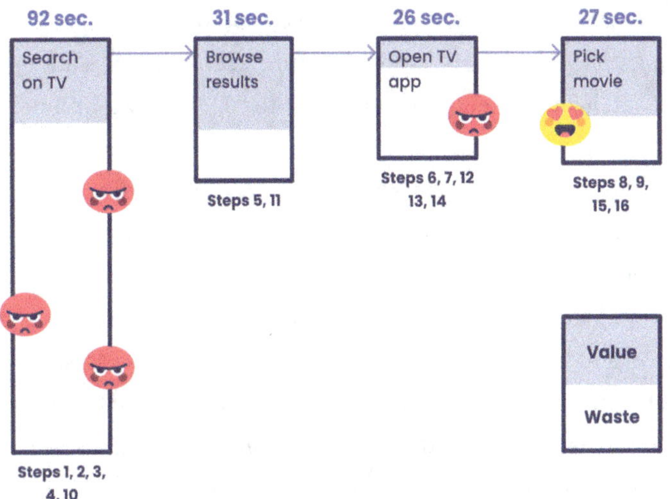

FIGURE 19. A customer consumption map illustrating Flavian's experience searching for a movie to watch on a smart TV. This diagram consolidates two sequences of actions that Flavian took on different streaming apps.

We grouped the 16 steps Flavian takes to find a movie he likes into four main experience phases, identifying both wasteful and value-adding steps. The ratio between the two is 8.5 to 1. The value-added parts of Flavian's experience occur when he's presented with a curated list of movies he enjoys, allowing him to quickly browse and choose a movie to watch (highlighted in the filled sections). These steps are primarily the last two in his process—step 15, "read the movie summary", and step 16, "click play". The first 14 steps, including opening apps, searching, reloading, researching, and waiting for results to load, add little to no value (represented by the empty sections). Ideally, Flavian would like to see a short list of science fiction movies he hasn't seen yet, with descriptions, and be able to pick one and start watching within 20 to 30 seconds. In contrast, many of us spend a significant amount of time searching for something to watch, only to end up turning off the TV after 20 minutes of fruitless browsing.

Mapping out Flavian's experience highlights clear areas for improvement. Repeated several times, the steps of navigating TV menus and opening different services are relatively time-consuming and mostly waste, not value. This mapping would provide the Chief Product Engineer of the "Smart TV" a deep understanding of their customers' frustrations and the risk of losing their loyalty.

At the same time, this customer consumption map suggests several opportunities for improving the product:

- Enhance the loading speeds of the most used apps (for example, the TV itself, Netflix, and Apple TV+) by addressing common issues caused by system incompatibilities.

- Eliminate the steps where Flavian has to wait or redo an action several times by enhancing the TV native app's search feature so it also displays Netflix content, potentially through a commercial partnership.

- Integrate film information directly into the search results could streamline the process, reducing clicks and load times while better capturing user preferences.

- Allow the TV to remember previous searches and share this data with hosted apps could significantly refine the experience, perhaps even eliminating step 15 entirely.

- Time software updates to avoid disrupting common viewing times.

The consumption mapping approach complements other customer discovery methods. It is especially valuable for assessing process efficiency and identifying wasteful actions in the customer journey. This methodology can be applied in any scenario where a customer or user is working towards accomplishing a Job To Be Done. We encourage you to try this approach yourself, by mapping out an activity you engage in daily, whether on your computer, at your workplace, or even in your personal life.

Now ask yourself:

- When did you last visit your client gemba? How did you approach the visit? What key insights did you gather regarding what truly matters to your clients?

- What stands out as the primary grievance from your customers? What actions have you taken to address it? Has it changed anything?

- What dominant emotions and frustrations do your customers experience? How did your observations at the gemba lead you to this conclusion?

UNDERSTAND HOW CUSTOMERS MAKE THEIR CHOICE

Designing a product that resonates with a broad audience and invites daily use is an intricate challenge. While many individuals can share a common problem, one that we hope our product will resolve, their specific needs are still shaped by their personal context and experiences. Marketing alone is not enough to persuade potential customers of our product's excellence. While promotion is always necessary, aligning our product's design and performance with the advertised benefits is vital to attracting and retaining customers.

Ideally, we aim to achieve universal satisfaction with a single product, without making it overly complex or too niche. To get closer to this ideal state, we need to understand the factors influencing people's choices when purchasing a product or service. Typically, there are a few consistent, fundamental preferences shared by a majority of individuals facing a similar problem (or Job To Be Done). These are the "must have, can't fail" characteristics we need to fulfill in our product design. These client preferences also act as choice criteria, providing a valuable perspective that allows us to:

- Identify areas where we are falling short compared to competitors.
- Build a customer model that informs our design decisions now and in the future.

How did you choose your last smartphone? For instance, Caroline prioritizes battery life because she makes heavy use of her phone during work hours and sometimes shares the internet with her laptop, both of which drain the battery quickly. Additionally, she has a keen interest in photography, so having good photo quality in her smartphone is important. These criteria, battery life and photo quality, represent Caroline's stable preferences that significantly influence her purchasing decisions. They are stable because they are shared by all the clients within the same segment and also because they change slowly over time. Figure 20 shows some other characteristics of smartphones that can be key customer preferences:

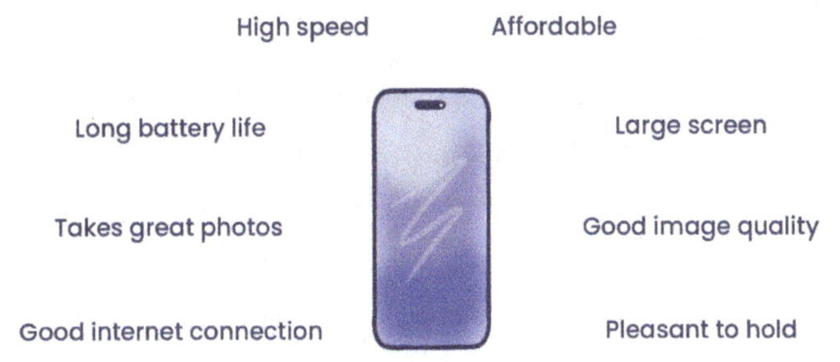

FIGURE 20. Key preferences for a new smartphone.

It is important to understand here that **preferences** are not the same as technologies. A preference like "long battery life" can be engineered into the product in several different ways, such as a bigger battery, lower-power components, or a smarter operating system. *A stable preference is always viewed from the user or customer's perspective, not from that of the engineer or the product.*

Another important point is that Caroline expects her new smartphone to satisfy *all* the stable preferences depicted in Figure 20 to a large extent. Her personal priorities are long battery life and photo quality, but any phone that fails on the other criteria will be rejected out of hand.

Any consumer product typically has only a few stable preferences per customer segment (or Job To Be Done). They can typically be counted on our fingers even for large and complex products. Think of these preferences as non-negotiables: they are the quality characteristics that we absolutely must satisfy to remain in the game. Our objective is to meet all of them simultaneously. To put a number on it, we can say that we need to achieve a minimum of 80% performance on each preference, compared to the current state of the art. For example, if the very best smartphone on the market has a battery life of 40 hours under "normal usage" (defined as some typical distribution of standby mode, phone calls, app use, and casual gaming), then our product must have a battery life of at least 32 hours or it is a non-starter. Of course, for some preferences we should surpass this threshold because we are also looking for a competitive advantage to differentiate our product.

Immersing ourselves in the world of our clients, using the techniques described in the previous chapter, allows us to pinpoint the consistent preferences that frame our product design. We can do this by creating a list of pros and cons for each existing solution from the customers' viewpoint. The pros do not necessarily reflect what is most important to them, because customers may like something, but not so much that they cannot live without it. The cons are the challenges that a solution imposes on customers, as well as their repercussions on the user's work, personal life, or overall experience. When a customer complains, it often indicates that the product is failing to provide something very important to them. The really important preferences are often the ones they take for granted.

Some of this information comes directly from the customer's mouths. During interviews and gemba walks, we are writing down their preferences, both likes and dislikes. We are paying special attention to what they love and what they hate, what causes frustration and what is satisfying. Another valuable source of information is online forums, reviews and ratings. For example, platforms like Trustpilot can offer insights for websites or services. Look carefully at the feedback of customers who have provided both the highest and lowest ratings. Both types of feedback are excellent indicators of what truly matters to our customers.

Devoting time up front to thoroughly understand customer key preferences enables us to make informed design choices, setting our service apart from the multitude of existing solutions.

Let's look at a concrete example. We want to build a supermarket website for older adults who are looking for an easy way to get their groceries every day. After doing a bit of gemba research, we discovered that many older adults love going to the supermarket in person, because they want to see the products before buying. It is also an opportunity for them to leave their home and have interactions with others. However, they do not like going to crowded places and they hate waiting in line at the cash register because it is physically exhausting. For some, making the trip to the store is getting more difficult, but at the same time they hesitate to get their goods delivered because it means letting someone they don't know enter their house. How can we resolve these difficult trade-offs and give ourselves a chance to satisfy the maximum number of older shoppers?

From our gemba research, we identify the following key preferences for their grocery shopping experience:

- They want to feel reassured (from order to delivery)
- They want to find their favorite products

- They need to be confident that products are fresh
- The shopping experience should be as easy as going to the store
- They do not want to be in crowded places
- They want to have some human interaction

For our online supermarket to succeed, we need to satisfy all these key preferences at least as well as existing alternatives. We force ourselves to think about ways to meet these criteria from the outset, *before drawing a mockup, writing a single line of code, or creating a backlog of features.* This handful of criteria will be our guiding principles during product design and development. Our commitment is to consistently satisfy and uphold these key preferences, diligently ensuring that each new change or update enhances them rather than compromising their fulfillment.

Immersing ourselves in the customer's world and committing to respect all their key preferences leads us to innovative solutions that might not have occurred to us otherwise. For example, to address the first key preference, "they want to feel reassured", we could propose an alert system that calls customers or sends them an SMS when their delivery is about to arrive, so they can prepare themselves to greet the delivery agent. We could also give delivery agents a confirmation number, similar to the Uber service, so that the customer can verify the agent. These simple steps can win over customers who have concerns about letting strangers into their homes.

Of course, at this stage the solutions we think of are just

hypotheses—we do not really know how customers will react to the product design, and the technical trade-offs we make might have unforeseen costs. It is good practice to simultaneously explore several solutions that address the key preferences in different ways. We could create low-fidelity prototypes (mockups) of various concepts and test them with a select group of potential customers before fully designing the product. Once we can successfully merge these concepts into one, we could develop a minimum viable product (MVP), deploy it in a real-world setting with potential customers, and then refine our client model based on their feedback. This means validating all design choices and any proposed product change against these key customer preferences. This ensures that the product remains aligned with what is most important for the customers over time, change after change. Section 14.4 will explore techniques for translating stable customer preferences into expected product behaviors (the "critical product performances"), as a way of guiding us throughout this process.

Finally, once our minimal viable product or a prototype is in the hands of customers, we need to measure its performance for each customer preference. We can do this by assigning ourselves a numerical score (say, on a scale of 1 to 5) and comparing our solution to existing alternatives. Figure 21 shows this assessment as a client radar chart. It clearly shows where the online solution is lacking, and where we must improve to satisfy customers. In this scenario, it is evident that customers would lack confidence in the service ("feel reassured"), worry about the freshness of their purchases, and would miss human interactions.

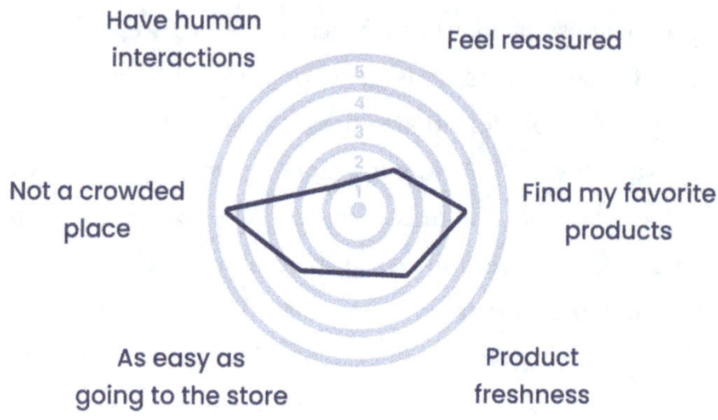

FIGURE 21. Radar chart of an online shopping solution.

Above we propose some innovative technology-based solutions to enhance the "feel reassured" preference, such as SMS alerts and a confirmation code for the agent. Naturally, adding these new elements to the solution is not free—it will incur build and run costs. Regardless of how much it enhances the product, any innovation requires comprehensive evaluation to guarantee that it delivers value in a cost-effective manner. In Section 14.5, "Plan for profitability", we will present some techniques to perform a detailed cost analysis, and determine the added value and profitability of such initiatives.

Technology is not the whole story either! The whole product includes numerous human and environmental factors, as we described in Chapter 6. We could also determine that the best way to make older shoppers feel reassured is to invest in more customer care. We could try to ensure that a given shopper is always served by the same delivery agent, so they form a stronger relationship with our proposed solution, and by extension the brand. Or we could create a service center that calls shoppers to go over their shopping list after the order is placed, and correct or amend it if needed, before sending the order on to fulfillment.

Do these human-based solutions make you nervous? One factor that often hinders tech startups from enhancing value is a strong inclination to automate customer interactions. Tech companies pursue automation to boost efficiency and scale operations rapidly. This strategy can be seen as a driver of higher valuations compared to human customer service, as streamlined and automated operations often yield a higher rate of return. However, this viewpoint overlooks the importance of personalized and human-centric interactions in delivering a superior customer experience and understanding individual customers' needs. The trade-off between automated customer service and human customer service is therefore not so clear-cut. We have all experienced personally the loss of value when we need support and automated tools fail to do the job. The theoretical value of automation can also evaporate when the tools in question are plagued by bugs or challenging for customers to use, a common occurrence in practice. Startups often prioritize speed at the expense of quality, and this trade-off tends to catch up with them in the end.

Now ask yourself:

- What are the stable preferences of your customers? What are the "must-do, can't fail" quality characteristics of your product?

- How would you rate your product on each of these aspects? Try making one radar chart similar to Figure 21 per customer segment or Job To Be Done.

- What would your radar charts look like for each of your client segments (or in other words for each of your Jobs To Be Done)?

CHAPTER 13
ANALYZE COMPETITORS TO IGNITE INNOVATION

Developing a product that truly engages our customers requires a profound understanding of the daily challenges they face. Observing them in their day-to-day environments and capturing their stable preferences is absolutely essential. It is equally important not to fixate on a single potential solution right from the start. Our first idea is rarely our best, and we need to give ourselves time to explore various options. In lean engineering, we refer to this approach as "set-based" design, in contrast with "point-based" design. Set-based design explores multiple solutions concurrently and converges on the one that best addresses the problem. Point-based design, the approach adopted by most startups, means building an initial solution and modifying it until a suitable market fit is found. *Set-based design is inherently less risky*, because it allows us to learn a great deal about the effectiveness of different technical trade-offs and the market reaction before engaging too many resources.

Studying multiple solutions simultaneously requires creativity and an open mind. Designers and engineers must regularly analyze competing solutions to broaden their horizons and think innovatively. They can challenge their own design decisions by understanding how competitors resolve hard technical trade-offs. The goal is not to thoughtlessly copy competitors, but to be aware of the possibilities and explore various avenues before committing to a single approach. True innovation occurs when the team ventures into uncharted territory with ambitious goals.

13.1 Decide which competing solutions to analyze

Complete immersion in the clients' world gives us the opportunity to understand how people work around their problems to the best of their abilities, and the array of products and services they turn to for help. We also see which products and services they prefer over our own, and under what circumstances. These observations on the gemba will show us which competing solutions are relevant for our analysis.

Lila and the team examined several comparable applications and tools before designing their app for nurses. They meticulously analyzed the alternatives, searching for shortcomings to enhance their own design. However, when they returned to the client gemba for a second round of observations, they made a significant discovery. Their true competitors were not other apps, but traditional media: medical reports filled out by patients on paper, voice messages exchanged among nurses, emails, and so on. The nurses already had functional workflows in place that didn't depend on a new app. Another striking revelation was that the nurses were already proficiently utilizing some advanced features of existing smartphone tools to facilitate these workflows. For example, some of them would take photos without even unlocking their phone. The standard camera apps were providing a partial solution already, but weren't on the designers' initial survey. In contrast, Lila's app demanded 7 steps just to add a photo of a wound, and even more to enter data on the specifics of its presentation and treatment. To many of the nurses, this approach to UI design was not just cumbersome but positively old-fashioned, especially since they were always on the move and carrying items.

This example illustrates how exploring *all* available alternatives enriches product design. Even when we think we are being creative, we all have tunnel vision and a confirmation bias towards solutions similar to the ones we are currently thinking about. Going to the gemba and immersing ourselves in the customer's world forces us to take a wider view of the solution space. While we may not be able to implement every idea in the initial version of the product, the insights gained from observing clients will inform future development. Some of these ideas can eventually lead to horizontal innovation: the creation of variant products within a family that are tailored to different segments (different Jobs To Be Done). Furthermore, as demonstrated by the nurses, the most competitive alternative solution may not resemble the product we envision building.

13.2 Competitor's teardown

When we think about older citizens who need to do their grocery shopping, a variety of solutions are already at their disposal. A customer does not necessarily stick to just one solution; they will combine solutions or switch between them as the situation warrants. Here are a few options:

- Shop in person at a nearby grocery store, but arrange for home delivery.
- Combine their shopping into a major trip and seek assistance from family members.
- Conduct frequent, small trips to nearby convenience stores and markets.
- Enlist a friend or family member to do the shopping on their behalf.
- Employ an in-home care agency for shopping and other tasks.
- Purchase essentials from a mobile grocery truck.
- Shop online, using a general service or a supermarket website.

Out of all these options, we choose one or two that are frequently used or look like interesting alternatives. These are the competing solutions that already fulfill several of our customers' stable preferences. We can then evaluate the performance of each one with respect to the preferences, for example using a radar chart like the one in Figure 21.

Finally, and most importantly, we "tear down" the alternative solutions. We try to understand why their designers made certain decisions and technology choices, the pros and cons of each choice, and the impact on customer satisfaction. For example, a competing website for online grocery shopping always displays the following warning at checkout: "If a selected product is unavailable at the time the order is prepared, it will automatically be replaced with a similar product." This rule allows the service to fulfill orders and deliver goods faster, but degrades the customer's control over what they buy. Both fast delivery and getting what they want are stable preferences for online shoppers, but which one should take priority? Did the designers make this choice because they were consciously trying to respect and optimize a key preference of their users, or simply to make fulfillment easier for their own workers? Or is this design merely a sales gimmick, designed to compel people to buy goods they did not really want?

Tearing down a competing solution is a multidisciplinary exercise. The goal is to find out:

- **How is the solution composed, and how does it work?** What are its functions, technologies, processes, and materials (if the product is a physical object)? How does it perform in different situations? How does the solution stack up in terms of quality, robustness, cost, ease of construction, and ease of maintenance?

- **How do all these components interact with each other?** Can we identify strong interdependencies? Are there any black-box components? Is human intervention needed to keep the solution working?

- **What are the notable pros and cons?** Which elements work well and which do not, depending on the situation?

- **What were the engineers' intentions behind some of the design choices?** Why do we think these choices were made? Are they related to cost or value? What breakthroughs did they achieve? How did they go about it?

- **Is it easy to assemble and disassemble?** To install and uninstall? To modify and integrate?

Creating a visual representation of a competitor's product, displaying its architecture and components on a wall, will help you understand the underlying logic of these design and technology decisions. Analyzing each part or component of the whole product will allow us to discern which aspects are executed well and which are less effective. It will help us see what elements are truly innovative, and how all these components work together. You can use Table 8 as a template to document your findings, and add other columns or details as you see fit. Feel free to add screenshots, pictures or even videos to illustrate the competitor's product when filling out the table.

Before we describe Table 8 in detail, remember that we are not just speaking of the core product or the digital platform. As we described in Chapter 6, the competing solution that we are tearing down is itself a whole product, that can have intangible, aesthetic, and human aspects as well as physical parts and software.

Product type and brand/make/name/version					
Component/ part/ function	Technical characteristics	Technical "how"	Cost	Notable innovations	Pros and cons
Assembly/integration:					
Key insights/discoveries:					

TABLE 8. An example template to record your observations when "tearing down" a competing solution into its component parts. For digital products, we are more likely to analyze software components or distinct functions of the solution rather than physical parts.

Here, the **technical characteristics** of a product refer to specific details and specifications that define its design, construction, and function. Dimensions, performance metrics, durability, and safety measures are examples of technical characteristics. Of course, the important characteristics will depend on the type of product you are tearing down, and whether the product is physical or digital.

The **technical how** describes the methods and choices that (we assume) the engineers used in constructing the component or part. Sometimes, the component or part is a third-party tool, a subcontracted service, and can be a black box. In this case, we don't need to understand how it is made so much as how the competitor uses it in their context. Often, third-party tools are flexible and can be configured to meet specific needs. When we need to tear down a web application, the server side is also usually a black box, but there are ways to make informed guesses about the server design. The underlying technologies and design patterns could be open source, or provided by well-known third parties such as Amazon Web Services. Understanding how a component is made and used is just as crucial as knowing what it does, because there are various ways of combining existing technologies and some are more effective than others. It is essential to grasp the reasoning behind the engineers' approach.

Cost represents the expense involved in making and maintaining or utilizing and integrating the component. You should consider both per-unit costs, such as raw materials, licenses or shipping fees, and fixed costs such as yearly subscriptions, labor or rent. Section 14.5, "Plan for profitability", provides a model for analyzing the cost structure of a product. If you don't know the details of the product cost, at least provide rough estimates. You can also use descriptive, relative quantifiers like "expensive", and "very expensive".

In the **Assembly/Integration** area, we detail how all the components or parts fit together during product assembly, pinpointing areas where the process is seamless and where it faces challenges. This can be thought of as understanding the "technical how" at the product level instead of the component level. Again, there is more than one way to assemble and configure a product while ensuring that the parts function cohesively. Understanding the designer's choice is critical, because often problems arise during integration that are not immediately apparent during design. It is easy to imagine a scenario where we follow the same methods and use the same technologies/parts as a competitor, yet get different results!

Finally, in the **Key Insights/Discoveries** area we summarize our main findings, highlighting what aspects of the product are particularly distinctive, where the product falls short, and what strikes us as truly ingenious.

The exercise of tearing down a competing product can take many forms:

- For a physical object, such as a mobile phone, we can acquire an example and work with engineers to interpret the disassembled components. We can also watch online videos of experts attempting to reproduce or reverse-engineer the product.

- For digital products, we can obtain the source code for open-source software components, or identify open-source libraries that are used by the solution even if the full source code is private. We can also look for information about the product's design and development by engaging with online communities such as developer forums.

- If the product is a service, or we are analyzing the service aspects of a whole product, then conducting "live my life" experiments will grant a deeper understanding of how it operates in different situations. For example, when calling the customer hotline for an internet service provider, what kinds of problems are diverted to automated response systems? How are customers able to talk to a human agent? The service is designed in a certain way to optimize specific preferences or performances, possibly at the expense of others.

You may have to undertake all three approaches. Remember that the "whole product" (Chapter 6) often has all three aspects: a physical device, the software that runs it, and support services to enhance the customer experience.

Finding the answers we need is a matter of searching every possible source of information: talking with engineers, attending conferences, reading articles, participating in online discussions, and more. Since competitors do not leave the doors wide open, the teardown exercise is challenging and sometimes requires creativity. Sometimes we can find answers in unexpected places, such as expert videos explaining how a product works[32]. The most crucial point to remember is that a teardown is a collaborative exercise: it should involve a team of specialists capable of understanding all aspects of the product's engineering development. This group is probably very similar to your design team, but don't hesitate to bring in outside specialists when you need them.

---

32 Video of how ChatGPT works: https://tktq.link/build-to-sell/how-chatgpt-works
Video of how a NASCAR Cup Series car works:
https://tktq.link/build-to-sell/how-nascar-works

FIGURE 22. The Chief Product Engineer and the team for a new online shopping service investigates a competing solution used by older citizens, and tears down the solution to understand its strengths and weaknesses.

When performing a product teardown, remember that our goal is to gain insights into the thought processes of the designers and engineers. How did they tackle some of the challenging trade-offs that we are facing in our own design? We may think their solution was short-sighted because it degrades some key preferences, or brilliant because they managed to satisfy multiple preferences simultaneously. Why did they choose this technology? We may think that it is old-fashioned or cutting-edge. Why did they choose this material? We may think that it is too costly, or robust and worth the expense. Why did they implement a process in this way? We may think that the process is too complex, or find out that it is much simpler than we initially imagined. We don't need to learn every detail of the competing product's engineering. We just need to learn enough to understand these types of design decisions and compare them to our own. This approach is the best way to transcend our ingrained beliefs and discover genuine innovations.

Let's return to our example of an online supermarket for older citizens. We have torn down a competing solution: the nearby grocery shop which provides the convenience of making frequent, small shopping trips. We can represent our findings as follows:

Bob's Market, near Main Park					
Compo-nent/part/ function	Technical character-istics	Technical "how"	Cost	Notable innovations	Pros and cons
Store	10m x 20m	• 5 aisles, 2 of which are refrigerated or frozen • Signs indicating each aisle's products • Fruits and vegetables at store entrance	• Aisle signs and price tags are all digital (significant cost?) • Fruit and vegetable bins are rattan. (cost?) Is it for freshness?	They mix cheese and meat in the same cold section. We don't often see this.	• Placing cheeses and meats in the same refrigerated section leaves more floor space for dry goods but also fewer brands of meat/ cheese. • Maintaining fruits and vegetables requires more work, since bins are far from the stockroom and close to a busy area (cashiers). Is there an upside we're missing?

Product listing	At most 5–6 similar products from the same brand on shelf	Re-stocking shelves every Friday	No big, expensive brands	Discounts on fruits and vegetables every weekend	Customers buy up fragile products (fruit and vegetables) more quickly, as long as they are still undamaged.
Cashiers	- 2 automatic checkouts - 2 classic checkouts	One line for automatic checkouts and 2 lines for the 2 conventional checkouts	We observed only 1 cashier, even at peak times. Why 2 checkout lines then?	Automatic checkouts with barcodes on the receipt for checkout. Security!	The barcode is a great security option because someone does not need to be present around the clock to check for theft at automatic cash registers.
Personnel	1 cashier, 1 manager who can help by opening second checkout line if needed	Friendly but busy and overwhelmed.	The staff wear a lovely designer uniform!		
Delivery	...				
Etc.	...				

Assembly/integration:
Central location on a pedestrian street. Clear product strategy: essentials, low-cost brands, focus on healthy ingredients although less choice than a major supermarket.

Key insights/discoveries:
Shelf positioning, replenishment and reduction of fruit and vegetables have been designed so that they go fast while they're still fresh and attractive.
The shelves are organized in such a way that cashiers can easily work on filling them during slack periods, for greater efficiency and lower costs.

TABLE 9. Teardown exercise for a local grocery store collecting our observations on the cost, strengths and weaknesses of different parts of its designed experience.

With all this information at our disposal, we can now prepare a client radar chart with our evaluation of two competing products: a big-box store's online shopping website, and a small grocery store at walking distance from a residential neighborhood.

This allows us to assess both products based on the same stable preferences of customers, so we can more easily detect opportunities for improvement.

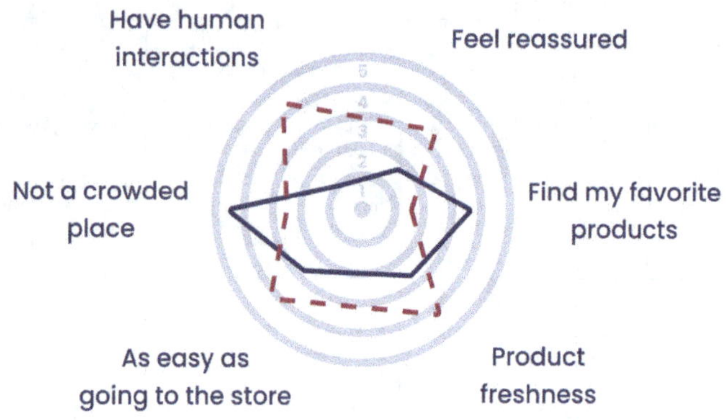

FIGURE 23. A radar chart of competing solutions for grocery shopping, comparing their performances with respect to senior citizens' stable preferences. The solid line rates a typical online shopping experience from a big box store as seen from the customers' perspective. The dashed line rates the experience of going to a local, small grocery store.

Figure 23 clearly illustrates the potential shortcomings of our basic product concept, an online grocery store for senior shoppers. Our customers tend to distrust online supermarkets, perceiving the products as less fresh, the platforms as difficult to use, and the overall experience as impersonal and unsafe. If we want to launch a new product in this space, we need to address these issues. The local grocery store has high performances where the online experience fails, but is more crowded and offers less choice.

After this analysis, we must ask ourselves whether online shopping is even a viable product for our intended customers. If we are just imitating existing websites, we will not satisfy all stable preferences. On the other hand, maybe this analysis unlocks our creativity. The design team can take it as a challenge to come up with novel ideas to shore up the weaknesses of online shopping and give customers a more personal and trustworthy experience. In Chapter 12 we already mentioned some ideas for improving the security of delivery and human interaction. Regarding the freshness of products, one strategy could be to entrust the delivery agent with a large basket of fruits and vegetables, allowing customers to select their items upon delivery. Another idea could be holding product tastings at local events or in retirement communities, to reassure senior shoppers about the quality of the products while also addressing their preference for real human interaction.

It is nearly always possible to find solutions—but each solution comes with its own costs and trade-offs. As we will see in the next chapter, quantifying and managing these is fundamental to engineering a product that is profitable as well as attractive to customers.

The analysis of competing products broadens the spectrum of possibilities. It inspires us to generate new ideas to improve our product, whether through superior technology, enhanced processes, or other means. It also enables us to identify which innovations proposed by competitors could pose a future threat. When we maintain a steady pace (takt) of product innovations, tearing down and analyzing competing solutions is a regular activity that lets us anticipate these market challenges early.

We close this chapter with a final anecdote from our industry experience. While working as a CTO at a successful health tech startup, Flavian spent three days analyzing the website of one key competitor, which was a medical appointment SaaS. He was assisted by the engineering manager, the Product Owner, and the UX Designer. Together, they mined network requests using browser development tools as a way to gain insight into the technologies, the data structures, and the visible surface of the backend architecture. One aspect of the website piqued their interest: it made extensive, almost ubiquitous, use of labels enabling customers to navigate easily between their appointments, notes, medication, and patient information. This observation sparked a productive discussion within the team, leading them to consider the role of labels in the company's service and the trade-offs of adopting a similar approach. Even more importantly, they applied this new insight to other aspects of their core product, such as using labels to enhance communication among the various medical advisors providing care to their customers.

Now ask yourself:

- What trade-offs are you struggling to resolve in your product? How have competitors addressed or attempted to address the same issues?

- When you last examined your competitors' products, what aspects surprised you? Why did their engineers make this choice? What specific performance metrics were they aiming to optimize?

- Is there a stable preference where a competing product outperforms your own? How did they achieve this? Does this insight give you any ideas for enhancing your own product?

PART
4

IMAGINING YOUR NEXT BIG IDEA

After a deep dive into the client world, you have completed the value analysis phase for this takt cycle. Now it is time to think about your next big idea. What will your new product deliver? How are you hoping to build loyalty among your existing clients and gain new clients?

Part 3 described how to build a robust client model and design a product that connects to their needs and emotions. Now, Part 4 will show you how to bring these insights together into a convincing product vision and strategy. Step by step, we will discuss the lean point of view to validating a new concept, and several tools that you can use to refine the design and economic model into a winning product. This process culminates in crafting the **concept paper**, a concise narrative that the Chief Product Engineer uses to discover and formulate their next great idea. The concept paper:

- **Ties all your insights into a coherent story** that explores how the product will win people over and what technical challenges the Chief Product Engineer and the team still need to resolve to bring the product to life.

- Details how the product will be **profitable**.

- **Describes the plan to deliver** the product before the next takt time.

- **Convinces everyone** that this is the best way forward for the product.

CHAPTER
14

ENVISION YOUR
NEXT GREAT CONCEPT

14.1 Resolve a difficult client trade-off

Sandrine has a cherished travel mug that accompanies her everywhere. She feels out of place without it, because having a cup of her favorite tea helps her think better, especially during work. Before finding this mug (and buying three in various colors), she used to bring her favorite porcelain mug to work. But it was not very practical: the tea would sometimes spill, the handle did not fit into her car's cup holder, and she worried about breaking it. For years she grappled with this trade-off between comfort and convenience. However, once she stumbled upon the right product, one that seamlessly blended comfort *and* convenience, she wasted no time in making the switch. She considers the product an excellent deal for the value it provides.

A remarkable product tackles a challenging problem, one that individuals are currently handling in a less than optimal way. This is why lean product engineers approach their next idea not just as a solution to an existing problem, but as a solution to a **customer trade-off**: two concurrent but conflicting preferences that no single product perfectly fulfills. We aim to resolve this trade-off by choosing technologies and innovations that provide high performance in both areas. Defining this trade-off and its solution is what we refer to as building a **product concept**. The final result is not just a bag of features—it is a **performance-based product**.

A product concept—the central trade-off to be resolved—provides a clear, shared vision that everyone can understand and rally behind. It prevents people from making changes based on their own preferences or pressure from the organization. This approach to product design is fundamentally different from building a feature backlog and deciding which ones, from an ever-growing list, should be implemented in the next release. Managing the feature backlog is always a painful exercise for the product team. Without a guiding vision for the product's core concept, they are pulled in all directions by internal stakeholders. They are never able to satisfy everyone, customers included. They are often forced to make compromises, and end up with half-baked or overly complex products as a result.

A product concept can be formulated as a *"yet* statement". For example, "it's fast *yet* energy-efficient" could be a good product concept for a data server or digital delivery service. The *yet* could be implicit or explicit, but it is always there to show how the concept stands out from existing solutions: the product does this (which might be true of others) *yet* it also does that (no other resolves the trade-off in the same way). Here are a few more examples of product concepts that encapsulate a client trade-off:

- An extra-light laptop with high battery life
- An environmentally friendly laundry detergent
- A 4x4 vehicle with city-style aesthetics
- An online bank that prioritizes people over profits
- An online dating service that connects like-minded individuals from the comfort of their homes
- A travel mug with a porcelain-like appearance and robust durability

Notice that we can easily rephrase each concept by incorporating a "yet": a laptop that is extra-light, *yet* offers high battery life. Describing the central trade-off sets the tone and an explicit design goal from the beginning, because underlying the *yet* is a real technical or engineering challenge that we are dedicated to resolving. For example, how can a product engineer conceive a mug that is sturdy yet delicate? "Sturdy" and "delicate" are not just a pair of features, they are technical characteristics or product performances that appear incompatible at first glance. Fulfilling the promise of the *yet* statement requires a unique approach to product design. Our goal for each product takt is not to roll out a new set of features (although that can still happen), but to enhance customer satisfaction and specific product performances by resolving difficult trade-offs. This requires innovative thinking from the entire team. Shifting the focus from the next feature to build to the technical challenge to overcome alters the nature of discussions among team members. In the case of the travel mug, the team could explore new materials, new handle shapes, and other design improvements depending on which trade-off they decide to work on.

> **By forcing ourselves to overcome difficult technical challenges with each product release, we maintain our competitive edge, and make it more difficult for competitors to imitate us.**

FIGURE 24. Sandrine's favorite porcelain mug fulfills two of her major preferences: it holds a lot of tea and has a comfortable grip. But it is not great for travel, because the tea sometimes spills and the mug could break. For a long time, she accepted the compromise because the travel mugs she saw on the market were simply not as comfortable to use.

Surya, a Product Manager at AutoRABIT, used this approach to rally her entire team. They were developing a digital solution to help Release Managers achieve their DevSecOps[33] goals within the intricate Salesforce development landscape. Surya's team framed the concept for their product as follows: "Achieve twice the user stories in half the time, without compromising customer data." Do you see the *yet*? Their concept revolves around the difficult challenge of allowing Release Managers to accelerate delivery within the Salesforce release process, while preserving quality (defined as data security). Immediately, the team's attention shifted from individual story development to collective, innovative thinking and experimentation.

In the context of the team's existing product, the technical challenge underlying this *yet* statement is to create a better visualization of live processes and outcomes for Release Managers, one that strikes the right balance between simplicity and completeness. Overwhelming the screen with information would make it difficult to navigate and interpret, but leaving out too much information would prevent Release Managers from making good decisions. Note that the product concept is not phrased in terms of data complexity or data quantity—it is phrased in terms of the value that Release Managers get out of the product, in terms of their preferences and the Job To Be Done. In fact, Surya and the team made a concerted effort to prioritize simplicity, recognizing it as the primary customer preference.

---

33 DevOps blends Development and Operations through Continuous Integration (CI), automating tests and deployment throughout the software development lifecycle. DevSecOps adds automated security checks into this process, ensuring security is continuously integrated and maintained.

By framing the product concept as a trade-off, Surya and the team achieved a remarkable feat: the latest version of their tool empowers Release Managers to respond swiftly to issues that could degrade data security and enhance collaboration with the various technical teams involved.

Now ask yourself:
- How would you articulate the yet within your product?
- Which trade-off does your product aim to address for your clients?
- What technical challenge must you confront to resolve the yet?
- In what way does this differentiation set your product apart from existing solutions?

14.2 Pave the way to emotion-centric design

The step between recognizing that we have a problem and actually buying a solution can be quite substantial. We readily express interest when shown a new solution, but hesitate to put our money on the line. Many startups have experienced the profound disappointment of enthusiastic focus groups followed by lackluster sales. This happens because the decision to acquire a product is not purely rational. It is always shaped by our personal circumstances, encompassing our past and present, and profoundly influenced by our emotions. Therefore, it is not enough to understand the problems people aim to solve and the essential characteristics of a solution. We also need to grasp which specific aspects of the product will *motivate* individuals to make the purchase and return for more.

The desire to purchase a product is rooted in our emotions. While conventional economics presumes that individuals are rational entities, who make purchasing choices strictly to maximize utility and profit, behavioral economics presents a contrasting view. It recognizes that the decision-making process is not always rational but frequently influenced by cognitive biases, emotional responses, and other psychological factors. Behavioral economics accepts that we perceive and interpret reality through our emotions and biases, shaped by our memories. It is easy to recognize the truth of this within ourselves. Our attachment to things (objects of course, but also places, activities, services, and experiences) stems from the positive memories, relationships, or events they evoke.

When creating a new product, it is essential to understand how it will resonate emotionally with specific customers. In other words, we need to determine how the product will establish a personal connection with people. Often, engineers downplay this aspect of design as secondary to function. A startup might wait until they have a working product before they start asking themselves how to reduce churn by better advertising or otherwise tapping into people's emotions, but by then it is too late. The connection between emotions and a product goes beyond marketing and advertising. From a lean perspective, the emotional connection is part of the product's utility.

A product concept embodies the emotion we aspire to evoke and infuse into the product design.

You might now be wondering, "Everyone has different lives and experiences, so how can I design a product that resonates with all their diverse emotions?" The answer is that we can still design for the *dominant* emotion, the one that is most prominent and consistent across various groups of people. Every product has such an emotion. You can observe this approach in TV commercials and billboard ads, both of which target very wide and diverse audiences. For example, consider a box of children's cereal. The dominant emotion in TV advertising is usually the child's *delight*, created by the bright colors and the toy inside the box. Commercials often depict a child opening the box with wide-eyed excitement. Beside them, the mom or dad is filled with satisfaction seeing their child so happy with a nutritious breakfast. The two customer groups are shown to experience different dominant emotions for the same product, but the focus is on the child.

Which product touches our emotions?

FIGURE 25. The decision to purchase results from an emotional connection with the product, not the other way around.

Every product evokes an emotion. Take Sandrine's favorite travel mug. It solves a genuine problem for her: it is as comfortable to use as her porcelain mugs at home, *yet* the travel mug is spill-proof and sturdy. But this technical solution is not enough to explain why she carries it everywhere and owns multiple copies in various colors. Simply performing a function consistently is not sufficient for a product to succeed and inspire loyalty. It must also elicit a positive emotion. In the end, Sandrine values the travel mug so highly because it recreates the experience of using a similar porcelain mug at home, which is a source of comfort and strength for her. When she holds it, it brings her the same sensation as the porcelain mug she uses at home. It makes her feel as if she's sitting in her armchair under a cozy blanket, wearing comfortable clothes, watching the fire crackle in the fireplace.

The insulation and spill-proof lid are technical considerations that allow the travel mug to perform its basic function. A legion of alternatives have the same features, but none of them resonated with Sandrine's emotions. What aspects did create this connection? They were the more subtle design choices. The travel mug boasts a wonderful grip that perfectly fits her hand.

It is lightweight and compact, making it easy to carry around. The surface is delicate and smooth, like the mugs she uses at home. Any alterations made to the design must preserve the emotional connection, or else Sandrine might stop using it and look for an alternative.

FIGURE 26. Sandrine's travel mug is a winning design not just because it conserves the performance of her porcelain mug (top left) without the inconveniences (top right), but also because of the positive emotions it brings her while she is away from home (bottom).

The dominant emotion of a product may not always be readily apparent. JB, the founder of the insurtech presented earlier, chuckled when Sandrine asked him what emotion he wanted to create with his short-term insurance products. He believed that insurance was primarily viewed as a commodity, so the people buying it were primarily concerned about price. He didn't think his products stirred any emotions at all. However, as he and his team started to learn more about their customers, they started to recognize different Jobs To Be Done and came to see the distinctive emotions linked to these jobs.

Encouraged by his sensei Sandrine, JB and several members of the team conducted a series of interviews to gain a deeper understanding of their customers' motivations. They discovered a number of genuinely personal stories. For instance, they learned about a father who purchased temporary insurance so that he could lend his car to his teenage child for a weekend trip. He viewed this trip as a rite of passage for his child and wanted to experience being a supportive father one last time before his child embarked on his adult life. Another customer wanted to borrow her parent's car and drive her best friend to the airport, hoping to capture a few more hours of quality time during the ride. For her, the act of purchasing temporary insurance was a gesture symbolizing this genuine friendship. From these two examples, a dominant emotion emerged: the desire to be a caring and supportive companion.

Designing to evoke specific emotions is a crucial responsibility for Chief Product Engineers. If they target the wrong emotion, or make changes that alter the dominant emotion associated with the product, they run the risk of disappointing customers. A lack of emotional connection or addressing the wrong emotion can ultimately lead to the product's failure. Developing a product concept means having a firm commitment to identify and incorporate emotions from the start, rather than simply designing to functional specifications provided by marketing or other departments. Considering a product solely in terms of its features, without taking into account the emotions it aims to evoke, is a surefire way to create a product that struggles to gain traction in the market. This perspective is one of the fundamental distinctions between a Chief Product Engineer and traditional roles like Product Manager or Product Owner.

Learning the language of emotions

To create an exceptional product concept, it is crucial to grasp the significance of emotions. Products have the potential to evoke a wide range of emotions, both positive and negative. An emotion typically originates as a bodily sensation, whether it is a fragrance that sends shivers down our spine, a familiar sound that brings tears to our eyes due to its personal meaning, or intense feelings linked to our moods and interpersonal connections. Naturally, our aim is to evoke positive emotions, such as the joy experienced when discovering the toy surprise in a cereal box, the warm nostalgia of being in grandma's kitchen, or the feeling of being a caring parent or close friend.

In his book *Emotional Design*, Don Norman defines three levels or layers of emotional response: visceral, behavioral, and reflective. He emphasizes the importance of designing products that incorporate all three layers.

- **Visceral.** Do I fall in love with the product at first sight? Is the product appealing and does it make me want to touch it, hold it, or play with it? First impressions matter.

- **Behavioral.** Does the product help me do the job I want to do? Does it do well as I expect it to? Is it easy to use? Do I feel joy and satisfaction when using it? Do I feel empowered?

- **Reflective.** Do I gradually develop an emotional bond with the product? Does it improve my own image and do I feel proud to use it? Do I want to share it with all my friends?

Translating these emotions into a clear concept is the challenge at hand. To deepen our understanding of the customer's emotional journey, we suggest the use of a versatile tool employed in various industries: the storyboard. It was developed for the film industry, where touching people's emotions decides the fate of the product. In other business settings, storyboards depict how our product will be used by real customers and the specific emotions we intend to evoke along the journey. Furthermore, storyboards are valuable and effective tools for communicating our vision to stakeholders and team members, providing a comprehensive perspective on the product.

Here is a storyboard developed by Claire from Productness, a CPO who took the "Build To Sell" training program[34]. Claire's product concept is a novel online resource for startup founders

---

34 The "Build To Sell" training program is based on the concepts outlined in this book, available at https://tktq.link/program

to validate their ideas before launching a business. Within the storyboard she outlines the emotional voyage of a woman with a product idea:

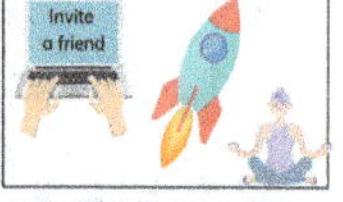

FIGURE 27. A storyboard illustrating the journey of an entrepreneur who needs to validate her idea, and gets the help she needs thanks to a new online resource (the product).

Here are some guidelines Claire followed to build her storyboard:

• **Show the problem.** Describe the "before" situation, which is the background of her story and highlights the value of the solution. What does the main character need to do, and how are they trying to resolve the problem?

- **Illustrate her first encounter** with the product. What is the first impression, and what emotion does the main character feel at this moment (the visceral response)?

- Present **the solution as an ongoing process**. This is the "during" situation, the experience of their Job To Be Done accompanied by the proposed solution. Show someone performing their task, and how they feel as they are using the product (the behavioral response).

- **Demonstrate the benefit.** This is the "after" situation, where we show how the person feels after using the solution several times and their attachment (the reflective response).

We can also use other storytelling models to illustrate our product concept. Pixar's storytelling model and the Hero's Journey are both compelling frameworks for showing the customers' emotional journey. The Pixar model is the one used by Uber to describe their product vision, according to Ebi Atawodi[35], former head PM at Uber, Netflix and now Google[36]. Here it is:

1. Once upon a time... (context)

2. Every day... ("before")

3. But, one day... (first impression, visceral response)

4. Because of that... ("during")

5. Because of that... ("during")

---

35 See this interview: "Crafting a compelling product vision | Ebi Atawodi (YouTube, Netflix, Uber)": https://tktq.link/build-to-sell/crafting-compelling-product-vision

36 You can find a detailed description of the Pixar storytelling model on Khan Academy's "Pixar in a Box" series https://tktq.link/build-to-sell/pixar-storytelling

6. Because of that... ("during", behavioral response)

7. Until finally... ("after")

8. And ever since then... ("after", reflective response)

9. And the moral of the story is... (product concept)

The Hero's Journey[37] is an effective way to create a first-person narrative and help people understand the product experience from the customer's point of view. Here it is, aligned with a few lean-oriented concepts to get you started:

1. Who is the hero? (the customer)
2. What is their greatest pain and longing? (the problem)
3. What is the quest they need to go on? (the Job To Be Done)
4. How can you help them on this journey? (the product concept or *YET*)
5. What is the gift you can help them discover? (the product)
6. How will discovering this transform their life? (the emotion)

You may select the model that best suits your expressive needs or even blend these models in your storyboard to offer different perspectives.

In Claire's storyboard, we clearly see the visceral, behavioral and reflective emotional responses of the protagonist:

---

37 For more details on the Hero's Journey model, you may visit the Joseph Campbell Foundation's website: https://tktq.link/build-to-sell/jcf-org

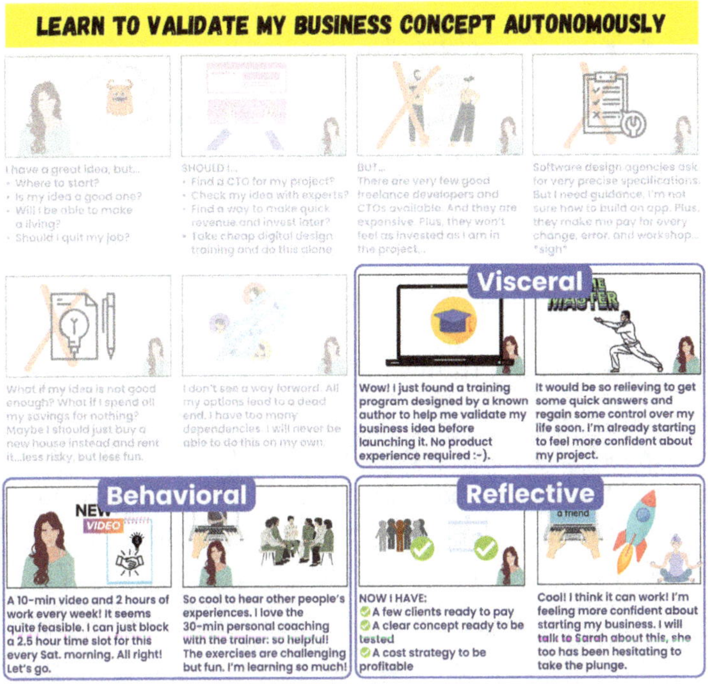

FIGURE 28. After setting up the initial situation and the problem, the storyboard highlights the customer's emotional responses at different stages of the product journey.

The customer will go through various other emotions before, during, and after using our product, but one dominant emotion tends to prevail in the end. Typically, the dominant emotion you aim to evoke is the opposite of the negative emotion that the hero feels at the start of their journey. In her storyboard, Claire emphasizes the emotions of "feeling in control" as the dominant emotion her product is designed to create for women entrepreneurs, in contrast with feeling overwhelmed and insecure at the beginning.

14.3 Assess the product's business potential

We see an increasing number of startup founders who rely on personal charisma and storytelling abilities to attract investors and achieve rapid growth. They pour their hearts into persuading venture capitalists and business angels to support their ideas, rather than creating exceptional products. This approach may have been effective a few years ago, when there were fewer entrepreneurs and the economic outlook was more favorable. However, now numerous startups and scaleups are being forced to downsize, pivot, or even cease operations because they are not living up to the initial promise. Today, a good story is not enough—investors want to see tangible evidence of both future growth and profitability. Furthermore, many are demanding that startups reach a break-even point within two to three years. To attract funding, entrepreneurs must establish a compelling case for sales *and* profitability from the outset. In lean product design and development, the financial viability of a new concept is a crucial factor. The viability of an idea determines whether we should proceed with development and can also change how to go about it. Introducing a new product always involves risk. It is often wiser to stop marginally viable concepts early, rather than creating a financial drain by moving forward despite misgivings.

Hence, once we have identified a compelling client problem to solve, the next step is to determine if the potential customer base is sufficiently large to justify the cost of development and production. The question becomes: *How many units of the future product do we think we can sell, and over what timeframe?* This means making an educated guess about how many people will actually purchase the product, and not just a revenue projection based on wishful thinking. Answering this question shifts the focus of discussion fundamentally, since it requires us to consider *who specifically* is likely to buy the product. Naturally, our guess will be influenced by the product's selling price.

Determining the right price, one that is neither too low nor too high, can make the difference between a viable concept and a nonviable one, between success and failure. This is precisely why the profit and loss of the product should be owned by the Chief Product Engineer, not by someone from the marketing or finance departments. Whether we are speaking of a brand new product or a new release with incremental improvements, *the price is inseparable from the design.*

The "price is right"

Several pricing strategies exist, but many of them are centered around how much profit we want to generate, rather than how much value we intend to create for customers. One of the most common strategies is the "cost-based" approach, which can be summarized as follows:

FIGURE 29. Cost-based pricing formula.

Notice that the market fit and customer adoption do not enter into this formula. The price is established by adding the desired profit for each unit sold to the production cost of one unit. This approach comes with significant risk, as there is no guarantee that customers will be willing to pay this price to acquire the product. If customers don't see its value immediately, the company will most likely have to spend substantial financial resources persuading people to make a purchase.

Another popular strategy is incentive-based. Here the idea is to deploy aggressive customer attraction techniques, such as temporary promotions or rock-bottom prices, then increase the price as demand rises and the product accumulates a base of "locked in" customers. A similar market penetration strategy frequently employed by SaaS companies is the "freemium" model, where the product line includes a free trial version and a more powerful paid version. We are also seeing the emergence of a hybrid approach, the "unlimited free trial".

Each approach comes with its own set of issues. The cost-based approach can result in overpricing, making the product difficult to sell. Some coffee shops apply a 300% markup to their beverages to account for rent and labor expenses. Nevertheless, not everyone is ready to spend five dollars just on a cup of coffee. The coffee shops who can get away with high prices have a strong brand and additional offerings, such as a comfortable workspace and reliable Wi-Fi. However, this pricing strategy is very risky when you are trying to build your brand and customer base. Incentive-based strategies, often used by internet providers, may be perceived as deceptive by customers and degrade the brand. As for the freemium approach, it can turn into a financial burden as free users still require support and converting them into paying customers is an arduous task.

Striking the right balance between value and profit is no easy feat: if your price is high compared to competing solutions, customers may perceive the product as luxurious and too costly. Conversely, if the price is too low then customers might question its quality. For this reason, Geoffrey Moore, in his classic book *Crossing the Chasm*, suggests establishing a price based on the market leaders.

Value-based pricing

Lean product development takes on this challenge in a different way: the goal is to find the optimal price that motivates customers to buy our product, based on its inherent value. This is the most efficient and accurate approach in most cases, but it does require a profound understanding of our customers, their behaviors, and their context. Without the detailed information obtained by conducting interviews, going to the gemba, understanding the Job To Be Done, and tearing down alternative solutions, estimating the value of your product is just guesswork. This heavy requirement could explain why many businesses don't choose this pricing strategy. In practice, based on all this evidence, we try to determine *how much the customer is willing to pay* for our product before setting the target profit. The formula can be summarized as follows:

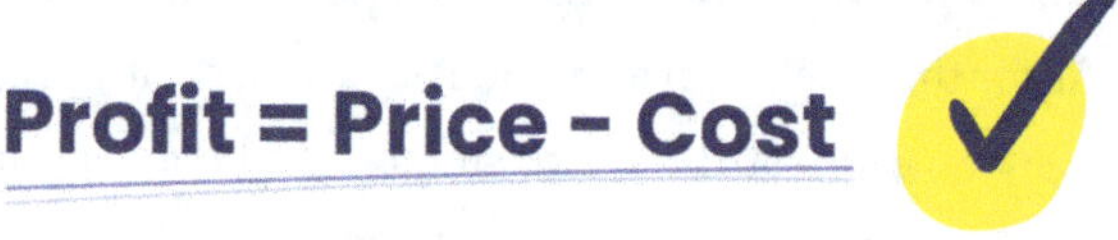

FIGURE 30. Value-based pricing formula.

This approach, which we recommend, is market-driven. We start by determining the price and the desired margin, and whatever is left is our target cost. **Price** is what customers are willing to pay for one unit of the product. It is set by the market, not by our own fiat. To estimate the price, we need to look at market conditions (competitors, growth rate, consumption habits, pace of innovation, etc.) as well as our customers' willingness to pay. **Profit** is how much profit we would like to make, but it must be coherent with industry benchmarks. For instance, a typical profit margin for a SaaS company is between 75% and 90%, ideally above 80%. Anything under 70% is considered worrisome.[38] The calculated profit must be large enough to cover operating expenses and enable continued investment in the product line. **Cost** in the above formula signifies the amount of money we have available to produce one unit of the product.

---

38 Source: https://tktq.link/build-to-sell/gross-profit-margin

This approach treats costs as variable, subject to the product's design. We aim to maintain a price that is acceptable to customers while minimizing costs to meet industry-standard profit targets. The key assumption is that if we want to increase profit, we can only do it by reducing costs, not by arbitrarily setting a higher price.

Let's look at an example to see how value-based pricing can be put into practice.

Alice is the co-founder of JamSpace, an online marketplace designed to help amateur musicians connect and form impromptu bands. Musicians who hire JamSpace pay a flat fee when they join the site, and pay again for each jam session they attend. A jam session is a few musicians playing together for a few hours in a studio, and all participating JamSpace members pay a fee for the event. JamSpace's services undeniably meet a real need, but the business has plateaued and Alice is contemplating the next steps. The matching and scheduling services are working well, expertly coordinated by Alice's team. The fee was initially estimated by Alice herself based on her market research of similar matching services.

As part of the "Build To Sell" training program, Alice conducted a thorough evaluation of her product's profitability. To her surprise, she discovered that the cost of supporting one musician was 1.5 times higher than the fee she charged for participation in a jam session. While she was dedicated to ensuring the well-being of musicians and organizing enjoyable jam events, running the service turned out to be more expensive than initially anticipated. Although increasing the price seemed like an easy solution, after studying the market, she realized this would not be a wise move.

She needed to check her initial assumptions by gaining a deeper understanding of her customers' needs and their current alternatives. To achieve this, she conducted interviews with several customers to uncover their primary Job To Be Done and how they were currently fulfilling it. She learned that a significant portion of her customer base were individuals with stable, well-paying jobs but not enough free time to commit to a regular band. These customers highly valued JamSpace and were willing to pay for a comprehensive solution. However, another customer segment was formed by musicians with lower incomes looking for a budget-friendly option to stay in practice. Although these individuals joined JamSpace to connect with other musicians, they rarely paid extra to organize an event. She considered simplifying her offering for this customer segment to lower the price. However, she first needed to find out whether this group would be willing to pay the reduced price regularly, given that JamSpace's primary competitor was informal gatherings with friends. Informal gatherings are free, but for this solution to be considered as an alternative, musicians had to have many connections already. Clearly this was not always the case. Alice concluded that it was worth exploring a new product concept with a lower price, aimed at this segment.

How many units can we sell?

Before we can answer this question, it is essential to determine what constitutes a unit of our product. In Alice's case, one unit could be a single jam session (for the amateur musicians with steady jobs) or a yearly subscription (for the full-time musicians with lower incomes). Alice needs to apply the "profit = price – cost" formula to both of her products. When evaluating the business potential of a new product, we often look at yearly revenue and total costs, but this viewpoint can obscure the details of individual purchasing decisions and make it harder to compare different offers. To gain a true understanding of the business model's effectiveness, a good rule of thumb is to bring the sales unit close to each individual customer. In Alice's case, this means developing a pricing strategy that works at the level of individual musicians, rather than jam sessions or concerts. Such events were bringing in big chunks of revenue, but the number of participants varied and each participating musician required different levels of support.

Alice's case is straightforward, but finding the appropriate sales unit is not always so easy. For instance, consider a consulting firm that provides expert teams of developers to build new digital products. What should be considered the sales unit in this scenario? Is it the contract, the project, the team, the individual developer, or even each day sold? Similar to JamSpace, I would recommend calculating the value-based price at the individual level. How many developers can we realistically place this year? How many days of their time can we realistically sell? Given that figure, what margin do we aim for? What will be the cost of supporting and developing each team member? All these questions present intriguing possibilities for exploring and validating the business model. We shall see in Section 14.5, "Plan for profitability", how to calculate real costs per unit sold and identify ways to reduce costs without degrading the value for customers.

Returning to Alice, she was faced with a challenging decision.

Should she invest her resources and effort in streamlining the full solution for well-off musicians, or develop a simplified version for the budget-conscious segment? Which path has the best business potential? The only way to answer this question is to estimate how many units she would sell over the next year and beyond, and whether this would lead to both growth and profitability. This estimation can't be arbitrary; it has to be grounded in actual data.

When she launched her business, Alice knew that over seven million people in the country played at least one musical instrument. She was confident that a substantial portion of these would share an interest in connecting with fellow musicians, just as she had personally experienced. However, this number just puts a ceiling on the size of her potential market. What Alice really needs to know is how many people are actively looking to join music bands each year.

This information was not readily available when she launched her business, but the recent emergence of numerous services facilitating connections among musicians indicated an expanding demand. Alice decided that she could assess the underlying demand and rate of growth by analyzing competing services as well as her own. She could analyze the different services offered, discover the technologies employed by competitors, count the number of members and events, and read the published customer feedback. She could also gauge interest in her simplified offer by conducting surveys within musician communities or testing cheap prototypes in a variety of situations. All this research permitted Alice to estimate the real sales volume and market price for her type of product.

Of course, we can never be 100% sure that the market is ready for a new product, but we must collect all the data we can to make an educated guess. Without access to this data, every decision we make is essentially a leap of faith.

Now ask yourself:
- What price are potential clients willing to pay for your product? What supporting evidence do you have?
- How does this price compare to your competitors' pricing?
- How many units of the product do you anticipate selling, and what evidence supports your estimate?
- What is your target margin per product sold, and does it align with the industry standard?

14.4 Conceive a performance-based product

Product Managers traditionally focus their efforts on creating roadmaps and curating a list of product features. These "wish lists", known as backlogs, can attain a truly massive scale. They are an inventory of all proposed changes, ranging from direct client requests to feedback from internal stakeholders. Some items in the backlog are scheduled for implementation in future versions of existing products, set to roll out over several months or even years, while others are placed on hold indefinitely.

The process of creating and maintaining a product roadmap is driven by pressure from top management and investors, who want a solid long-term plan to reassure them that their investment is safe. They mistakenly believe that the more features get crammed into a product, the more customers it will attract and the bigger the return on investment (ROI). This approach often leads startups down the wrong path, resulting in products that don't quite hit the mark with any segment and accumulate technical debt. Take a peek at your product team's feature backlog and you'll find a mountain of unaddressed requests gathering dust. Some of them may be so ancient that no one on the team remembers creating them.

After a subset of features and bug fixes has been selected for the next release, often through a somewhat painful process of negotiation, the delivery team starts working through them. Success often boils down to getting as many features as possible out the door, rather than thinking about how much value they bring to our customers and the business. It is rare to remove items from the backlog, even when we have doubts about their worth. It is even rarer to check the actual value brought by the delivered features. Once a feature is in the product, it becomes a permanent resident even if it is not doing much for our users. This leads to bloat and technical debt. To echo Marty Cagan and Chris Jones in their book *Empowered: Ordinary People, Extraordinary Products*, product teams tend to prioritize output over outcomes.

While we often agree that product teams should shift their focus towards solving customer problems instead of churning out features, identifying the next critical problem for our customers remains a major challenge. Going to the client gemba provides us with insights into their lives and changes in tastes and behaviors. By seeing where our product falls short, the gemba can help us understand where we need to focus our energy. However, it does not tell us *which problem we need to tackle next*. How can we set priorities without letting our personal biases and preferences get in the way? The title of this section holds the answer: by breaking the feature mindset and refocusing our attention on the most critical performances of the product that are creating value for its users.

The feature frenzy syndrome

The feature frenzy syndrome, as we affectionately call it, comes with a couple of hefty downsides:

The first is the need for speed, which paradoxically tends to transform the delivery pace into a sort of slow-motion race. Because the product team is juggling a haphazard mix of unrelated features, delivery is split into siloed work streams. Some developers can even end up working in isolation. The result is fewer opportunities for effective collaboration and slower delivery of individual features. It's a well-established principle that working on multiple tasks simultaneously can significantly delay the completion of each task. This division of focus not only hampers the speed of execution but can also affect the quality of the output. If the release contains an ambitiously large number of features (to achieve the team's performance targets for example), this trend only intensifies. The team's lack of focus also takes a toll on quality. Features rushed into the product lead to endless rounds of rework, client complaints, and in-house headaches. To get through the feature backlog more quickly, developers may feel forced to take shortcuts, piling up technical debt and potentially spawning a backlog of defects, perpetuating the vicious cycle.

The other downside of feature frenzy syndrome is that it is easy for product teams to get wrapped up in clearing the backlog as an end in itself. Every completed story, every delivered feature feels like a success, sometimes against terrible odds! But by keeping their noses to the grindstone, product teams and even the Product Owner can lose sight of the bigger picture. What is most important to our customers? How are market needs evolving? Do the features in this release really support the customers' Job To Be Done? By rushing through a bloated backlog, product teams often end up missing the mark entirely: the new release fails to meet or improve their clients' stable preferences and loses the opportunity to forge an emotional connection.

Cynthia, working for an international non-governmental organization, embarked on a mission to develop a new application aimed at inspiring her country's population to embrace a more eco-friendly lifestyle. To realize her vision, she collaborated with a consulting firm who provided her with a wealth of data from surveys and competitive analysis, complete with persona profiles and pain points. Cynthia built a list of features for the future app, using the consultant's report as her North Star. With a clear goal in mind, Cynthia enlisted DevCraft, a digital development firm, to turn her dream into a tangible product. Paul, DevCraft's CPO and a seasoned lean practitioner, understood the importance of real-life validation, so he insisted on meeting potential users, which Cynthia readily agreed to. The experiences of these users echoed the findings of the consulting firm's report, providing further validation. Cynthia and Paul then conducted another prioritization exercise to streamline the list of features, recognizing the potential challenges of a large backlog. However, after the session they still faced an impressively long "wish list". In the end, they decided to include the majority of identified user problems in the first release of the product.

On an individual level, Cynthia and Paul were confident that each proposed feature addressed a genuine problem. However, the large backlog led them to create an overly complex application, essentially combining three products into one. While it took a long time to build, the team had a great feeling about the final product design and felt that development was going well. Furthermore, they conducted multiple rounds of testing with potential users, each time getting positive feedback that bolstered their confidence in the app's success. However, the first release had disappointing results. Six months later, despite a large number of downloads, users were not using the app regularly. Less than half had succeeded in creating a habit around the application. One major feature that everybody thought would create great value ended up with an adoption rate of merely 15%. These results prompted Cynthia and Paul to decommission several modules of the application and rethink their approach.

Their mistake was succumbing to the common temptation of trying to cram every possible feature into the product. This decision may be driven by the belief that since it is difficult to prioritize we should not choose, instead relying on our clients to provide feedback on their preferences over time. Like many startups, they ended up with a "jack of all trades but master of none", and the product failed to fully resonate with customers.

Betting on numerous needs simultaneously without a profound grasp of stable customer preferences led Cynthia and Paul astray. As previously highlighted in chapter 12, understanding stable customer preferences before starting development is paramount.

Product behaviors NOT product features

To hit the sweet spot with customers, it is essential that we remain focused on what matters most to them. The saying "Perfect is the enemy of good" is particularly relevant in product design. Cynthia and Paul overlooked the crucial step of identifying stable customer preferences for the segment they wanted to address first. This was not a matter of negligence—as stated at the beginning of the story, they had lots of high-quality research to draw on—they just missed the essential step to consolidate this data into a useful product model.

Before diving into feature development, we first need to know how the product must behave to fully satisfy all customer preferences.

Customer preferences act as guardrails for our product development team, so they make design choices that fall within the acceptable limits expressed by our customers. Some of these limits may hinge on emotions rather than quantifiable characteristics, which underlines the need to master the art of observation in order to put them into practice.

Take, for example, our discussion of an online shopping service for older shoppers in chapter 12. One of the fundamental preferences that emerged from interviews was "easy access to their favorite products". Recognizing this factor as non-negotiable compels us to establish design boundaries. What does "easily" really mean? It might translate into a streamlined product selection process (such as a window to view previous, favorite, or recurring purchases), or it might mean raising the visibility of store-featured options. We can also establish a performance target to showcase only three or fewer products in a category, so the shopper is not faced with choice paralysis. Notice that this design requirement is *not* a feature—it is a statement for how the application should behave. Respecting the customer preference can therefore modify the design choices of several related software features, such as product search and the user interface.

This behavior-first approach ensures that our application aligns with our customers' most important quality criteria and fulfills their expectations for the resulting shopping experience. The result is what we call a **performance-based product**, which we can contrast with the "feature-based product" that results from following a traditional product roadmap and backlog. After our design fully satisfies the most widespread needs, we can consider other preferences that might be more personal, such as allowing customers to declare other criteria for product selection (low sugar, gluten free) or automatically detecting such factors in their purchasing history.

Shifting our focus from product features to product behaviors transforms our work environment entirely. Developers have a new mission: to propose innovations that fully align with customer preferences while respecting predefined performance boundaries. In stark contrast with just picking a feature from the backlog, this *call to innovate* sparks dynamic and engaging conversations within the team. In an article on the Taktique blog[39], Surya Dashrath discusses the evolution of her role from writing user stories for developers to providing a framework that guides collective decision-making. Surya is a PM at AutoRABIT, the company that we presented in Section 14.1. This shift revolutionized the dynamic between the product and development teams, replacing frustration with invigorating design discussions that the teams sometimes voluntarily extended into lunchtime.

Surya built a **critical performance table** to structure and facilitate these discussions with the tech teams, which is illustrated below. Table 10 offers just a glimpse of the content, which is a strategic tool for AutoRABIT products.

---

39 Surya describes her experience in a must-read article on the Taktique blog: https://blog.taktique.com/stop-fearing-product-backlog

Key client preference	Critical product performance		Technical trade-off	Wow effect
	Critical product function	Function performance target		
Ease of use	Drag-and-drop visual system to build pipelines	< 5 actions to create the pipeline from source to destination		
etc.				

TABLE 10. Structure of a critical performance table used at AutoRABIT to inspire innovative ideas from designers and developers in meeting the key preferences of their customers.

One customer segment has a consistent preference for "ease of use", aligning with the product's main goal: to make Salesforce more user-friendly and manageable, converting common user jobs into a more streamlined experience. Through meticulous observation of clients at work and analysis of their feedback, Surya and the team translated this stable preference into a desirable product behavior. The system for building deployment pipelines needed to be not just intuitive but fast: users set a clear limit of *fewer than 5 manual actions* from start to finish. This measurable constraint on the product design is what we call a **critical product performance** which the table decomposes into two parts: the **critical product function** (drag and drop system) and the quantified **function performance target** (fewer than 5 actions). Satisfying this preference and the corresponding critical performance was a genuine challenge for the team! Existing products, including their own, all struggled to deliver this level of performance despite its significance to users.

Note that while "ease of use" is a clearly stated customer preference, it is also a subjective criterion. In contrast, writing down a critical performance of "fewer than 5 manual actions in the drag and drop system" sets a clear goal. Defining critical performances for all their customers' stable preferences paved the way for this team to explore various design possibilities, clearly see which ones had a chance of satisfying customers on all fronts, and innovate together to resolve trade-offs between the performances while keeping acceptable limits in mind. In short, this approach to design empowered them to make optimal choices for the customer.

A critical performance table does more than just help the team innovate and build consensus around the best solution. It guides them toward identifying the next challenge to improve customer satisfaction and bolster their competitive edge. By listing all the client stable preferences alongside the product's current performances and behaviors, it shows which preferences are still unmet or have opportunities to improve. At the start of each new design phase, dictated by the product takt (refer to Chapter 5), the critical performances of the product are re-evaluated. This process allows the team to explore various solutions to enhance the product while ensuring they do not compromise the customer experience.

Resolving trade-offs to trigger innovative thinking

Shifting the focus from features to critical performances redefines the mission for the whole product development team: Product Managers, designers, developers, and other specialists. Instead of checking a feature or user story off their list, their goal becomes to explore diverse technical solutions together. Hitting performance targets that align with every stable client preference is a real puzzle, one that will take everyone's brainpower and expertise to solve.

A product is a network of interconnected systems and components that need to work together seamlessly to create the right behaviors. Like instruments in an orchestra, each subsystem fills a unique and necessary role, but also imposes its own constraints on the whole product. A change made to one component can also impact others, for better or worse. The effects of this intricate balancing act are experienced on the design level as **technical trade-offs**.

Framing the design problem as a set of performances to achieve and trade-offs to resolve, rather than features to build, provides us with an opportunity to differentiate our product based on what is really important to customers: their stable preferences.

For example, for a search engine users typically have two stable preferences: speed and relevance of results. If we express these as critical performances, we might require a response time under 100 ms, and also ask for at least one of the top three results to be the most relevant content for the searcher. Satisfying the second preference fully might require comparing the search query to more data, which increases the response time. In this case, we say that there is a technical trade-off between the two performance criteria. Clever engineering might enable us to improve relevance significantly with very little impact on speed, but this doesn't change the fundamental nature of the trade-off.

A smartphone is a product with several interconnected preferences, performances and trade-offs. Improving battery life (a stable preference) could be achieved by using a battery with a higher energy storage capacity (a product function with a critical performance), but this would increase the phone's weight (low weight is another critical performance) and hence degrade its ergonomics in terms of size and ease of grip (another stable preference).[40]

Below, we diagram these relationships: boosting battery life leads to an increase in weight, so we can identify a negative relationship (–) between the two functions "energy storage capacity" and "lightweight". The arrow goes in both directions: trying to decrease the weight of the phone makes it harder to provide a large capacity, and vice versa. The product engineering team will need to resolve this conflict, or trade-off, if they want to make an impactful change to the product.

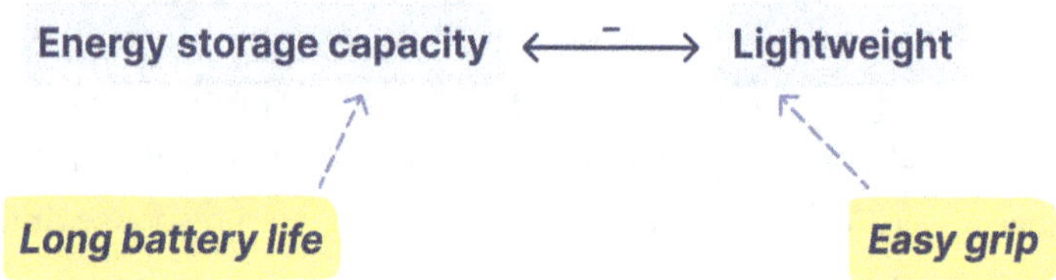

FIGURE 31. Diagram of stable preferences (italic, bottom) and critical product functions (normal, top) for a smartphone design. The negative relationship between the two product functions indicates a challenging design trade-off.

---

40 This example is greatly simplified compared to the real complexities of smartphone design. In reality, there is more than one way to increase battery life, so we would define a critical performance in terms of how many hours the battery lasts under normal use.

Figure 31 provides a bird's-eye view of the critical performances and their trade-offs. We can also summarize this information in a table similar to the one used by Surya:

Key client preference	Critical product performance		Technical trade-off
	Critical product function	Function performance target	
Long battery life	Energy storage capacity	At least 20h battery life	Lightweight (–)
Easy grip	Lightweight	Between 140 and 160g	Energy storage capacity (–)

TABLE 11. A critical performance table for two stable preferences of smartphone users.

The interconnectedness between client preferences and related components or functions makes it difficult to design to specific values of the performances, especially for complex products. This is why we express the performance targets as ranges ("between 140g and 160g", "at least 20h battery life") instead of values ("140g" or "20h battery life"). Performance ranges give the engineers room to maneuver and test different technical solutions to find the best compromise for the customer.

The benefits of posing customer preferences as a design challenge extend far beyond the delivery of a single product. Resolving technical trade-offs both feeds and orients experimentation by the engineers. Each envisioned solution provides valuable insights into what works and what doesn't, and how the different components of the product interact on a macro level. This knowledge becomes a reusable asset in shaping future product evolutions.

Resolving technical challenges involves numerous factors, not just technology considerations. We also need to take into account customer knowledge, cost, scalability and safety, to name a few. Implementing a technology change is a delicate process where many things can go awry. Hence, another advantage of performance-based design is that it offers clear visibility into the repercussions of decisions across the whole product. By mapping the full network of critical product functions as in Figure 31, and identifying the positive and negative relationships between them, we gain reassurance and a level of insight that is difficult to achieve with a feature-centric approach.

The table below shows another example of a trade-off, this time in a digital product: Sandrine's online "Build To Sell" training program:

Key client preference	Critical product performance		Technical trade-off
	Critical product function	Function performance target	
Does not take me too much time	Short concept videos	Less than 5 minutes	Low-effort practical exercises (–)
Can immediately apply it to my situation	Low-effort practical exercises	- Between 1 and 3 hours of work total - No more than 2 exercises per concept	Short concept videos (–)

TABLE 12. A critical performance table for "Build To Sell" training program materials.

The first column of Table 12 lists the key preferences of a customer segment: startup founders, CEOs and CPOs who are keen to learn but short on time. In response to their stable preferences, her product concept is to provide "learning units that are not too theoretical *yet* provide insights that can be immediately applied in my situation." There are various types of course materials that Sandrine could create, but she must manage the trade-off implicit in the product concept.

Sandrine then defines two critical product functions of the course content that respond to the preferences: concise videos and practical exercises. If the training videos are too brief, they may not help participants understand course concepts well enough to apply them in their own context. Practical exercises would definitely help in applying the concepts, but her target audience might have difficulty finding time in their busy schedules. This trade-off between length and practicality is shown in the last column of Table 12 and illustrated in Figure 32.

Many other online training programs and courses struggle with the same challenge. Fulfilling both preferences simultaneously is no small feat, and Sandrine has been actively exploring diverse solutions. Some of them are already providing good results! Cracking this technical challenge will give her training program a unique advantage, setting it apart from the alternatives.

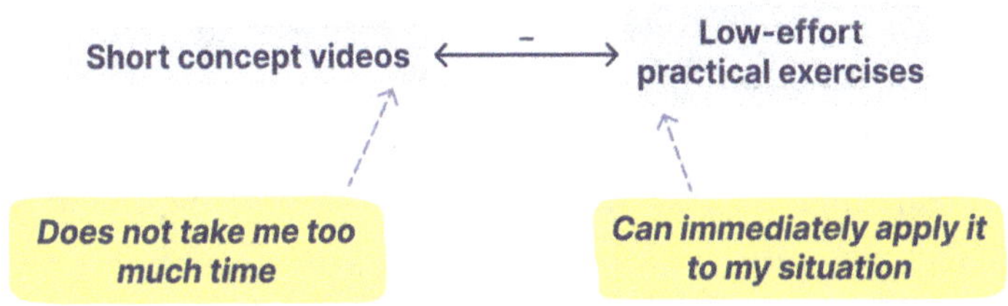

FIGURE 32. Diagram of stable preferences (italic, bottom) and critical product functions (normal, top) for "Build To Sell" training program materials. The negative relationship between the product functions indicates a challenging design trade-off.

After making the diagram above, the next step is to quantify our design goals. For each critical product function, we need to also define a range of values that we are sure will satisfy the corresponding customer preference: the function performance target. In this example, we aim to produce videos *under 5 minutes long* to match our students' preference for easily digestible content, without compromising the practical side. For the "low-effort practical exercises" function we set two performance targets: 1 or 2 exercises per video, and total effort of 1–3 hours. Explaining the concepts well *and* providing clear instructions for the practical exercises in a 5-minute video presents us with a significant technical challenge!

Wowing clients

Some product performance criteria need to stay within defined boundaries to meet client preferences, while others have the flexibility to exceed expectations, potentially sparking a "wow" effect. Throughout the design phase, the team might discover ways to wow clients without compromising any aspect of the product or drastically escalating costs.

Cécile Roche and Luc Delamotte, in their fantastic book on lean engineering[41], describe this concept using the Kano model. According to this model, the wow effect can only occur in two cases:

---

41 *The Lean Engineering Travel Guide: The Best Itineraries for Developing New Products and Satisfying Customers,* by Cécile Roche and Luc Delamotte

- If we introduce a new function that the client does not expect, assuming it satisfies a real customer preference.

- If we improve the performance of an existing function beyond the client's expectations.

For example, one critical performance for an e-commerce website is page-loading speed. A speed of 1 second feels a lot more satisfying than 3 seconds. In 2006, Data Scientist Greg Linden shared that Google's traffic was growing by 20% for every 200 milliseconds decrease in page loading times. In other words, a one-second reduction doubled their traffic. He also shared that Amazon was able to gain 1% in sales for every 100 milliseconds decrease in page loading times. In 2006, that was an extra 100 million dollars for just 0.1 seconds![42]

In the Kano Model, the critical performances of a product fall into three useful categories. Page loading speed is in the "performant" category, meaning that there is a linear relationship between speed and satisfaction (at least within a reasonable range). In the examples of Google and Amazon cited above, satisfaction translates directly into increased traffic and revenue. The two other categories of performance are "attractive" and "must have". They both have exponential relationships to satisfaction: attractive performances generate increasing satisfaction if they exceed expectations, while "must have" preferences generate increasing dissatisfaction if they fall below expectations. The three relationships are illustrated in Figure 33.

---

42 See the slides by Data Scientist Greg Linden:
https://tktq.link/build-to-sell/greg-linden-study

A fourth type of performance, "indifferent", has no effect on customer satisfaction at all.

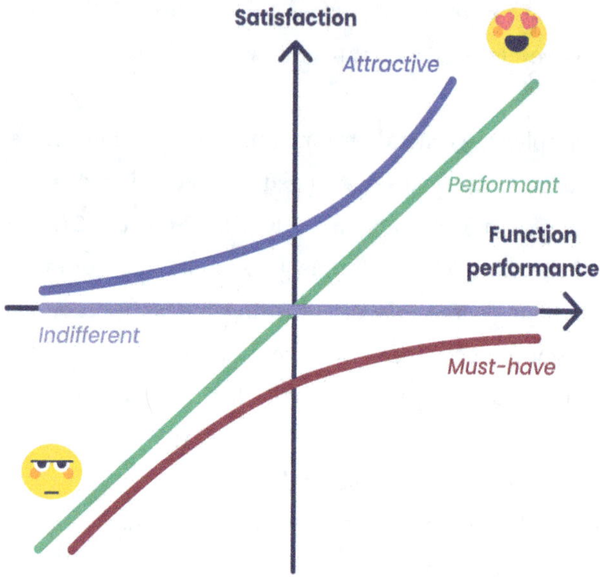

FIGURE 33. The Kano model of customer satisfaction as a function of product performances. If a must-have performance is below expectations, the resulting dissatisfaction is likely to negate any benefit from exceeding expectations in other categories.

The Kano model tells us that as the performance delivered by a product function increases beyond expectations, it can generate immense customer satisfaction. This is the "wow" effect in a nutshell—exceeding expectations on the right performance can have a game-changing impact. Likewise, underperformance on an essential function causes strong disappointment. This is why it is crucial for our design to meet customer expectations in all categories. Failing to do so will cancel out any gains from our innovations.

Returning to the example of page-loading speeds, improving this performance often comes with trade-offs. For instance, speeding up an e-commerce website might require reducing the number of catalog items displayed on a page, potentially making it harder for customers to find specific products. Therefore, it's crucial to balance enhancements with the need to maintain or improve existing functionalities, ensuring that efforts to impress or "wow" customers do not inadvertently degrade their overall experience. One crucial aspect of product design is identifying which performances can be enhanced together, without degrading others.

Key client preference	Critical product performance		"Wow" effect
	Critical product function	Function performance target	
Long battery life	Energy storage capacity	At least 20h battery life	· 30h battery life
Easy grip	Lightweight	Between 140 and 160g	· Close to 100g

TABLE 13. Examples of "wow" effects that we could introduce into smartphone design, provided that all other performance targets are maintained.

For instance, consider the smartphone scenario where 20 hours of battery life meets a customer's expectations. Typically this level of performance translates into a workday of heavy use, with the phone recharging overnight. However, if their new phone lasts more than a full day, it brings a delightful surprise. Even if the customer forgets to recharge overnight, they still have a few hours of battery life remaining. This factor can significantly impact the perceived value of the product, assuming we also fulfill other key preferences. For an e-commerce website, a surprisingly smooth shopping experience can also create that crucial "wow" factor. But caution is key—our primary focus should always be achieving solid performance for all critical product functions. Only when we are sure of this do we aim for exceptional performance in a specific area.

Concurrent prototyping to resolve trade-offs

Improving a product's critical performance always involves development and innovation. This is an opportunity for the team to consider new solutions to navigate the inevitable trade-offs, not just return to the ones that worked before. The lean approach to product design, whether a brand-new product or the next release of an existing product, involves exploring multiple solutions concurrently. This accelerates the discovery of the most compelling solution, and at the same time builds valuable engineering knowledge to inform future product designs. The team simultaneously tests multiple prototypes that address the trade-offs between key preferences in different ways. The weaker solutions are eliminated fast, allowing the team to converge on a design that is both technically and financially feasible, and has great market potential. This practice, called "set-based concurrent engineering", is widely adopted in the manufacturing realm. *The Lean Engineering Travel Guide* mentioned in Chapter 13 also discusses set-based engineering in detail.

Set-based engineering stands in contrast to a range of "point-based" approaches, where a single solution or product is built, tested in real conditions, then iterated upon. Digital startups under pressure from investors to generate revenue often turn to point-based engineering in order to release quickly. While businesses working this way might bring their products to customers a little faster, the process is more costly and time-consuming in the long run. In point-based engineering, the journey from the first release of a product to an optimal market fit by incremental releases often turns out to be long, expensive, and dissatisfying to customers. What's more, the engineers might find themselves constrained by technical choices made early in the project, making it difficult to adopt superior solutions discovered later. It doesn't take long for a team to become entrenched in feature frenzy syndrome, especially when the product is critical to the company's success.

At Toyota, a Chief Engineer might examine dozens of prototypes resolving a single trade-off in different ways, aiming for improved outcomes in two or more key performances, before making a decision for the final design. In fact, the prototypes are a series of experiments—each one generates a data point on a "trade-off curve" that visualizes the boundary of technically feasible solutions and serves as a repository of knowledge for future projects. More specifically, a trade-off curve is a visual map of the possible values that can be achieved for two conflicting performances simultaneously, based on real experiments or prototypes conducted by the team. These curves are essential for both guiding the team's design experiments and making decisions about the product. They are also useful for training new joiners, helping them quickly understand what solutions the team has tried before in the context of the product's key constraints.

To illustrate the concept, consider a team tasked with designing a question answering system with a chatbot-type interface. We can imagine that the system will be used to help customers troubleshoot problems and get detailed information from product manuals via the company's website.

We can easily imagine the excitement of the team when this project is initiated. The software engineers are tempted to use the latest and greatest technology for chatbots, GPT-4, because they know that it can respond appropriately to almost any question a user might ask. After some experiments, they realize that GPT-4 and similar large language models (LLMs) can also look for specific answers in a database of technical manuals. These experiments make the team confident that a major LLM would give the best results in terms of flexibility and accuracy. However, when they start to analyze its sustainability, they realize that major LLM services also have high computational and environmental costs. The data centers that run the models consume an enormous amount of energy and fresh water, and sometimes they are called on for trivial tasks. The company will also pay a non-trivial cost for each user query, which must be taken into account since they expect to have millions of users.

Not satisfied with just one proposal, the Chief Product Engineer encourages the software team to explore other options. When we study the real needs of the customer, how likely is it that deploying the full power of GPT is justified? Would a smaller LLM, one that they can host themselves, do just as well? Also, if the technical manuals use a lot of jargon and are very similar to each other, will an LLM really be able to tell them apart reliably? If not, would customers be happier with a traditional search engine, enriched with labels and categories relevant to the product line? Or would something like a FAQ with a traditional, scripted chatbot fulfill 99% of user requests, while ensuring that users are only given certifiably accurate technical advice?

After conducting several experiments to find answers to these questions and others that come up, the team draws a diagram with the flexibility and general knowledge of the solution on one axis, and sustainability/cost on the other. The result is shown in Figure 34.

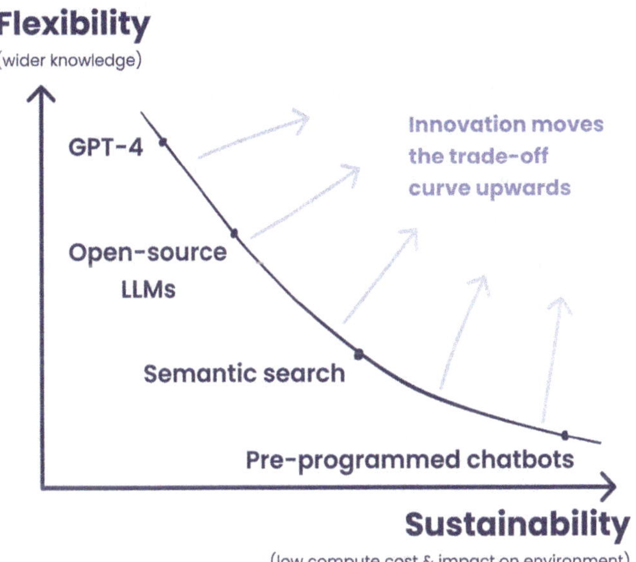

FIGURE 34. A trade-off curve for a question-answering chatbot designed to provide technical information and solutions to customers. Large language models (LLMs) capable of understanding a wide variety of questions posed in different ways, such as GPT-4, are energy-intensive and costly, especially when the number of users is large. Pre-programmed chatbots, on the other hand, are little more than automated FAQs and have very limited scope. The other technologies on the curve represent compromises between these two extremes.

In this trade-off curve, the team has tested four different technologies for the system. They need the solution to be sustainable (in terms of operating costs and environmental impact), while providing a great experience to millions of users (in terms of flexibility and accuracy). Currently, the best compromise appears to lie in the middle of the curve, a solution including elements of both open-source large language models (LLMs) and semantic search engines. To achieve a solution with performances above the curve, the team would need to innovate. At the time of writing this book, such technologies do not exist, highlighting a significant opportunity for future development.

In the set-based concurrent model, engineers build multiple trade-off curves to evaluate future and existing prototypes to discover the most effective overall solution. In the digital world, trade-off curves are not yet widely used. Perhaps this is because both the waterfall method and Agile software development strongly encourage point-based engineering. They share the flawed assumption that digital products can be redesigned cheaply over successive releases, when in practice poor design choices at the start of a project often snowball into a major drain on time and resources, as well as creating a bad first impression with would-be customers. By adopting a set-based approach to prototyping and building trade-off curves for major technology decisions, product teams can start developing the product from a well-considered design and predict the consequences of any technology changes proposed down the road.

A prototype, or a mockup, serves as a cheap and simplified design, providing the team with the opportunity to validate their hypotheses before diving into a full-fledged product development. Working on several prototypes before settling on a final product design reduces the risk of major corrections down the road. By sparking creative discussions among engineering and design specialists seeking to resolve difficult trade-offs, set-based engineering can make a significant difference in avoiding technical debt. In the digital realm, it is often easy to get current or potential clients to participate in tests related to user experience and product usability. Beta testing and A/B testing are common practices that can be extended to support concurrent prototyping.

80 + Alpha

With each new design cycle, our goal is to make the product better and better. To outpace the competition, we aim to not just maintain all product performances, but also introduce one key improvement or innovation in each release that grabs our customers' interest. This concept is known as **80 + Alpha**, where Alpha represents the new element and 80% denotes the minimum level of performance for all other aspects of the product (emphasizing that we cannot fail to deliver on any key customer preference). The term originates from the automobile industry, specifically Toyota, where designing a safe and durable vehicle is always a complex challenge. The "80 + Alpha" doctrine implies that the Product Engineer and the team need to master existing engineering standards in order to systematically reach the minimum level of performance (80%) without reinventing the wheel and potentially introducing new problems.

Every time we make a change to one part of a product, we touch the whole product, so this mastery implies a deep understanding of how various elements of the product work together and the design boundaries that the team should not exceed. Then, operating within these constraints, the team can innovate to achieve exceptional performance in one area or introduce a new feature (the Alpha). By adhering to the "80 + Alpha" principle, companies can repeatedly upgrade their products while ensuring they remain reliable and competitive. It fosters a culture of consistent improvement and innovation, driving the product's evolution in a way that is both manageable and forward-looking. Industries are often disrupted by companies maintaining a regular and frequent pace of innovation, known as product *takt* (see chapter 5). A consistent pace of innovation led by one company compels competing companies to innovate also, if they want to remain relevant. This dynamic pushes the entire industry forward and can lead to rapid advancements in technology, services, and consumer offerings.

The "80 + Alpha" concept is perfectly applicable to digital products. Websites, peer-to-peer platforms, smartphone apps, and custom AI services all have critical behaviors and performance thresholds. They must meet user expectations (80%) and function flawlessly to remain competitive. New versions of a digital product can include an innovation, a new component, a performance boost, or simply a behind-the-scenes technical change that reduces costs or enhances quality (the Alpha). Assuming all critical performances are met to at least 80%, the Alpha is what users will notice and find appealing in the new version.

To summarize, the lean product engineer consistently views their product as a collection of critical performances whose consistent delivery is essential to fully satisfy the key preferences of customers. The product must be updated regularly to maintain its competitive advantage, so the design team generates a regular stream of new ideas designed to capture attention following the 80+Alpha principle.

Let's look at an example based on the authors' design of their e-learning training modules. In the latest version, here's what their "80 + Alpha" included:

80%:

- **Optimize the video length.** Keep instructional videos between 2 and 5 minutes. This brief format helps maintain student attention and improves retention of information.

- **Limit weekly workload.** Reduce the total amount of student work to less than one hour per week. This approach respects students' time and prevents work from piling up, making the course more manageable and appealing.

- **Quick response time.** Aim to answer any student queries within half a day. Rapid responses improve student satisfaction and support effective learning by addressing questions and concerns promptly.

Alpha:

- **Introduce "learning bites".** Offer short sessions on theory topics, with videos and quizzes that last no more than 5 minutes each. These "learning bites" allow students to quickly absorb new concepts, making the program more flexible and accessible.

Now ask yourself:

- When you buy your next home appliance, computer, phone, or any other product, pay attention to how you compare your options. How do your own key preferences influence your choice?

- Have you seen engineering teams stuck on a technical trade-off that seemed impossible to resolve, such as speed versus accuracy? How did they manage to move forward without proposing a complete software redesign?

- When was the last time you were "wowed" by a product you bought? Can you point to the function and performance behind this emotion?

14.5 Design to cost

The Lean Startup approach, which emphasizes building a Minimum Viable Product (MVP) and continuously improving it to find a market fit, faces some challenges. While it promotes a healthy dynamic of "build fast and break things" to innovate quickly and grow sales, it is important to balance this speed against the realities of bureaucracy and cost rationalization. These factors inevitably become more significant over time as the business scales, necessitating a thoughtful approach to growth and efficiency. We have witnessed many startups falter mid-flight as they were unexpectedly overtaken by the "big company diseases" from which they could not easily recover, because they were not fully aware of the costs involved in manufacturing and delivering their product.

In Section 14.3 we explained that it is essential for the *product team* to analyze the market to determine the true price, and take charge of anticipating, calculating and minimizing production costs so that the product is profitable. If the product team does not do this, the financial team may implement arbitrary cost cuts when issues arise, potentially harming the product and its customers. Expanding on those principles, this chapter introduces a strategic approach to creating profitable products from the outset, through an activity known as **target costing**. Target costing is an ongoing process overseen by the Chief Product Engineer alongside technical and functional specialists. Its focus is not on cutting costs so much as identifying opportunities to enhance value throughout the entire product flow, with cost reduction being a natural outcome.

Building a product cost model

Recall that in Section 14.3, we introduced the value-based pricing formula, where profit is calculated as "price − cost". "Profit" is determined using industry benchmarks, "price" is aligned with the actual value we create with the product and market rates, and "cost" is the variable we aim to optimize. Since profit and price are set by the market, together they determine the target cost for the Chief Product Engineer. The target cost is a major constraint. Any change to the product should always trigger a detailed cost analysis, a practice that is often overlooked during design and engineering discussions. To develop a plan for profitability, we first need to establish a cost model for our product. Let's consider a fictional example to illustrate how to construct this model.

Imagine you are the Chief Product Engineer of a storytelling box for children called the Lyra Box, produced by Lyra, a fictional company. Your product concept is simple: a way for children to listen to high-quality stories, *yet* one that is independent of smartphones and screens. The product includes three distinct elements:

- The Lyra Box: a hardware box to play stories, either pre-recorded by Lyra storytellers or recorded through an app.

- Lyra Leafs[43]: wooden, leaf-shaped cards that allow you to play one or a set of short stories when inserted in the box. Technically, they contain a secure digital key that allows the Lyra Box to download a story from the internet. Leafs can include about ten short stories.

- An app that can record stories and also play them (useful when kids want their favorite music in an unlikely place).

In addition, Lyra has put in place an e-commerce site where users can buy the Lyra Leafs and a back office where professional storytellers write and record stories played via the Leafs.

---

43 The variant plural is trademarked by Lyra.

FIGURE 35. The Lyra Box and Lyra Leafs.

Lyra sells their box for $100, and stories are available for download at a fixed price of $10 (we use rounded numbers for convenience). You are aiming for a 20% margin on the Leafs, an 80% margin on the app, and to break even on the box. This means that your target cost for producing the box should not exceed $100, the target cost of a story played on the app should not exceed $2, and the target cost for a Leaf should not exceed $8.

Now, here is how you can build Lyra's cost model and see how far you are from reaching these target costs. In this example, we only calculate the cost structure of the Leaf element to provide you with an understanding of the process. However, as Lyra's Chief Product Engineer, you would need to repeat the process for the box and the app.

1) **List the product's functions.** Functions describe how the product works to meet your client's stable preferences. For instance, for an e-commerce website, functions include the product listing, the basket, the payment system, and the suggestion system. Since a product involves various

user experiences in different situations, we need to examine the functions of a Lyra Leaf across the entire product flow, including design, development, delivery, maintenance, support, and recycling. (End of life functions are especially important for physical objects.) In this case, we can identify four main functions for the Lyra Leaf: story production, story download, production of the physical Leaf, and assorted functions linked to the purchasing of Leafs via the e-commerce site.

The Story Production function creates stories, while the Story Download function generates story downloads. The Wooden Leaf function relates to the manufacturing of wooden Leafs, and the e-commerce website facilitates Leaf purchases. We shall compute the total production cost for the Lyra Leaf based on the number of Leaf purchases, the unit selected for our product cost calculation.

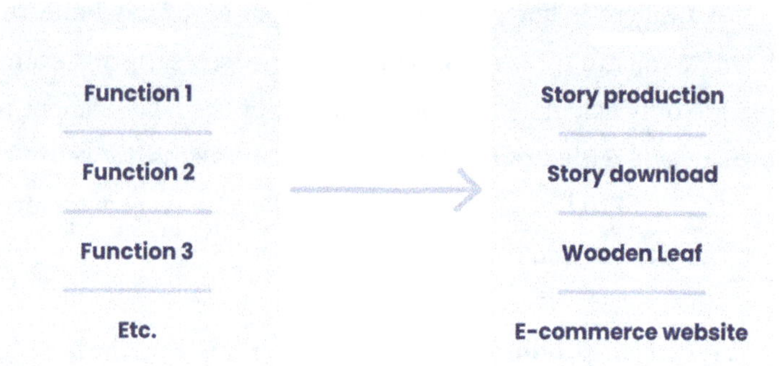

FIGURE 36. Listing major functions that contribute to the product life cycle of a Lyra Leaf.

2) Identify the different types of costs associated with each function. When developing a product, we typically require various types of resources: *labor*, representing the workforce engaged in design, manufacturing and distribution; *materials* utilized in production; *intangible inputs* used in design and development; *infrastructure* expenses like buildings, cloud services, and utilities; and *third-party services*. To these we can add R&D and product design, including software development, especially for digital products. Additional resources may apply to your industry, such as intellectual property and logistics. To produce the Leafs, you consider the following types of costs (we're keeping it simple but you will probably need to be more comprehensive):

- **Labor:** the storytellers who create the stories, the developers who code the story into the Leaf, the e-commerce site designers and developers, the operators who manufacture the Leafs

- **Raw materials:** the materials needed to produce the Leafs, including the wooden cards and the chips

- **Intangibles:** any non-physical resources required to design and produce the Leafs, such as paid datasets or images

- **Infrastructure:** buildings, utilities, on-premise servers

- **Third-party services:** cloud services, payment processing, emails, search engine for the e-commerce site

Below, Table 14 suggests a cost breakdown for the e-commerce website function:

Labor		
	Website developers (x2)	
	Website designers (x1)	
	Content writers (x2)	
	Site Reliability Engineer (x1)	
Third-party services		
	Emails	
	Cloud infrastructure (servers)	
	Cloud infrastructure (serverless)	
	Cloud infrastructure (storage)	
	Payment processing	
	Emails	

Table 14. Different costs involved in selling Lyra Leafs through Lyra's e-commerce website.

3) **Classify these costs as "fixed" or "variable".** Some of these resources take the form of recurring payments, such as monthly rent or yearly salaries and subscriptions. They are classified as "fixed" costs since they do not depend on production volume. (We could argue that some of these costs vary slightly based on volume, but they are dominated by time rather than quantity.) Other resources are procured as required and depend on production or sales volume, such as third-party services, raw materials or even licenses, so we call them "variable" costs. In order to calculate our product unit cost, you categorize all the

listed resources for each function as either "variable" or "fixed". Table 15 shows this classification for the e-commerce website.

Labor		Fixed or variable?
	Website developers (x2)	Fixed
	Website designers (x1)	Fixed
	Content writers (x2)	Fixed
	Site Reliability Engineer (x1)	Fixed
Third-party services		
	Emails	Variable
	Cloud infrastructure (servers)	Fixed
	Cloud infrastructure (serverless)	Variable
	Cloud infrastructure (storage)	Variable
	Payment processing	Variable

TABLE 15. Fixed and variable costs involved in selling Lyra Leafs through Lyra's e-commerce website.

4) **Calculate the product unit cost.** For variable costs, simply record the cost per unit. For fixed costs, first convert each one to the same period: yearly or monthly for example. Then divide these amounts by the number of units you expect to sell during that period to get another cost per unit. Finally, add the variable and fixed unit costs to get the total unit cost. In the Lyra Leaf example, the two website developers are a fixed cost, so we calculate a yearly amount ($400,000). Then we divide this amount by the number of projected sales (500,000) which equals $0.80. This means that the

web development cost for the e-commerce site is $0.80 per Leaf sold. The cost breakdown for the whole function "e-commerce website" of the Lyra Leaf element is $3.07, based on the projected sales of 500,000 units over one year:

Labor		Fixed or variable?	Yearly cost	Unit cost
	Website developers (x2)	Fixed	$400,000	$0.80
	Website designers (x1)	Fixed	$200,000	$0.40
	Content writers (x2)	Fixed	$400,000	$0.80
	Site Reliability Engineer (x1)	Fixed	$200,000	$0.40
Third-party services				
	Emails	Variable	n/a	$0.009
	Cloud infrastructure (servers)	Fixed	$60,000	$0.06
	Cloud infrastructure (serverless)	Variable	n/a	negligible
	Cloud infrastructure (storage)	Variable	n/a	negligible
	Payment processing	Variable	n/a	$0.06
			Total	$3.07

TABLE 16. Product unit costs involved in selling Lyra Leafs through Lyra's e-commerce website.

Once you repeat this exercise for the other three functions (story production, story download and Leaf manufacturing), and add all the functions' unit cost, you get a total unit cost of $7.70 per Leaf based on the current sales projection. Therefore, compared to your target cost of $8, you decide that the product design is financially viable. Of course, if the production volume increases, economies of scale may further reduce the unit cost. But the reverse is also true, which is why your sales projection needs to be based on concrete data rather than wishful thinking (see Section 14.3, "How many units can we sell?"). Producing a high volume to keep costs down, then not selling them, would result in a large stock that poses an even bigger financial problem. Note that some resources and costs can be shared across several functions. For example, the labor cost of software developers contributes to both the basket and the payment system of an e-commerce site. In such scenarios, we can apply a ratio based on their distribution across functions.

5) **Build a cost breakdown bar chart.** Visually represent the calculation in step 4 using a stacked bar chart, as illustrated below. Notice that the heights of the bars are proportional to the cost amounts. This type of chart helps you see at a glance whether some expenses are unexpectedly large. On this graph, it is evident that the majority of costs come from the production of stories and e-commerce activities. You can delve deeper into these layers to identify opportunities for value improvements, by finding out which sub-functions incur the highest expenses. For instance, in Lyra's e-commerce activities, most of the cost can be traced back to labor. This serves as a clear indicator of where you should concentrate your efforts to identify and eliminate waste: by going to the gemba to speak with Software Engineers about their problems.

FIGURE 37. The result of the target costing exercise for the Lyra Leaf production.

When our entire product cost breakdown is done, we can compare the actual unit costs of our product with our initial target costs to check if they are lower, higher, or the same. This will clarify our profitability prospects and reveal opportunities to add value. Note that in most companies costs are the responsibility of the Finance team, who manages them in bulk. For example, labor costs are managed for the company and its departments, but Finance doesn't care about the distribution of labor on the level of a product, let alone the cost per unit sold. Product specialists need to do their own calculations if they want to gain insights into the true cost drivers of development and delivery, and find opportunities to improve value at the core.

This basic cost model is a great starting point for planning your product's profitability, but you will want to tweak it to fit your specific product, industry, or situation. Often, it reveals that our planned economic model for the product just won't work (because it is not profitable) or the need for big changes in the value chain where costs are out of control. Catching these issues early and taking action is crucial for ensuring your company's long-term success.

This was the case of Lucie and Julien from Ocus, the scaleup we presented in Chapter 3. Already a leader in brokering photography sessions for the online food delivery market, they wanted to break into the hospitality industry. They wanted to propose a high-quality photo service for renters (for example, Airbnb hosts) in isolated locations that would be cost-effective using their current platform and operations. They did a thorough analysis using the target costing strategy we present in this chapter, which confirmed that their existing model was not totally adapted to this new segment. Their margin would be reduced because their real costs would significantly exceed the target cost. However, the cost breakdown structure showed the potential to improve value on at least two functions: the amount paid to photographers (including travel costs and premiums for experience) and the cost associated with canceled photo shoots. This pushed them to come up with new ideas, some based on technology and others geared more towards improving the process.

Improving value to reach the target cost

With a clear understanding of our product cost structure in place, we're ready to work on enhancing value to reach our target cost. To do this, the team must find the right mix of technologies and systems that can achieve the desired product performances while simultaneously finding smart ways to remain below the target cost. This activity is known as "target costing". It is radically different from "cost-cutting", which aims to reduce the highest costs in response to budget overruns without considering the overall economic model. Target costing aims to either create value or eliminate waste within the economic model. In fact, the Boston Consulting Group (BCG) also refers to this target costing activity as "design to value", emphasizing that it's an ongoing effort focused on adding value rather than merely cutting costs.[44]

Throughout the conception phase, the role of the Chief Product Engineer is to mobilize the whole team around the target cost. Target costing is always a *team activity*, not the sole responsibility of the Finance department. Target costing is accomplished through collaborative work sessions with specialists involved in the product flow, because waste can build up at any stage including product design. During these sessions, the collected experts explore ideas for enhancing value across the different functions and develop a collective plan to achieve the target cost. Ideally, this should be an ongoing exercise, but it must occur at least once per product design iteration (or takt cycle).

---

44 See BCG article: https://tktq.link/build-to-sell/design-to-value

This is a critical moment, when technical decisions are made that impact the entire value chain all the way to the customer.

Therefore, the first step in "target costing" is to identify and assemble the most relevant people. We gather experts from various departments who contribute directly or indirectly to the product flow. These are individuals with hands-on knowledge of the product's technologies and functions: experts hailing not just from design, development and delivery teams, but also marketing, support, maintenance, logistics, and even external partners. In the Lyra Box example, we could involve specialists from hardware, packaging, storytelling, e-commerce, and back-office operations.

The people involved in target costing must be prepared and willing to engage at the gemba to uncover facts and test multiple solutions. Remember, the gemba is where value is created throughout the product flow. In this exercise, the gemba includes the workplaces of every specialty that comes together to manufacture and deliver the product. The team also analyzes competitors' products to understand the rationale and impact of their design choices. These people should think outside the box and have a growth mindset, each member contributing from their area of expertise.

The target costing team embarks on a waste hunt to enhance value throughout the product flow with the goal of reaching the target cost. For this activity, understanding the language of waste is crucial. There may be:

- **Labor-related waste**, such as rework, defects, excessive movement of materials, and unnecessary motions.
- **Material-related waste**, including scrap, unused materials, and poor collaboration with suppliers.
- **Equipment-related waste** might be characterized by breakdowns, slow problem-solving, and variable performance.

We also refer you to the seven-waste model presented in Section 11.4. You can record the waste you find in the following table:

Product function	Waste description	Idea for value enhancement

TABLE 17. A template for observing and recording sources of waste in the product flow.

Identifying areas for improvement along the product flow is just the beginning. After spotting these opportunities, the team, led by the Chief Product Engineer, collaborates to eliminate waste in the selected functions. Together, they set a new cost target and devise a plan to achieve it. They continue to monitor progress, ensuring that each step brings them closer to the new cost objective, and they learn from failure along the way. For instance, we see below the cost structure of a large e-commerce website and the team's goal to improve value in the "product listing", "search" and "order picking" functions:

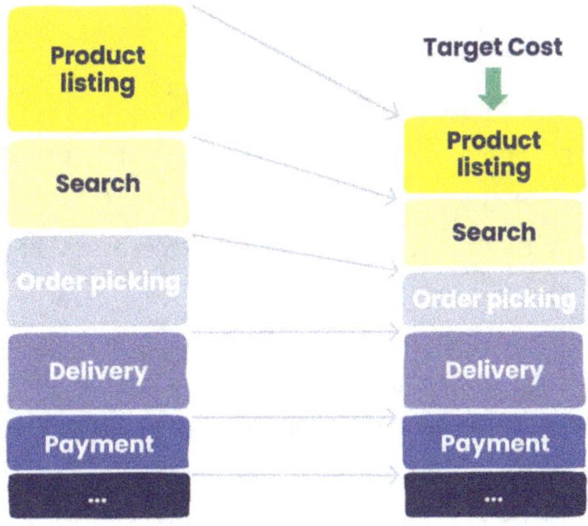

FIGURE 38. Current cost breakdown of an e-commerce site (left), and the desired outcome (right) after implementing improvements to the product listing, search, and order picking functions. By looking for opportunities to remove waste or enhance value in these functions, the team hopes to bring the total cost below the target cost.

Outside these specific target costing improvement sessions, the Chief Product Engineer ensures that the target cost is respected with every new change. Throughout the design and development process, they prominently display and track the target cost alongside client stable preferences and critical product performance metrics.

Now ask yourself:
- What are the functions of your product?
- What resources are required for each one? Which are fixed? Which are variable?
- What is the unit cost for each function and your whole product unit cost?
- Is your real unit cost higher than your target cost? Where do you see opportunities to improve value in your product cost breakdown?

14.6 Keep the heritage, drop the legacy

Do you remember when Facebook really began to increase its popularity? From 2007 to 2008, it seemed like every millennial was joining. Back then, it was hard to imagine that this generation would eventually move away from Facebook, but that's exactly what happened[45]. What led to this extraordinary shift?

Several factors contributed to the decline in Facebook usage among millennials. They shifted towards more engaging social media platforms like Instagram, which offers a more visual and streamlined experience focusing on high-quality images over text. As Facebook became more about passive content and less about interactive and meaningful personal connections, it lost its appeal. Younger users began to perceive it as outdated, even

---

45 We suggest this analysis by a Media expert: "5 reasons millennials are quitting Facebook", https://tktq.link/build-to-sell/millenials-quitting-facebook

nicknaming it the "parents' social network". Meanwhile, growing privacy concerns and the implementation of the EU's GDPR law in 2016 made millennials wary of Facebook's handling of personal data. All these factors, combined with an expanding array of social media options, led millennials to choose platforms that supported active engagement and better privacy controls. Facebook's failure to adapt to these changing preferences accelerated the shift among younger internet users.

What were Facebook's strengths? In retrospect, it is easy to see that we valued it mainly for an engaging daily feed of our close friends' and family's activities and updates, with some fun interactions through comments and reactions. What is interesting is that this hasn't really changed: the feed and our friends' posts are still there on Facebook. But the overall experience of Facebook has changed. As a result, so has its attractiveness as a provider of this core experience. Each new feature added was gradually eroding this core experience instead of improving it. At the same time, Facebook failed to offer significant protections for our personal data in response to the cultural shift, so even users who still valued the core experience became wary of the platform.

Choosing what *should not change* in a product can be as difficult, or even more difficult, than deciding what *should change*. Telling the two apart requires a profound understanding of value from the customers' point of view, and of all the technologies that go into making the product. It involves identifying the elements of your product and the user experience that customers have come to appreciate, as well as recognizing those aspects that no longer capture their interest. This understanding allows for more targeted improvements and updates that align with customer preferences and market trends. Degrading your core experience—your heritage—can cost you your market, as we saw with Facebook. If your product is a hit, then you need to understand what makes it a hit and protect that experience. You wouldn't put makeup on the Mona Lisa, would you?

Many companies fall into the same trap as Facebook, because they don't know the difference between heritage and legacy. They spend most of their time trying to outpace the competition by delivering new features. They forget to check in regularly with customers to see what works and what doesn't. They lose sight of what their customers really value, until the market forces their hand. But by then, it might be too late.

Product *takt* to test market trends

One way to avoid falling into this trap is to see our product as a flow of incremental releases and impose a **product *takt*** (see chapter 5), a steady pace of innovation that will allow us to test the market frequently without taking huge financial risks. Adopting a product takt forces us to take a hard look at the value proposition of previous product releases. What aspects of the current version must we keep, so as not to disappoint customers? What aspects do we need to remove or change, so that customers remain interested? We call these two sides of the product **heritage** and **legacy** respectively. This approach, which views the product as more than just a "bag of features", helps prevent us from making knee-jerk reactions in response to market trends. Focusing on the overall user experience and value rather than reacting to internal and external pressures, encourages more strategic and thoughtful decision-making. Too often, startups rush to release new features, praying that some or all will hit the mark, while failing to 1) protect the performances that drive customer satisfaction, and 2) understand how the market is changing. Over and over, we see digital products lose loyal customers as they twist themselves into knots looking for the perfect market fit while ignoring evolving tastes.

A product takt cycle starts with revisiting our customers, to understand what they value about the current version of the product and what Jobs To Be Done still need help. At the end of a takt cycle, the immediate market response to a new release quickly indicates whether we have impacted our product's heritage and if we are clinging to legacy features. This feedback is crucial for understanding how well the updates align with both the evolving market expectations and the foundational elements that define our product.

Without keeping an eye on our heritage and legacy, after a few releases products can evolve into complex mixtures of highly specific features. This is especially true for digital products, which have no physical constraints to slow down this trend. Often new features are requested by a small but vocal minority of users, and end up adding complexity for the silent majority of users as well as the developers. We must constantly adapt our products to evolving tastes while ensuring that we don't change or remove the things that really matter. Our product stands a better chance of remaining pertinent and interesting over time, and keeping its leadership on the market.

> **Even features originating from direct customer requests can degrade the product's heritage if they are not implemented thoughtfully.**

But how do we continuously adapt the product to keep pace with social trends while preserving whatever it is that customers expect?

If we want to make the right choices for product improvements, we have to understand exactly which aspects of the whole product are heritage and which ones are legacy. Our heritage consists of technologies or features of the user experience that make the product useful and unique, which must be preserved and enhanced. These are the design choices that bring the fundamental value on which customer loyalty is based. Legacy, on the other hand, refers to technologies or user experiences that we need to renew if we want to respond to our customers' changing tastes and eliminate the weak points in our product. Sometimes, a legacy technology forms an integral part of our product, simply because we have never thought of doing things differently. Then, when we want to improve the product, it gets in the way. At this point we must ask ourselves if it is still fit for purpose. Are we attached to that aspect of the product simply because it has always been there, or does it really create value in and of itself? Traditional is not the same as good.

Apple earned its reputation as a trend-setter in the personal computing sector for good reasons. Their products are attractive and easy to use, and they are not afraid to test out new ideas.

But an equally important aspect of their success is their willingness to let go of legacy features that they consider outdated. For example, in 1998 they released the first all-in-one PC without a 3.5-inch floppy disk drive: the iMac, which gave rise to a very successful product line. This design choice was shocking at a time when most people still had boxes full of disks at home carrying their purchased software and personal data. But Apple had seen the writing on the wall. More and more people were downloading software and media from the internet instead of buying physical media, and soon iMac users realized that the missing floppy drive was not a handicap at all. To take a more recent example, in 2016 the iPhone 7 was the first major smartphone[46] to drop the 3.5mm headphone jack.

Returning to the example of Facebook, we see that their heritage experience is still present in the product, if degraded. Collecting and reselling private data was a legacy feature—not of their product, but of their business model. Users initially ignored this practice, and it certainly did not prevent new users from appreciating the core experience or adopting the product. However, Facebook failed to update this aspect of the product as data privacy became a growing concern for most users.

Additionally, we need to see what our rival companies are keeping when they update their product. What was thrown away? Taking a step back, what design choices do we see most frequently in the market? Has the market agreed so completely

---

46 The first smartphone manufacturer to remove the jack was Oppo in 2012, but Bluetooth headphones were not as common at the time so these models made less of an impression on the market. The new iPhone, on the other hand, abruptly changed the behavior of manufacturers and consumers.

on a heritage design that it has become a common standard, like the steering wheel and pedal control system for cars? Or the keyboard for computers? Or is there still room for innovation even in what seems to be a common practice?

Once you start viewing your market through the lens of heritage and legacy, you can begin digging for gold. When a competitor discards a feature, technology or design, figure out why they made the change. Was it a legacy choice that they removed to make way for some other improvement? When you see the same features appear over and over, do they respond to a common customer need? Are some competitors preserving these features as their heritage?

Knowing where to draw the line between heritage and legacy is an essential skill for the Chief Product Engineer, but also for company managers and CEOs, since this is a highly strategic question. If we are going to change the product, we need to do it in the right way. The product takt forces us to revisit the question of legacy versus heritage in each release cycle. Customer preferences can change, so our definitions of legacy and heritage will change too.

There are many reasons why we might want to avoid changing the DNA of our product. We run the risk of disappointing our customers and losing their trust (and therefore their business). We can also become emotionally attached to certain aspects of the product and resist changing them for their own sake. Perhaps an engineer cleverly innovated a core technology, or the original design team included a feature based on the founder's passion. In some cases, we want to get the most out of the current version of a product before investing in a major update or in new products. We might be afraid of cannibalizing our flagship product's market. However, not innovating is worse than all these outcomes. The world outside changes too fast, much faster than companies can pivot. To be successful, the design team of a product must always keep one step ahead by working on the next release.

Seeing our product as a flow paced by the takt allows us to track heritage and legacy across all iterations of our product, and also understand this distinction in our competitors' products. A product has a history, and seeing it through the eyes of legacy/heritage over time, gives us a sense of its future trajectory. Each new innovation cycle offers a chance to observe which elements were retained (heritage) and which were altered (legacy), allowing us to gauge the rate of change in consumer preferences, what aspects have maintained enduring appeal, and how societal shifts are occurring and their speed. Each legacy change should be associated with an Alpha, the major innovation of a given product release.

For instance, the following graphic illustrates the timeline of Sandrine's training products over the years leading up to the current "Build To Sell" training program. For each product we see its name, the major innovation (Alpha) that Sandrine introduced, and the reason for the change.

In this product timeline, we clearly observe a shift in market tastes from in-person to shorter, remote training sessions. This change can be attributed partly to the COVID-19 crisis, which accelerated some ongoing trends. Particularly in the tech sector, online learning platforms were already well established and remote work was gaining momentum.

This understanding helps differentiate what may soon become outdated (legacy) from what continues to be valued as part of our heritage. If we consider the history of all training products that Sandrine has developed over the years, a common factor is that a renowned expert in lean practices teaches the course. (Not always Sandrine!) This aspect has stayed constant even as the course format and content have evolved with the times. Recently, the post-COVID world has amplified students' demand for more mobility, flexibility and autonomy, leading Sandrine to introduce the concept of e-learning bites in the latest iteration. Such insights are essential for strategically planning future updates and innovations, to ensure they align with both evolving trends and timeless elements.

Now ask yourself:

- What aspects of your product have changed over time, and which have not? How do these changes, or lack thereof, reflect shifts in societal tastes and technological advancements?

- What features of your product are customers particularly fond of, and how can you tell? Conversely, which features are used less frequently, and do you understand why this is the case?

- Examine your main competitor's latest product iteration. What features were removed, and what might the reasons be for these changes—were they legacy? Conversely, which features continue to be included in each new version, and why do they remain—are they valuable heritage?

14.7 Blend fixed and flexible technologies

In the previous section, we talked about dividing the product into heritage and legacy aspects. Sometimes these aspects of a product are specific technologies, but just as often they are properties that emerge from several technology choices (for example, long battery life in a smartphone is driven by energy management software as well as the physical battery) or are functions of the overall user experience (like impeccable customer service). Therefore, heritage and legacy are ultimately about how customers use the product to generate value.

But as product designers, we also wrestle with individual technologies, their trade-offs, and their integration. This section proposes a classification that can help us make the right technology choices faster: dividing the product design into components that are *fixed* or *flexible*. This perspective can also help us avoid the common trap of allowing a product's complexity to increase over time.

Technology encompasses all the tools, processes, and materials that contribute to enhancing a tool's functionality, efficiency, or user experience. For simplicity, we propose to use the term **technology** to describe all the concrete elements that make up a product, whether or not they are commonly referred to as "tech". Hence, a technology is not just a software or hardware component. It can also be an impactful choice or designed workflow that enables the product to perform a certain task or solve a specific problem. For instance, if we consider a consulting practice that sells software development, the technologies defining its service-based offer could include specific programming languages, product design methodologies, and project reporting tools. These technologies are carefully selected or built to fulfill the functions and performance targets we have determined for the product, ensuring they align seamlessly with our clients' stable preferences.

The **fixed technologies** of a product are those essential to its fundamental operation. They have been standardized and are often proprietary. They should not be modified or replaced without exceptional justification. In software development, a fixed technology might be a fundamental software library, a third-party service like Google Pay, a set of machine learning algorithms, or a delivery solution. In physical products, a fixed technology might be a standard part (fasteners, electrical components, programmable circuit boards, and so on), an engineering standard that must be respected, or a patented device. Regardless of their nature, fixed technologies undergo thorough testing, demonstrating their effectiveness across various scenarios. When a technology is deemed fixed, the strategy is to stabilize it.

Creating the conditions for maximum reuse of standard technologies is a way to ensure that the team does not have to reinvent the wheel for each new release, which would create uncertainty and drastically slow the pace of delivery. This approach does not mean that the fixed parts can never be improved for better performance, but it is done with more care and planning. No new technology is introduced into the fixed scope unless it has fully been tested in different situations, including outside of the existing product. Even for an improvement as simple as changing the material of a screw to a more durable alloy, auto and airplane manufacturers ask their suppliers to go through a long qualification process including multiple tests of quality and variability in the new part. The decision to replace or update one of the core software libraries in a digital product should be just as rigorous.

Flexible technologies, on the other hand, can be modified, replaced or upgraded without significantly altering the product's core functionality. They allow us to innovate and adapt to new quality requirements. Flexible parts are tailored to meet the unique or evolving demands of different market segments. In software development, a flexible technology might be a Wi-Fi module that can be replaced with a new version, or a mobile app that can be regularly updated to align with new releases of Android OS. An example for a physical product would be the bands and straps of a wristwatch, and for a service-based product it might be a loyalty program. Incorporating flexible technologies is a crucial aspect of effective product design, as they enable the product to maintain relevance across diverse market segments and over time. They enable what we refer to as "industrial customization", where we can address specific customer emotions and circumstances while maintaining a robust and stable core.

Finally, by standardizing the interfaces between fixed and flexible technologies, we can quickly and cost-effectively propose new creations, sidestepping the need to start the design process from scratch each time. This is a savvy (and cost-effective) approach to product strategy that keeps us on the fast track to innovation.

Fixed technologies are safeguarded by engineering standards that every team member should comprehend and receive training on. Fundamentally, an engineering standard represents the best known method of accomplishing a task or of using a technology for a given purpose. The product design team builds a new or optimized solution out of fixed and flexible parts, creating an engineering standard that represents their best solution to fulfilling the key performances and resolving the trade-offs. At least, this is the best solution known to the team as of now!

Since engineering standards are not to be altered carelessly, it is essential to apply the lean principle of kaizen: we want to improve the performance of the product by achieving continuous improvement over time, ensuring that enhancements are made without unnecessary alterations. Establishing a library of reusable parts, components, services, and modules with standard interfaces streamlines product development and enhances consistency. It also facilitates the training and onboarding of junior engineers.

While manufacturers of physical products are used to working with standard parts, software designers must learn to strike a balance between generalization and customization. Before writing a single line of code, certain components, libraries, or functional subsets of the solution should be clearly designated as flexible and modular, while others remain fixed and immutable. This will permit the development team to adapt the product to new contexts without extensive modification. The discipline of software engineering has established numerous standards and practices to encourage the creation of reusable and resilient code, ensuring both agility and scalability: modularity, dependency injection, design patterns, and unit testing to name a few. While a comprehensive exploration of these practices is beyond the scope of this book, our key point is the necessity of formulating a well-defined fixed vs. flexible and reuse strategy from the outset, and incorporating these discussions into the product release cycle as an integral part of the discovery phase.

Mapping technology value

To identify the fixed and flexible technologies within a product, the first step is to clearly define the technologies that the product uses to perform the various functions. This can be effectively organized using an architecture diagram. This diagram helps in mapping out how each technology used relates to the product's critical performances and aligns with stable customer preferences. By visually organizing and connecting these elements, you can critically assess whether the chosen technologies allow you to reach the performance targets and fully satisfy what customers value most (their stable preferences).

The next step involves evaluating which technologies are flexible—those that can be easily changed or adapted—and which are fixed, meaning they are integral to the product's core functionality and harder to modify. This evaluation is crucial for shaping the technical strategy of the product. It enables teams to recognize areas where technology can evolve to meet changing market demands or where it must remain consistent to maintain the product's integrity and functionality. This process is fundamental in aligning technological decisions with strategic business goals and customer satisfaction, ensuring that every technological choice directly contributes to delivering value to the customers.

Figure 39 shows an example of an architecture diagram linking technologies to critical performance targets and stable preferences. The product is an earlier version of the "Build To Sell" training program, for which Sandrine is the Chief Product

Engineer. Fixed technologies are clearly highlighted, such as Sandrine herself as the sensei who will teach the course and respond to students' questions. For this product, which is mostly service-based, a fixed technology is any aspect that customers are strongly attached to, so it should not be altered without careful consideration. For instance, several students said that they would only join the group and individual coaching sessions if they were facilitated by Sandrine, rather than one of her partners who was less recognized in the field of lean product development. Other reasons we can classify a technology as fixed are because it implements a well-known industry standard, or because we have turned it into a reusable and valuable component of the design (in other words, an internal standard). In the "Build To Sell" training program, we see this kind of technology represented in the lean engineering core concepts and tools, which form the foundation of the course and address customer preferences for innovative and proven methodologies.

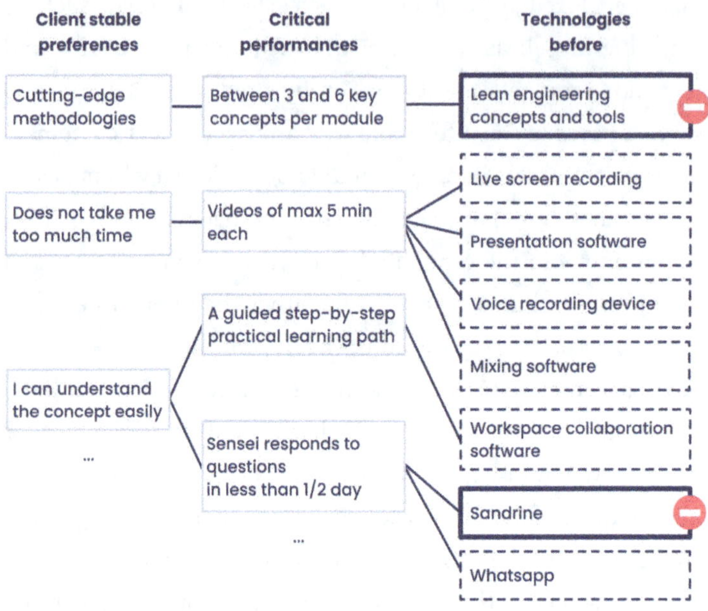

FIGURE 39. Architecture diagram showing how each technology used in a product supports the critical performances and stable use preferences. The fixed technologies are identified with bold outlines.

In earlier releases of the "Build To Sell" training program, Sandrine personally recorded and edited the videos using inexpensive tools, albeit with suboptimal quality. The technologies she used for creating videos remained flexible, due to constantly evolving and diverse requirements for the content and the delivery platform. Initially, Sandrine viewed her training product as complementary to her Sensei practice, hence her low-cost strategy. As demand grew and requirements diversified, Sandrine and her team expanded the program to encompass new topics and formats, catering to emerging needs and Jobs To Be Done.

By now the training program has evolved into a fully-fledged product, prompting the team to prioritize value for students while managing costs more effectively. This led to new technology decisions such as adopting voice editing software for the training videos, investing in higher-quality recording devices, and developing customer-centric software to streamline video creation while preserving the sensei's personal touch. These decisions were made collectively to facilitate rapid industrialization of video production without sacrificing authenticity. Similarly, the collaborative workspace for readings and coursework went through several transformations over time, transitioning from basic software such as Google Workspace or Notion to more professional learning management systems. For this function, the team chose technologies to meet the stable preferences of mobility and guided, autonomous learning. Figure 40 illustrates the evolution of technologies implemented in response to the increasingly ambitious performance goals and evolving customer preferences of the training program.

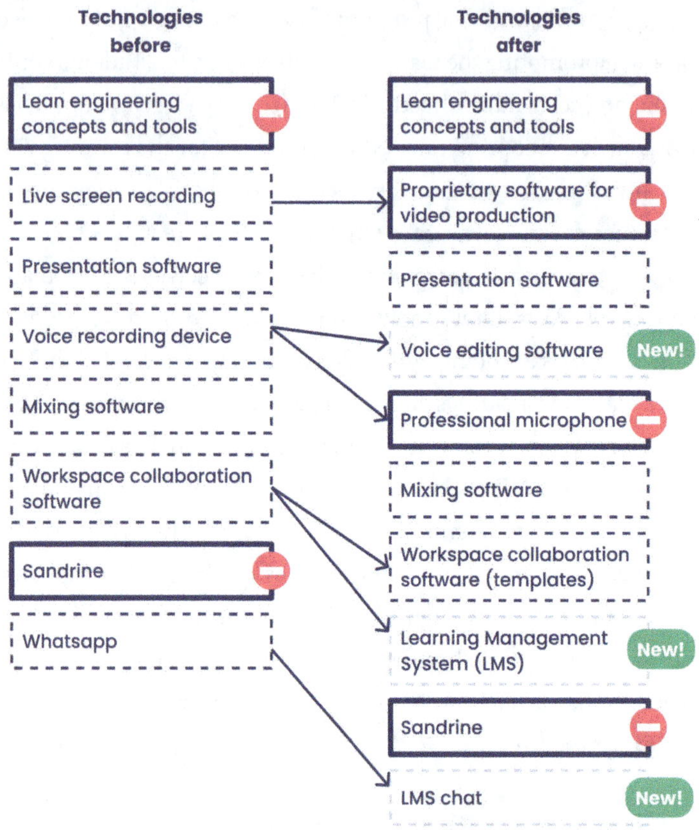

FIGURE 40. Changes to flexible technology components in the "Build To Sell" training program. Note that the fixed technologies did not change.

Agreeing on which components are fixed and which ones are flexible with all members of the team encourages a balanced approach, avoiding extremes of over-caution or excessive innovation, while also avoiding haphazard changes. It also prevents individual team members from including technologies solely because they are trendy or popular. It is imperative to have a shared understanding and consensus on which technologies should remain fixed so as to prevent any disturbances to the product when reusing elements.

In their excellent book *Designing the Future*, Jim Morgan and Jeff Liker argue that the concepts of "fixed vs. flexible" are complementary forces which intensify the innovation spirit:

> *Far too many product developers take sides in the conflict between the unlimited potential of human innovation and the incredible power of good standards. In one camp, the "free spirits" fear that standards limit creativity and lead to painfully boring products. In the other, the "technocrats" are haunted by visions of cost overruns and operational chaos that result from unconstrained imagination run amok.*

Engineering roles may prioritize caution, while product/marketing roles may lean towards boldness, although the opposite may occur as well. Regardless of the scenario, engaging in discussions about fixed and flexible technologies encourages team members to challenge each other, aiming to find the optimal balance. See Chapter 15.2 for more information on keeping a healthy balance between innovation and stability.

Now ask yourself:

- What are the fixed elements of your product? Are they fixed because you don't have control over them, or are there other reasons?

- What are the flexible parts of your product? Are they flexible because they allow you to accommodate different and evolving customer tastes, or are there other reasons?

- Do you have a strategy for reusing technologies in your product so that you can release new versions more easily? How do you select which technologies to standardize and reuse?

TRANSFORM YOUR IDEA INTO AN INSPIRING NARRATIVE

15.1 Articulate your bold vision in a concept paper

Many of us have grown accustomed to crafting or reviewing indigestible PowerPoint presentations to highlight upcoming projects. We write countless slides filled with personas, market data, technology details, development schedules, and budget information. While this research and planning is essential for any new product, a 100-page information dump does not make for a compelling business case. The fact of the matter is that most of our presentations, whether targeted at internal or external stakeholders, focus too much on *ourselves*. "Look at all the work we did!" they say, or "Look how creative and innovative we are!" Consequently, obtaining the necessary level of support becomes challenging and the final product often fails to meet customer expectations.

In their book *Working Backwards*[47], two former Amazon executives describe how Jeff Bezos challenged them to come up with more customer-centric and innovative pitches because their fancy presentations did not provide answers to half of his questions about the viability and feasibility of their ideas. This is how the famous "product press release" method was born at Amazon. The Product Manager writes a press release for their future product, before doing anything else to launch the project. This document serves two objectives: 1) it describes the product from the customer's perspective, not from the company's perspective; and 2) it makes a very clear statement about the product and the direction. The press release should demonstrate that customers will feel compelled to buy the new product and that the team has considered all potential scenarios before any resources are engaged to embark on the project.

If you follow all the practices we suggest in this book, you will have gained the right insights to craft a compelling story for your new concept. You will have visited your client's gemba to observe customers in their real environment. You will have identified their essential needs and dominant emotions, and understood how your product can truly help them. You will also have grasped their key preferences and seen where current products fall short. You will have identified the key quality

---

47 Colin Bryar and Bill Carr: *Working Backwards, Insights, Stories, and Secrets from Inside Amazon* (Pan Books, 2022).

criteria and performances that your product needs to provide to truly impress them. Finally, you will have several ideas on how to tackle the technical challenges and navigate some of the pitfalls in design.

Now, how can you then summarize your findings into a captivating visualization of the customer experiences and the technological feat you and your team propose to undertake? The Chief Product Engineer develops a **concept paper** for this objective. In fact, they write the concept paper throughout the discovery phase, as a means to think more deeply about the vital aspects of their upcoming product. They iterate on it multiple times, until they are confident in the viability and feasibility of their project.

Like Amazon's press release, a Chief Product Engineer writes the concept paper with input from their team of experts, and completes it before design and development start. Like the press release, it is a written narrative of the product concept and business case, rather than technical documentation or a collection of statistics and charts. However, a concept paper takes this idea a step further. Its narrative should reflect the Chief Product Engineer's most audacious ideas and intentions. Thanks to all the deep insights they have gained from the practical exercises we suggest in this book, Chief Product Engineers have earned the right to dream big. Accordingly, the concept paper makes a bold, assertive, and persuasive case for the product, resulting in a personalized document. No two concept papers are alike: each is the brainchild of a Chief Product Engineer's unique vision and approach.

Typically spanning two to six pages, a good concept paper should visualize:

1) **What the successful product will look like** from different angles: market, technology and cost, what the product will do concretely for the customer, what quality requirements we insist on, and what will be the impact on the customers' lives.

2) **What are the tough technical problems we must solve**, focusing on what challenges we need to tackle head on and how we propose to overcome them. This is where the Chief Product Engineer describes the defining technical trade-offs and any unknowns still to be resolved.

3) **What pitfalls we must avoid** and any other factors that we need to pay attention to in order to succeed.

> **Writing the concept paper inoculates the development team against "feature frenzy syndrome", because it encourages thinking in terms of value enhancement rather than functional scope.**

The concept paper offers a rationale for the decisions we plan to make and the trade-offs we need to resolve to create a product that is both marketable and profitable. Because concept papers are inherently strategic by nature, you will not find many public examples. However, we can offer guidelines for crafting your own concept paper. As a good starting point, write down your findings and arguments for each of the subjects below.

What the successful product will look like:

- **Describe the proposed concept.** Craft a compelling client trade-off statement (a *yet* statement) that highlights the value of the product and the problem not effectively addressed by alternative solutions, encapsulating the proposed concept in one attractive sentence. Follow up with a more detailed description of the final product, showcasing its bold, radical, and ambitious nature. Consider including a visual representation or mockup to enhance clarity and visualization. (Section 14.1)

- **Describe the value proposition** of your product in terms of customer problems and emotional responses. Explain how customers will use the product, what benefits they will derive, and any potential drawbacks. Designing a storyboard can help illustrate this. Drafting the product press release or a fan letter[48] are other effective methods to clarify the real benefits we expect the product to bring to clients. (Chapters 9 & 10, Section 14.2)

- **Justify your choice of performance requirements** by listing the stable, non-negotiable preferences of your clients for their satisfaction and your success. Discuss whether your product aims to surpass competing solutions, address areas of dissatisfaction among customers, or maybe both. (Chapters 12 and 13)

---

48 The concept of a "fan letter" in product management describes a written document or message that expresses enthusiastic praise or appreciation for a product, similar to a letter a fan might write to their favorite celebrity or artist. In product management, a fan letter can be used as a tool to articulate the anticipated benefits and value proposition of a product in a compelling and persuasive way.

- **Provide context about your clients**, including whether you are targeting one segment or multiple segments with distinct Jobs To Be Done and preferences. Use *real people* representative of their segment, rather than generic types or personae. Real people have real Jobs To Be Done and clear preferences backed up by their specific circumstances. (Chapters 9, 10 and 11)

- **Estimate the price and business potential.** Estimate the projected number of units sold and revenue generation. Discuss market evidence for the intrinsic value of the product and profit margin. Assess whether the product aligns with the company's overarching goals and objectives. (Section 14.3).

What tough technical problems you must solve:

- **Identify which critical performances of your product** you will improve to meet the stable preferences of your clients. Quantify these improvements and justify your decisions. Articulate the "wow" factor that will differentiate your product from competitors. (Section 14.4)

- **Detail the technical trade-offs** necessary to achieve the desired level of performance. Identify which challenges are difficult to overcome, and explain the reasons for their complexity. (Section 14.4)

- **Discuss the options available to address these trade-offs**, including any experiments already conducted to inform decision-making. Explore various solutions along with their respective benefits and drawbacks. Consider including trade-off curves to illustrate the challenges and your chosen direction. (Section 14.4)

- **Summarize the key improvements and innovations** planned for the new product, the "80 + Alpha". Describe the main changes intended for the product and outline any knowledge gaps that need to be addressed. Provide a plan for acquiring the necessary knowledge and expertise. (Sections 14.4 & 14.6)

- **Describe challenges linked to the target cost.** Highlight the technical challenges that may arise in maintaining the product target cost and how you plan to address them. Explain your strategies for staying within this target cost by improving value, either through innovation or by reducing waste, or both. (Section 14.5)

What pitfalls you must avoid:

- **Describe your product's heritage.** Identify which aspects of the product (technologies, features, design, or other factors) are essential to its identity and must remain unchanged. Provide reasons for their significance. (Section 14.7)

- **Outline any limitations or constraints to be mindful of.** Define boundaries that must not be crossed, whether they are technical, regulatory, or otherwise, and explain the rationale behind each restriction. (Section 14.7)

The Chief Product Engineer builds a new concept paper at the start of each product change cycle. (Remember, a lean company's drumbeat is the product takt time.) Even if the new product is an iterative release, the goal of this exercise is to avoid making assumptions about what will be delivered. Whether our goal is to improve an existing product, introduce a new variant within an existing product family, or launch the first product of a new family, we *do* know that we will deliver something new.

The takt cycle starts with research, returning to the gemba, and understanding how our customer's preferences might have changed. The first section of the concept paper summarizes our new understanding of their world, and how our proposed improvements reflect and fulfill their preferences. Returning to the gemba will also highlight any learning gaps that still need to be resolved, so that we can minimize uncertainties before starting to build the product.

When it is ready, the concept paper becomes a key input of the product "obeya": a dedicated space (physical or virtual) where the Chief Product Engineer and their team come together to conceive and build the product according to their vision. Obeyas are a key topic covered in this book's sequel, *Build to Scale*.

The concept paper, coupled with the practices outlined in this book, empowers anyone in charge of conceiving a new product or a new version of an existing product to:

- Identify genuine opportunities for value creation, leading to the conception of a superior product—one that is appealing, cost-effective, and innovative.

- Quickly assess the viability of a new idea before significant time and resources are invested.

- Clearly communicate their vision, streamline technical decision-making and enhance team engagement.

Creating a concept paper is an iterative process that involves thinking, observing, analyzing, experimenting and changing our mind. If while writing the concept paper we realize that an idea is not workable, it is better to change direction than invest resources into the project.

Now ask yourself:
- How would you describe your product's bold concept? What would be a good "yet" to introduce this concept?
- What is your product meant to do for your customers? Which quality requirements did you decide to emphasize and why?
- What problem or trade-off did you crack in order to succeed? Which one would you like to crack next? Are there any trade-offs you are still struggling to resolve? How do you plan on going about this?

15.2 Keep a healthy balance between innovation and stability

Sometimes, carried away by our ambitions, we decide to implement a drastic change or cram in too many changes simultaneously. Doing so raises significant risks around technical feasibility, production costs, and altering customer behaviors. One reason we research and write a concept paper with our team of specialists is so they can ground us, highlighting challenges that the Chief Product Engineer is unaware of or tempted to ignore. But they are also there to encourage innovations that are valuable and justified. In product design, it is crucial to balance stability against innovation, to find the middle ground between excessive and insufficient risk within a single release cycle.

In every new product release, even minor ones, we need to provide enough innovation to excite our customers and enough stability to reassure them that they will not have to change their habits. As Product Managers, Product Owners, and Chief Product Engineers our role is to define and promote a product vision that achieves this balance and presents a good business opportunity. We do this by assembling a team of experts who will challenge or extend our initial vision, and come up with a balanced design. This is how we can ensure that the delivery team builds the best possible product. The same approach and tools can be applied to any type of product and at all scales. We go through the same process whether we want to release a slightly better smartphone in an established product family, or an entirely new platform that we hope will be the next Instagram.

In every product design and development project, a dynamic unfolds among the team of product, design and technology specialists. The people involved will subconsciously sort themselves into two camps. One side is innovative, more willing to incorporate brand-new technologies and make major changes to the product design. The other side is reluctant to change a winning formula and favors small, incremental improvements. For example, the Product Owner might want to add a cool new feature such as an AI-powered interface, even though this would require major changes to the data model used in the back end. The Technical Lead is reluctant, because changing the data model would affect many other subsystems and the AI itself is untested.

FIGURE 41. A product team will include both enthusiastic innovators and conservatives who prefer incremental change. The Chief Product Engineer's role is to help the two sides find a balance that both excites the product's customers and reassures them that the change is not too great.

This difference in points of view can create conflicts and frustrations. But when it is well managed, this same tension drives healthy debate. As a Chief Product Engineer, someone who is wholly responsible for the success of the product, your goal is to guide the team in finding the right balance between product innovation and product stability. This will happen naturally if you provide them with a clear product vision, and challenge the technical specialists to find the best solution for the customer and the business. When everyone in the team agrees on the problem to solve (Job To Be Done) and the criteria for success (critical performances), then they are free to innovate where necessary without throwing out what already works. Using the "80 + Alpha" approach outlined in Section 14.4 will facilitate this process by providing a structured framework for the team, encouraging innovation within a clear set of boundaries.

Tech teams are often more proactive and eager to experiment with the latest software tools on a product, even without a clear business case. While this enthusiasm for cutting-edge technology can sometimes be excessive, sometimes such innovations are warranted and beneficial. Below we provide a real-life example of what can happen if innovation is allowed to stagnate.

An e-commerce company delayed upgrading its main search engine for years, due to concerns about potential disruptions and the product team's relentless focus on fixing bugs and adding new features. The aging architecture is now putting the tech team in a difficult position, as they struggle to implement new tools that could significantly improve the consumer search experience. The current version of the website's search engine simply lacks crucial features needed to support these improvements. As a result, the company is faced with an unpleasant choice: let the performance of the search function fall far behind their competitors, or invest major resources in a complete redesign. This situation underscores the importance of maintaining a healthy balance between maintaining stability for customers and pursuing necessary technological advancements to meet their evolving demands.

All innovation carries cost. Excessive innovation doesn't just create higher R&D costs, it can also bring unforeseen challenges (like technical integration) and increase the risk of encountering market resistance. On the other hand, too little innovation can lead to product stagnation, leaving an opportunity for competitors to swoop in with the next big thing. This balancing act means that the choice of *where to innovate* must always be a well-reasoned one. It is not just about what we think is trendy or reasonable. It is about what level of investment will create value without breaking our target cost model.

Surya, AutoRABIT's Product Manager featured in Section 14.4, sought to simplify the release job process for their users because the main platform had become overly complex. However, AutoRABIT's developers were hesitant, citing the lack of suitable APIs and the risks of making significant changes at that stage. Surya engaged with her team, considering their constraints and concerns, and urged them to explore viable alternatives, knowing the positive impact this would have on their key users (Salesforce Release Managers). They deliberated over which aspects of the current product were essential to AutoRABIT's identity and which were a hindrance. Their investigations, including gemba walks and support ticket analysis, underscored the importance of a simpler interface to re-engage users, while recognizing that the ARM backend was a crucial heritage element to retain and enhance. They applied a "80 + Alpha" approach and ultimately, the team struck a balance, leading to the development of their successful new flagship product, Flow Center, in just a few months.

Maintaining the right mix of innovation and stability is a crucial aspect of the Chief Product Engineer's job, but one that can be easily disrupted if hierarchical relationships are in play. The design team must be free to brainstorm, push back, and negotiate as they find their way to the best solution. Hierarchical relationships among team members or with the Chief Product Engineer impede this free exchange of ideas. Even the Chief Product Engineer's global vision must always be subject to challenge. A Chief Product Engineer usually does not even have a stable team over time: they compose a different team of experts to build each new product they are tasked with. They have a transverse role in the organization, and their main objective is to ensure the success of their product.

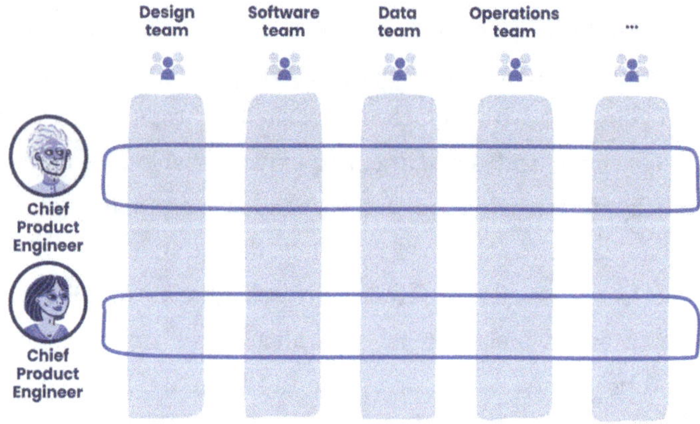

FIGURE 42. In a scaleup with multiple products, two Chief Product Engineers compose their teams from the common pool of specialists. They have authority over the product they have committed to delivering, but they have no hierarchical role with respect to team members.

Without hierarchical influence, the Chief Product Engineer must cultivate other qualities to recruit and engage specialists and engage the whole team with their vision. This is the ideal situation, since it allows the team to find the right equilibrium without undue influence. In startups, the first product lead is often the founder, and the whole company is their team. This situation may be dressed up as a non-hierarchical and collaborative organization, but team members will still hesitate to push back. No matter how casual the culture, the founder's authority is a risk factor for the success of the product and the company. Founders need to be aware of this risk and take steps to foster a safe environment for collaboration. Then, as their product line grows, they need to find and train their successors: leaders with an open mindset and passion for customers who can carry the Chief Product Engineer tradition forward.

Now ask yourself:
- Who decides where and when to innovate in your organization? Is there someone responsible for protecting a stable core?
- When deciding the nature of a new release, do the innovators usually win out or is it the technical conservatives? How do you ensure that design decisions have input from both camps, and that decisions are fair?
- What is your strategy for keeping a good balance between innovation and stability?

15.3 Create a convincing product manifesto

An irresistible product is the outcome of healthy and dynamic collaboration among individuals with diverse expertise and perspectives. However, once we gather several people in a room and task them with making a decision, some conflict is inevitable. Rarely does consensus appear without some intervention. Discussion can stagnate when people defend their own domain instead of looking for opportunities to compromise, and working relationships can become chaotic, emotional and sometimes personal. At times, the Product Manager lords over the tech team, overriding their recommendations despite lacking direct authority or relevant expertise. This is common in organizations that view product design as a delivery process, with developers operating somewhere downstream of the product team. Whatever the source of conflict, in traditional companies, a CEO or some other top leader typically has the final say. In a lean organization, it is the Chief Product Engineer, but with a crucial difference: Rather than choosing sides or dictating a solution, they exercise their leadership skills to get everyone working towards a common vision.

Consider the example of Elsa, the CPO of the health tech firm we presented in chapter 4. She faced many challenges in aligning her C-suite and other company stakeholders on the product roadmap. This is understandable given the complexity of her company's product, which was a platform that had to serve both medical professionals and patients while protecting private medical data. But ultimately, instead of decisions being made by a balanced consensus, the Chief Growth Officer emerged victorious in most debates. This group dynamic did not result in much improvement to the product or sales, causing Elsa endless frustration. Elsa eventually left, prompting the company founder and CEO, who was the original Chief Product Engineer, to step in and reduce the overbearing authority of the CGO.

Preventing, recognizing and defusing such situations is a crucial skill in product design. A Chief Product Engineer must possess excellent negotiation skills or else cultivate this ability. First of all, they need to propose a product concept that inspires and attracts the right team of specialists, people with a passion for problem solving and an open mindset, to keep politics to a minimum. They will need to charm external stakeholders who hold authority or influence over members of the team, such as department heads, business leaders, and external partners. This requires not only the skill of convincing others, but also the ability to listen and compromise when necessary. None of this is possible unless the Chief Product Engineer can clearly articulate their vision.

In lean organizations, the Chief Product Engineer follows a specific process for decreasing friction and speeding up decision-making, called **nemawashi**. This process is frequently used at Toyota to build consensus around a new concept or change. Getting everyone on the same page before settling on a plan is a surefire way of making faster decisions. The product leader collects the input and suggestions of everyone involved, one by one, and attempts to resolve any conflicts. The Chief Product Engineer must persuade others that their intention is good, that their product strategy is fantastic, and that they will use the company's funds wisely. People will push back, and if they don't do it immediately then they surely will after resources have been committed. The nemawashi approach may appear old school and slow, but it prevents different interpretations and conflicts down the line, ultimately accelerating the project significantly. This process will be more effective if the Chief Product Engineer has good negotiating skills and is supported by the company leader, because it circumvents the current hierarchy (unless they are also the founder). Product design is inherently strategic, so it is crucial that the Chief Product Officer has the autonomy to pursue new opportunities for the company. This backing not only aligns efforts with the broader company objectives but also empowers the Chief Product Engineer to innovate and make impactful decisions.

The essence of nemawashi is to align everyone before finalizing any action plan, whether it is a minor change to a process or a whole product design. The product leader methodically gathers individual inputs and suggestions on the current solution, addressing any conflicts among the team along the way. Then they can propose a new solution incorporating the feedback, and repeat the process if necessary. The aim of nemawashi is both to refine the concept and to secure universal support prior to implementation. At Toyota this approach has proven effective in achieving consensus on the product vision before starting development, bypassing many time-consuming and counterproductive negotiations. Nemawashi must be completed before any public announcement of a new product.

The Chief Product Engineer should already have written the concept paper for the product, so they can use it as a support for nemawashi. Specifically, they undertake the following actions:

- Conduct one-to-one meetings with each stakeholder (not just their own team) to present the product vision and business case, collect feedback, and propose refinements that respect existing constraints.

- In case of conflicting feedback, invite the concerned parties to another meeting to resolve the conflict.

- Hold individual meetings with each specialist in their team to share the stakeholder feedback and ensure their continued commitment to the revised concept.

The Chief Product Engineer can also go through this process with members of their team while the product vision is still being designed. These one-to-one meetings are vital for ensuring that every voice is heard and to strike a balance between excessive innovation and maintaining the status quo.

To succeed in keeping everyone committed to the same vision and working together toward the same goal, here are some key behaviors to follow:

- **Be attentive.** Focus not just on your customers, but also on what your team members and stakeholders are saying. Good listening skills are essential, as is a good dose of empathy. You can apply the same techniques you used researching your customers to understand the different points of view and needs expressed by your team. Try to frame these internal discussions with insights from the gemba. Don't hesitate to share customer feedback and real situations that relate to the issue at hand and inform your choices.

- **Identify your allies.** As you interact with your team, gauge who is likely to support you, who may create obstacles, who might outwardly agree but cause issues indirectly, and who could be an excellent performer once convinced, despite initial resistance. For those who need more convincing, leave room in the product vision to incorporate their good suggestions and encourage their buy-in. Being able to anticipate the individual attitudes and dynamics of the team is crucial for negotiations and effectively steering the project.

The outcome of this nemawashi process is a succinct summary of the concept paper, just one or two pages, that all stakeholders may sign to approve. We like to call this summary the "product manifesto" because it serves as a declaration of principles, values, and intentions behind the product concept. It can be bold and visionary, emphasizing the importance and significance of the new concept. The product manifesto includes the most crucial information to expedite the final validation of the project, including the problem we aim to solve, the underlying reasons, the proposed concept, the technical challenges, and details regarding cost, planning, and a go-to-market strategy. Providing all this information in the manifesto guarantees that everyone has the same comprehension of the concept paper and fosters engagement.

In some organizations, formal agreement is essential to prevent conflicts and misunderstandings later on, which can jeopardize the success of a project. Flavian and Sandrine have experienced situations in small startups where this bottom-up validation process would have been immensely beneficial. It is known that the act of signing a document has psychological and sociological effects, influencing individuals' commitment, engagement, sense of responsibility, and trustworthiness. Of course, this signature process is not essential and should be avoided in settings where stakeholders already enjoy a high level of mutual trust. However, in highly political contexts or large organizations, signing the manifesto can foster greater engagement and commitment from individuals.

Although our team didn't feel the need to sign it, we share below our product manifesto for *Build to Sell*. Writing it down was a great help in achieving early alignment among the three authors. In your own product manifesto, feel free to include visual elements such as a client radar chart, a trade-off curve, a consumption map or anything else that enhances the clarity and impact of your concept and business case. Just make sure to keep it concise, no longer than two standard pages, as many stakeholders may not have the desire or energy to read longer documents.

Product manifesto

Build to Sell book, Sandrine, Flavian, Caroline
May 30, 2023

What will our successful product look like?

Our bold concept:

A captivating and beautiful handbook brimming with user-friendly tools and engaging narratives, that also serves as a practical guide to transform products into irresistible offerings (Yet). The book introduces an innovative concept (Alpha)—the Chief Product Engineer—who bridges the realms of technology, product development, and finance.

Build to Sell will be the ultimate companion for product enthusiasts across all roles and organizations. With easy access to information anytime, anywhere, readers will confidently share it with colleagues, managers, or friends, believing it will inspire a fresh approach to product development. The guide is designed to free companies from the "feature frenzy" trap, emphasizing the creation of digital products and services that truly connect with customers. It advocates for a lean approach to product design, treating it as a problem-solving journey rather than a checklist of features. Innovative topics:

- **Emotion-centric design:** Create products that leave a lasting impact by tapping into dominant market emotions.

- **Chief Product Engineer:** The "super Product Manager" responsible for product strategy, technical design, AND financial outcomes. Nurtures an "artisan" mindset.

- **Performance-based product:** Optimize product performances and navigate technical trade-offs instead of focusing all your energy on writing, prioritizing and delivering features.
- **Design to cost:** Balance agility and cost control for long-term profitability using "target costing" techniques.

Who will be interested in reading our book?

Entrepreneurs who want to grow fast and attract investors, but who also want their businesses to last. Many startups fail because they don't understand their market or have trouble preparing their company for growth. These entrepreneurs are busy and don't have time to learn new methods. They might read e-books or hire teams to develop their products. We want to help them and their team members use *Build to Sell* as a simple guide to understand their market and build sustainable businesses.

Top quality requirements for our product:

- **Beautiful design:** Inspiring, desire to share it with others. Appealing cover and illustrations; light cover; nice quality of paper for printed copies; appealing even in digital versions.
- **Portable:** The traveler's companion. Fits in a coat pocket; is available on kindle, e-book and audio formats.
- **Universal audience:** Attract a large variety of people around the world. Should speak to agilists, product specialists, tech people and leaders.

- **Thought provoking:** Avoid stereotypes and "déjà vu"; strive to evoke "aha" moments. Each new concept features a real-life example showcasing a problem readers have likely faced, along with compelling arguments and fresh perspectives.

- **Great for book clubs:** Book clubs offer a popular avenue for spreading the movement. Incorporate in the book thought-provoking questions, engaging exercises, and practical tools to enrich the discussion and deepen understanding.

Price and business potential:

Books of similar size and content typically sell for around $25–31 in paperback and $15–22 as e-books. We've set our prices at $29 for paperback and $19 for e-books. Based on past sales in the lean community, we know we can sell 10,000 copies, with a 50/50 split between paperback and e-book. However, our goal is to have a transforming impact on a wide audience, so we want to keep the book in the spotlight for at least two years and grow our community by tenfold. This means we need to sell over 100,000 copies worldwide.

What tough technical problems must we solve?

Key technical trade-offs we need to tackle:

- **Thought provoking vs. self-explanatory chapter titles:** Chapter titles featuring action verbs and impactful terms.

- **Relatable content vs. the size of the chapters:** Use real-life examples from our own experiences in tech, product, and top leadership, and obtain people's consent. Include examples from diverse contexts. Test the concepts, examples and tools in the Taktique training group sessions (universality, ease of understanding, actionable).

- **Appealing illustrations in digital formats vs. visual, step-by-step examples:** Conduct tests on color, font size, and weight in degraded conditions, prioritize readability on various Kindle devices.

- **Fits in a pocket vs. clear and comprehensive:** Less theory, more examples to reduce the size of the chapter, making the book smaller but still rich with insights.

- **Thought provoking vs. universal audience:** Check that vocabulary used is acceptable and inclusive via feedback from book editors and via a Python program developed by Flavian.

Challenges linked to the target cost:
Having all graphics created by a professional designer would exceed the target cost, so we budget for a few visually pleasing cartoons. Flavian and Caroline, leveraging their expertise, will produce all other figures and illustrations. This allows us to allocate more resources for professional layout and cover design.

What pitfalls must we avoid?

What we must keep:
Although this book is first and foremost a product design and development book, the essence of lean and lean engineering remains central. We're incorporating concepts and tools from our

successful "Build To Sell" training program. Foundational product design concepts from popular books such as *Inspired, Continuous Discovery,* and *Crossing the Chasm* are retained, along with insights from business literature like *Competing Against Luck, Change or Die, 9 Lies About Work,* and *Working Backwards.* We aim to maintain a style and tone similar to esteemed product books like *The Mom Test* and *Empowered* for their appeal.

What we must be mindful of:

We need to acknowledge the limitations of the Silicon Valley model, which relies on recruiting top-tier talent and pouring vast sums of money into the product—approaches that aren't feasible for most companies. Our goal is to be more inclusive and resonate with all types of entrepreneurs. Furthermore, while the lean methodology is valuable, it can also seem intimidating at first glance. It's crucial to highlight the differences in how lean companies operate and ensure that our methods, rooted in lean principles, are accessible and not obscured by jargon that readers may not fully grasp or identify with.

Now ask yourself:

- How are you sharing your product vision and strategy with the team members and stakeholders? Collectively or individually? What do you do to make it inspiring for others?

- How do you know that everyone is committed to your vision of the product? Are there persistent points of conflict?

- How would you describe your "bold product concept"? What is your next "Alpha"? What are the top three to four critical performances you want to achieve?

15.4 Front-load the design and development process

In product development, the design phase sets the foundation for the entire project. Decisions made during this phase have far-reaching consequences. Ill-considered choices can snowball into complex problems during the development process and post delivery, sometimes persisting over several release cycles. Software and digital product teams have become very familiar with the concept of technical debt, which is an overhead of bug fixing and rework caused by rushed or convenient design choices made early in the development process. Of course, physical products can also suffer from shoddy design! The authors have personally bought a washing machine whose motherboard has malfunctioned twice in five years, a hybrid car whose lidar sensors constantly fall out of alignment, and headphones whose most vulnerable part, the audio cable, can't be replaced. The list goes on and on. In the industrial realm, it is commonly accepted that between 70% and 90% of the total manufacturing cost can be attributed to issues arising from the design phase[49]. This insight underscores the financial impact of early decisions, and applies not just to the automotive industry but across all sectors, including the digital realm.

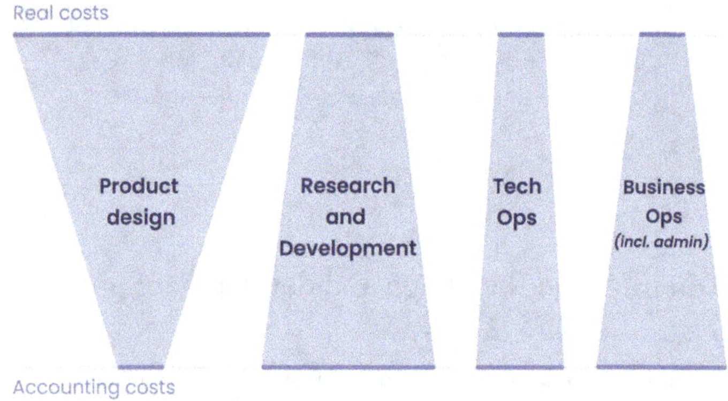

FIGURE 43. Decisions made during product design influence the entire product life cycle and have by far the largest impact on total costs.

While no similar statistic has been published for the digital industry, it is widely recognized that design and development decisions significantly influence both direct and indirect costs. In software development, poor design choices regularly lead to expensive and time-consuming rework.

To see the impact of rework in your own context, we suggest the following exercise. Take your most recent development iteration

---

49 Does Product Design Really Determine 80% of Manufacturing Cost?
https://tktq.link/build-to-sell/product-design-manufacturing-cost

and place a red sticker on each card that represents repairing an error from prior iterations. Then calculate the ratio of value-repairing to value-creating activities. This provides an initial insight into the cost implications of poor design decisions. For example, a common figure in software development is that 20% of each development sprint is bug fixing. On top of that, we should add the cost of quality control activities and rework during other phases of the product life cycle, as well as customer support. The same is true in manufacturing. How many products don't pass final inspection? How many are returned by customers because of defects? What is the associated cost of these quality repair activities?

According to the American Society for Quality[50], the "cost of quality" summing all these activities typically accounts for 15-20% of sales, but it can reach up to 40% in certain organizations. While it is unclear how much of this could be mitigated by focusing on quality earlier in the process, these percentages are quite telling. Additionally, there can be a substantial impact on the user experience due to bad design decisions, potentially resulting in lost sales and a damaged reputation.

Nowadays, software teams often start work without extensively addressing knowledge gaps, opting instead to integrate this learning directly into the delivery process. Their strategy involves building the product in small increments, allowing them to adapt flexibly to changes in requirements. This approach allows teams to deliver and demonstrate functional software early, but also adds considerable uncertainty and variability to the overall project, often introducing new errors and prolonging

---

50 https://tktq.link/build-to-sell/cost-of-quality

timelines as a result. Aware of this, developers often refrain from giving upfront work estimates, which can sometimes frustrate management and customers. Sometimes, under pressure, they might offer unrealistic estimates, ultimately leading to disappointment. For this reason, in the software sector teams commonly resist providing delivery timeframes, citing the abundance of unknowns. While this concern is valid, it should not deter them from minimizing these unknowns upfront. Doing so allows for more informed decisions early on and helps prevent the accumulation of technical debt in their designs.

Agile, we argue, is still better than the alternative "waterfall" methodology, which commits vast resources to building a fully specified, rigid product design that may not meet the needs of customers when it is finally delivered. Agile teams deliberately front-load key design elements, delivering them early in the development process to diminish knowledge gaps while maintaining a satisfying pace for stakeholders. Some Agile projects allocate R&D time boxes during delivery to explore aspects of the product that require deeper investigation, such as choosing the optimal database for the back end or experimenting with algorithms. Usually these research tasks are purely technical, not customer-oriented; for this they already have regular meetings with the Product Owner (who is supposed to represent the end user). In contrast with waterfall, Agile recognizes that customer needs may shift and that many facets of the design can be significantly improved during implementation by trial and error with feedback from end users.

However, it is feasible to commit to project timelines and meet customer expectations without constantly soliciting their feedback on our designs. For example, when you purchase a TV, the product is complete and thoroughly tested, and salespeople don't require you to submit Jira tickets for issues. This suggests that TV engineers must resolve as many unknowns as possible before they finalize the design, manufacture the product, and sell it. This raises the question: Why can't a similar approach be applied in software development, or perhaps a hybrid of both methodologies? Lean product design is a major part of the solution: all the work described previously in this book to understand the customer and their preferences allows the design and development teams to make much better initial guesses about the technical details of the product. As we have seen, identifying and addressing knowledge gaps in the early stages of the design process is more cost-effective than addressing them later. Nevertheless, even after the concept paper is written and all stakeholders have committed, some knowledge gaps will remain. (Recall that a section of the concept paper was reserved for listing these unknowns!) At this stage, we've gathered enough insights to create an initial project scenario and prepare for concurrent set-based experiments to address the biggest unknowns. The next step is to collaborate with all specialists involved to develop a more accurate project and cost plan, and then launch development. Moving forward, we can adopt an iterative approach to address unexpected problems during development using kaizen.

The first task of the development team at this point is to gain a deeper understanding of the product, as well as its foundational technology and processes. This approach is known as front-loading the development process. For instance, they may need to understand new technologies they want to use, address uncertainties about an aspect of the product, get acquainted with complex changes, demystify any unclear processes, experiment with various solutions to resolve a technical trade-off, or acquire knowledge about a new method they intend to adopt. These early insights and decisions will influence how the team implements changes down the road.

The goal of this pre-development phase is to anticipate and tackle potential problems and uncertainties that the specialists on the design team have foreseen. This is a fantastic way to build enthusiasm among the developers, foster learning, and disseminate specialized knowledge for later re-use. A Chief Product Engineer with whom Sandrine has worked starts every new project by leading sessions with their team to bridge these knowledge gaps together. Sometimes they and the team spend several weeks exploring key topics without making any change to the product. In these learning sessions, the Product Manager encourages every technical and functional specialist to state their knowledge gaps and propose strategies for addressing them, fostering an environment where no one needs to pretend they know everything and everyone contributes valuable insights.

Traditional software projects using only proven and mature components may be forgiven for spending little time on research and discovery before launching into development. However, lately more and more software projects incorporate Artificial Intelligence (AI), which is experimental by nature. Companies specialized in AI such as Sicara from the Theodo group (a trend-setter for lean design and development in the digital sector) have learned that traditional Agile development is too risky. Their teams often spend some time testing the performance of various AI algorithms and related technologies on the customer's data, before deciding whether a new application is worth building or guiding the client in another direction. The software development only starts after learning which AI technique can reach the desired performance, if any. AI is ideally suited for the performance-based product development approach we advocate in this book.

Of course, learning needs to continue throughout the project, and it is the job of the Chief Product Engineer and everyone in the development team to keep the product vision and technical design up to date as new information comes in. Even when development is well underway, the team will need to spend time investigating solutions and addressing technical trade-offs. A good strategy for making the development plan more predictable is to maintain two distinct work streams: one for R&D aimed at cracking new, complex technical challenges, and another for delivering the product using tested technologies and processes. New technology is only moved to the delivery stream after it has been vetted and proven by the R&D stream.

Minimizing unknowns as much as possible before starting development is a smart strategy. The techniques in this chapter have shown how to establish the necessary knowledge base and consensus prior to building the actual product. Starting development without properly addressing all the knowledge gaps laid out in the concept paper can be very risky, or even a showstopper. But even more important, it forces the team to widen their field of knowledge about the product, the technologies, what works in what case, and what does not, where are the boundaries and how to push them safely in the future.

Now ask yourself:

- Reviewing your current iteration backlog, how many action items still have uncertainties?

- In your most recent interaction, did any task turn out to be harder than expected? What unanswered question would have let the team estimate this task correctly?

- What strategies do you employ to reduce these uncertainties? Does the team tackle them proactively or simply treat them as a margin of error on their capacity?

- How do you ensure that your team continues to capitalize on new insights?

CONCLUSION

Entrepreneurship involves taking massive risks, but as we have seen most startups get into trouble for one simple reason: they are not proposing the right product for their market, or if they have found a market they are not focusing their efforts on improving the right parts of the customer experience. Constructing a truly effective product design and development culture, the core of any business that hopes to scale, is a two-step process:

1. **Customer exploration and strategy design:** Before a single line of code is written or any physical product is built, identify and flesh out a compelling product concept. This includes crafting a vision and strategy based on gemba data, one that not only engages but also secures buy-in and motivates stakeholders.

2. **Superb execution and preparation for growth:** Transform this concept into an irresistible product that not only meets market needs but gears your company up for

the next phase of growth. This involves considering every aspect of the product: the user experience, technical feasibility, and market readiness.

Both steps are underpinned by robust, *continuous learning* methods. Learning about our customers ensures that our products not only meet but exceed market expectations, and that our design and business strategy for the products will drive long-term profitability. This book has focused mainly on Step 1: front-loading the development process with robust discovery and evidence-based strategy, a crucial yet often overlooked component of product design. Our next book, *Build To Scale*, will cover Step 2. It will discuss lean concepts such as obeyas, radical quality, trade-off resolution, set-based design, go-to market strategy, product ramp-up, and more.

The performance-based product

In this book we have seen the most important practices used by learning organizations to develop strong product strategies. Briefly, they are:

- **Set a regular innovation pace.** Establish a consistent rhythm of product innovation, defined by the product takt, which aligns with what the market can absorb. This rhythm acts as the heartbeat of the organization, ensuring that all activities from sales to support are synchronized.
- **Grow leadership in innovation.** Appoint a Chief Product

Engineer to lead the product innovation cycles. This role is crucial for developing an extraordinary product vision, rallying experts and stakeholders around the vision, and achieving financial success for the product. Remember, the first product engineers are often the founders themselves, and they play a pivotal role in finding suitable successors, not just in crafting the perfect process.

- **View the whole product as a collection of client experiences.** Look at your product as a series of user experiences across different scenarios, recognizing that a company's offering includes a set of services enabled by both technology and human effort.

- **Deeply immerse yourself in your customers' world.** Go beyond mere appearances by actively engaging with customers, taking their complaints seriously, and understanding their needs and preferences from the perspective of their gemba. Learn to navigate around your own and others' cognitive biases to root your product development in genuine user insights.

- **Manage your product as a set of performances and technical trade-offs to resolve**, rather than just a collection of features. Always be mindful of evolving tastes and societal trends to ensure that your product remains relevant and interesting. Develop a sound financial strategy based on value-based pricing and industry-aligned profit margins, and empower your product team with a clear cost target to spur innovation and ensure long-term profitability and adaptability.

- **Craft a persuasive narrative.** Engage both internal and external stakeholders by creating a detailed concept paper. This document should articulate a vision that balances cutting-edge innovation with the need for organizational stability. It should outline strategic goals, potential impacts, and practical steps towards implementation, thereby rallying support across the board.

By embedding learning deeply into the product development process, companies can more effectively adapt to changing client needs and market conditions, significantly increasing the likelihood of developing products that are not only aligned with user desires but also capable of exceeding their expectations. This approach ensures products that are truly irresistible to consumers, continuously refined based on solid feedback and insights.

Where to start based on your role

If you aren't sure where to start implementing the ideas in this book, here are some good first steps depending on your role and responsibilities.

- **Startup founder:** Draft a concept paper to refine your product vision and validate your strategy. Engage with our community of experts and practitioners to gain insights and accelerate your project.

- **CEO of a scaleup:** Collaborate with your product and development leads to identify team members who can undergo specialized training to enhance their skills and potentially become Chief Product Engineers. Implement a weekly session with your leadership team to analyze a customer complaint, aiming to cultivate a genuinely customer-focused culture by centering discussions on improving client satisfaction.

- **Head of product (including CPO):** Assess potential candidates for Chief Product Engineer roles within your team, including yourself. Encourage them to develop a concept paper for their product, deepening their understanding of customer needs and market dynamics, and establish a routine of visiting the client's gemba.

- **Head of tech (including CTO):** Identify potential Chief Product Engineers among your team, particularly those working on reusable tools. Task them with creating a client/competitor radar chart to define value, and a table of product critical performances to frame and quantify the technical trade-offs faced by developers.

- **Product Manager/Product Owner:** Begin by analyzing your customer feedback and complaints to pinpoint the primary Jobs To Be Done of your main client segments. Develop a client radar chart reflecting their stable preferences, then review how your current product measures up against your accomplishments and vision so far.

Our final word

Crafting irresistible products is an exhilarating journey of continuous learning and adaptation. This journey starts on day one, when we first start talking about the concept, and continues throughout the product life cycle: design, development, delivery, and beyond. This book has taken you on a tour of product design as it is practiced in lean companies from all sectors, from manufacturing to pure digital. A lean company doesn't build anything without these learning practices in place, and a clear, adaptable vision of what resonates with their customers.

In contrast, many traditional product development methods claim to incorporate learning, but only do so on a superficial level. Workshops and interviews are common, but the lessons learned usually do not come from the gemba: the design is based on what users *say*, not on what they *do and feel*. During development, the learning that takes place is more about ticking boxes than enhancing the product with actionable insights. These learning rituals might take the form of feedback loops (getting the PO or some other customer representative to sign off on features) or iterative testing (demonstrating an early version of the product with fanfare but no expectation to be challenged on the basic concept). In short, these methods of learning about the customer are not deeply woven into the design and development process.

This narrow focus on the initial design, roadmap, and development schedule leads product development teams into the trap of "feature frenzy", where delivering new features as fast as possible overshadows the need for meaningful improvements based on deep customer insights. Products delivered in this way often don't resonate with customers. Startups stuck in this mode soon notice symptoms such as inefficient delivery by teams struggling with technical debt, or declining sales due to lukewarm reception. The only way out of this vicious cycle is to break free from the feature-centric approach. The lean alternative is to center every decision on customers and their preferences. Instead of delivering a list of *features*, the goal is to deliver a product with the critical *performances* that support and delight your customers. A startup that succeeds in embracing adaptive and learning-focused product development will find itself able to face new challenges and make a significant difference in the market.

As we look to the future, the landscape of product development is riddled with significant challenges—resource scarcity, rapid technological evolution, and dynamic societal changes. Each of these elements calls for a forward-thinking approach to product design that not only anticipates changes but leads the way in sustainable innovation. This book aims to empower you, the reader, to navigate these complex waters with agility and vision. Use it as a dynamic toolkit, revisiting chapters as you face new challenges or when inspiration strikes. By embedding learning deeply within every stage of the design and development process, you'll be better equipped to create products that not only meet but exceed the demands of tomorrow's market. You will be able to mold products that anticipate environmental constraints, leverage cutting-edge technology, and resonate deeply with evolving consumer behaviors. Through this approach, you can transform challenges into opportunities to innovate and thrive in an ever-changing world.

ONE LAST THING

More *Build to Sell* resources

You will find more resources around the book at
https://www.taktique.com/books/build-to-sell

Help others discover the book

Many readers rely on reviews to decide if a book is worth their time. Your thoughts can help others find the right book for their needs. If you found this book helpful, please consider leaving a review on Amazon and Goodreads (we provide direct links below). Your feedback can guide them in making an informed choice. Thank you for sharing your experience and helping others discover this book!

Amazon

https://tktq.link/build-to-sell/book-review-amazon

Goodreads

https://tktq.link/build-to-sell/book-review-goodreads

Taktique bite-sized courses

If you would like to go further, we invite you to come practice the book's concepts (and more!) in our "online" and "in-person" training courses, and join our thriving community. Our customized training journeys are designed to meet your unique needs and situation. Find out more at:

https://tktq.link/program

Follow us on social networks at:
https://tktq.link/socials

GLOSSARY

80 + Alpha

Originating from Toyota's automobile industry, this concept emphasizes continuous improvement while balancing consistency and innovation. It entails maintaining a minimum level of performance (80%) across all aspects of a product while introducing one key improvement or innovation (Alpha) in each release to captivate customers' interest. This principle ensures that the product remains reliable and competitive while fostering a culture of consistent improvement and innovation. In the digital realm, the same principle applies, with new versions of digital products incorporating innovations or performance boosts while meeting critical performance thresholds. (Chapter 14.4)

Andon

Andon is a visual tool that signals issues immediately upon detection, encouraging a "stop as soon as a defect occurs" approach. It relies on a chain of help, ensuring swift responses to prevent problems and waste downstream, benefiting both the organization and the clients. (Chapter 3)

Big company disease

Big company diseases, a concept first introduced in *The Lean Strategy*, are common issues that arise during scaling and can start very early, affecting not just big companies but also startups and scaleups. These issues lead to increased complexity and rigidity in processes, hindering innovation and agility, and making it difficult for organizations to adapt and respond to changing market demands. (Chapter 3)

Chief Engineer

At Toyota, the Chief Engineer, or shusa, oversees the entire product development process. They lead a small team to create the product concept, manage design, and coordinate with production and sales. Chief Engineers cultivate an artisan mindset and integrate the team's efforts around a compelling vision through influence and innovation. Though they don't directly supervise all team members, this setup fosters innovation through productive tension. We use the term Chief Product Engineer throughout the book. (Introduction)

Chief Product Engineer

The Chief Product Engineer, often the company founder in early stages, plays a pivotal role in ensuring the profitability and success of the product. Responsible for coordinating interdisciplinary teams and fostering a product-centric culture, they harmonize team efforts and ensure cohesive product design. Despite lacking formal authority, they wield influence through persuasion and collaboration, driving vision and business case transformation. Operating at the intersection of client needs and technological advancements, they exemplify a growth mindset and venture beyond role boundaries. This crucial role is indispensable for achieving financial success and ongoing value enhancement. As the company grows, the founder's role evolves to perpetuate the Chief Product Engineer's artisan spirit, instilling a culture of excellence and innovation. (Chapter 7)

Client radar chart

A tool used to define value and track competitor benchmarks based on key customer preferences. It visually represents how well a product satisfies these preferences compared to existing alternatives. (Chapter 12)

Client stable preferences

These are the pivotal quality characteristics that clients rely on when evaluating solutions and comparing alternatives. They are consistent and enduring within the same segment, serving as the essential criteria that must not be overlooked to remain competitive. These preferences profoundly influence the success of a product, evolving over time and molding design approaches. Typically, they manifest as a few stable preferences per segment, encapsulating what truly matters to customers. Understanding these preferences before embarking on development endeavors is paramount, providing guidance to teams and shaping technological choices to ensure continued relevance and customer satisfaction. (Chapter 12)

Concept paper

A concept paper is a key tool used by the Chief Product Engineer and their core team to think through and translate customer preferences into a product idea. It outlines the vision, profitability, technical strategy and delivery plan in a coherent story, spanning two to six pages. Serving as a written narrative rather than technical documentation, it grounds ambitious ideas, identifies feasibility, and highlights what needs to be learned and the risks to pay attention to. The concept paper is essential in the early stages of product development. (Chapter 15.1)

Consumption and provision mapping

Originating from *Lean Solutions* by Dan Jones and Jim Womack, consumption and provision mapping focuses on both sides of the customer experience: consumption and provision. This approach involves mapping out the journey from the customer's perspective as well as from the provider's angle. By analyzing these dual perspectives, organizations can identify inefficiencies, improve processes, and enhance the overall customer experience. (Chapter 11.6)

Critical product function

This element of product design is essential for ensuring the product behaves as expected and aligns with key client preferences. It defines specific design criteria that must be met to fulfill the product's purpose effectively. Without these critical functions, the product may fail to meet customer expectations or perform as intended. They serve as the foundation upon which the product's design and features are built, ensuring that it meets the needs and preferences of its intended users. (Chapter 14.4)

Customer complaints analysis board

This structured framework enables organizations to dissect and understand individual customer complaints thoroughly. By analyzing complaints daily, organizations foster a culture of careful consideration, challenging biases, and avoiding hasty judgments. This strategic approach ensures that every customer concern is taken seriously, contributing to continuous improvement and enhanced customer satisfaction. (Chapter 11.3)

Customer experience

Customer experience encompasses all interactions a customer has with a company and its products, impacting their overall perception and satisfaction. It is crucial for customer loyalty, retention, and business success. This includes every stage from purchase to support and affects brand perception, product appeal, and sales growth. Focusing on customer experience in different situations helps improve products and reduce churn, ultimately driving growth and profits. (Chapter 2)

Emotion-centric design

This approach focuses on crafting products that deeply resonate with customers by tapping into dominant emotions in the target market. Recognizing that purchasing decisions are heavily influenced by emotions, rather than purely rational factors, emotion-centric design aims to evoke positive emotional responses and establish personal connections. It emphasizes considering emotions from the outset of product development to ensure that every design choice aligns with the desired emotional response, transcending mere functionality to create products that evoke meaningful emotions in users. (Chapter 14.2)

Feature frenzy syndrome

This common phenomenon, affectionately named in this book, carries significant drawbacks. Firstly, the rush for speed often results in a paradoxical slowdown in delivery. The team's focus on a myriad of unrelated features leads to fragmented work streams and isolated developers, hampering collaboration and prolonging feature delivery. This fragmented attention not only slows execution but also compromises the quality of the output. Moreover, the fixation on clearing backlogs can obscure the bigger picture, causing teams to lose sight of evolving market needs and customer priorities. By hastily pushing through a bloated backlog, teams risk missing the mark entirely, failing to address or improve upon stable client preferences. (Chapters 4.1 & 14.4)

Fixed costs

These are expenses that remain constant regardless of production or sales volume, such as rent, salaries, and subscriptions. (Chapter 14.3)

Gemba

Gemba is a Japanese term meaning "the real place," where value-adding activities occur. It is a key concept in lean design, referring to where products are conceived, built, and used. In lean, going to the gemba involves direct observation to gain accurate insights into customer interactions and real issues. Regular visits help leadership and team members address delays, understand Jobs To Be Done, and uncover client work-arounds, providing deep insights and acting as a reality check against cognitive biases. (Chapters 9 & 11.4)

Gemba walk

Gemba walks are indispensable for removing cognitive biases and delving into the realm of customer emotions, which may not be visible elsewhere. These walks offer an unparalleled opportunity to understand the intricate nuances of customer experiences in real-life situations, allowing product creators to tap into the emotional aspect of their offerings. Recognizing that products are not merely functional but evoke profound emotions, gemba walks become the primary activity for anyone conceiving a product, providing invaluable insights for empathetic design and innovation. On the gemba, we uncover what customers often don't explicitly express, gaining crucial insights that guide product development towards meeting unspoken needs and desires. (Chapters 9 & 11.4)

Heritage technologies

These are unique features or technologies that distinguish the product from competitors and should be preserved and improved to maintain its competitive edge. (Chapter 14.6)

Horizontal innovation

Horizontal innovation is the addition of new products to a product family to address different customer needs. As one of the two main takt times, it focuses on expanding product variations to cater to diverse customer preferences and Jobs To Be Done. This approach is informed by customer insights, ensuring tailored solutions that align with evolving market demands. (Chapter 5.2)

Iron law of scaleups

The Iron law of scaleups, a concept from *The Lean Strategy*, refers to the inevitable problems faced during rapid growth. It highlights the challenges and complexities that arise as organizations expand quickly, necessitating adaptive strategies and continuous improvement. (Chapter 3)

Job To Be Done

Jobs to Be Done (JTBD), a framework pioneered by Clayton Christensen and his colleagues, guides product design by understanding specific customer goals and circumstances, including social, emotional, and functional aspects. It defines genuine client needs, facilitating user-centered design and segment-specific solutions. JTBD focuses on real people and their contexts, prioritizing customer value and driving innovation. (Chapter 10)

Job To Be Done interview

An interview to understand the Job To Be Done goes beyond understanding how customers use our product or what features they desire. The interviewer must delve deep into the customer's lived experiences, uncovering the circumstances, steps, and motivations behind their actions. These interviews focus on the tasks customers want to accomplish and the journey they undertake to fulfill those tasks. By exploring the context and intricacies of customer behavior, Job To Be Done interviews reveal valuable insights that shape product development and innovation. (Chapter 11.5)

Kaizen

Kaizen is a Japanese term meaning "change for better" or "continuous improvement." It encourages ongoing development and optimization, focusing on enhancing performance without unnecessary alterations. Central to Toyota's success, kaizen is a key principle of lean methodology, ensuring continuous improvement in all areas. (Chapters 14.7 & 15.4)

Kanban

Kanban is a tool for managing work that visualizes customer demand across the organization and highlights issues. It is essential for practicing kaizen, as it helps people focus on the right problems—those that prevent the company from delivering the right value at the right pace to customers. (Chapters 3 & 5.4)

Kano model

This framework helps identify how exceeding expectations for critical performances in the "performant" or "attractive" categories can enhance customer satisfaction by creating a "wow" effect. For instance, improving page loading speed on an e-commerce site beyond what customers anticipate can lead to a significant boost in satisfaction and traffic. (Chapter 14.4)

Lean

Lean is a business strategy focused on creating value for customers while minimizing waste. Waste refers to any activity or process that doesn't add value to the final product or service. By eliminating these non-value activities, lean aims to streamline processes, making them more efficient and cost-effective. Lean emphasizes the importance of people development, believing that building great products starts with building great people. This means developing and empowering employees at all levels to continuously solve problems and improve processes. Lean encourages innovation and iterative development, promoting continuous improvement throughout the organization.

A key role in lean is the Chief Engineer (called Chief Product Engineer throughout the book), who acts like a super Product Manager, spending significant time where value is created to understand and improve processes. Tools like concept papers and obeya (large open workspaces for project teams) are used to enhance collaboration and efficiency.

Overall, lean aims to deliver irresistible products by focusing on value creation, efficiency, and the continuous development of both people and processes. (Chapter 8)

Lean sensei

A lean sensei is a Japanese term for a teacher who is crucial in lean transformations. They combine coaching with teaching to help navigate and apply lean principles in practice. (Foreword, Chapter 8.1)

Legacy technologies

These are features or technologies that, while possibly integral or traditional, no longer resonate with customers and may even generate annoyance or disinterest if retained unchanged. They can impede progress but may still play a crucial role in the product's functionality. (Chapter 14.6)

Live My Life

When gemba walks aren't feasible, the "Live My Life" approach enables team members to step into the shoes of customers. This immersive method involves experiencing the product as customers do, adopting their lifestyle, and gaining firsthand insights into their daily routines, challenges, and preferences. By living the customer's life, team members gain deep empathy and understanding, which inform product development decisions and drive customer-centric innovation. (Chapters 6.2, 10, 11.4)

Nemawashi

A consensus-building method employed to garner agreement on a new concept or change. It entails collecting input and suggestions from all relevant parties involved. By involving everyone in the decision-making process, conflicts are minimized, and project decisions are expedited. (Chapter 15.3)

Obeya

An obeya is a physical or virtual space that facilitates idea exchange and enhances transversal collaboration. It contributes to a cohesive vision and supports the conception of high-risk product changes. This dynamic space is essential for effective teamwork and innovative problem-solving. (Chapter 7.3)

Performance-based product

Introduced for the first time in this book, the performance-based product is a comprehensive methodology for designing products that satisfy all stable customer preferences while capturing their emotions with innovation. It encourages product teams to explore creative and diverse solutions in search of the best way to optimize performance targets aligned with client stable preferences. It shifts the focus from feature delivery to creative problem-solving, inspiring teams to devise novel approaches to resolve technical trade-offs and enhance product performance. (Chapter 14.4)

Point-based design

An approach to find the best market fit for a product iteratively, often starting with a minimum viable product then pivoting or enhancing it in response to feedback. Compared to set-based design, it potentially leads to higher costs and longer development cycles due to the need for frequent iterations and adjustments. (Chapters 13 & 14.4)

Product concept

Remarkable products go beyond delivering features; they resolve customer trade-offs through innovative solutions, encapsulated in a product concept's "yet" statement. This clarity not only guides development but also prevents arbitrary changes, ensuring focus on addressing the core issue. It motivates teams to tackle technical challenges and deliver solutions that truly enhance the customer experience. (Chapter 14.1)

Product flow

In the context of product development, "product flow" refers to the continuous evolution of a product through a series of innovations that adapt to shifting market conditions and changes in consumer preferences. Rather than viewing a product as a static entity, this concept emphasizes its dynamic nature, with each iteration responding to evolving market demands and customer tastes. By embracing this perspective, businesses can maintain relevance and competitiveness by consistently delivering new and improved versions of their offerings that resonate with their target audience. (Chapter 5.3)

Product manifesto

A concise declaration outlining the principles, values, and intentions guiding a product concept. It condenses the essence of the concept paper into a brief document, typically one or two pages long. Its primary function is to foster alignment and commitment among all stakeholders involved in the product development process. (Chapter 15.3)

Product ramp-up

The process of scaling production and marketing efforts to meet increasing demand or to launch a new product successfully. (Chapter 15.4)

Product takt

A product takt is a cadence of new product releases within the same product family. A new release might aim to resolve a different problem for another customer segment, or it might be an upgraded version of an existing product to keep customers interested in the brand. Each release cycle is an opportunity to analyze the value we created or destroyed with our previous releases (value analysis), so we can more easily decide what new change will improve value (value engineering). The product takt forces us to check our product bets on a regular basis and minimize the risk of disappointing customers. It also prevents us from burning our cash on several wrong ideas at once. A product takt is more than just a product release rhythm; it's a disruptive force in industries. By imposing a pace of innovation, it not only drives progress within the organization but also compels competitors to innovate. This dynamic reshapes industries, fostering continuous innovation and continued relevance in a rapidly evolving market landscape. (Chapter 5)

Product teardown

Examining the various solutions available in the market, we select competitors that align with our clients' stable preferences. Tear-down analysis involves deconstructing these solutions, scrutinizing their design choices, and assessing their impact on customer satisfaction. This collaborative effort uncovers technical characteristics, costs, innovations, and assembly processes, providing a comprehensive understanding of each competing product's strengths and weaknesses. Through this exercise, we identify areas for improvement and potential threats, guiding our own product development strategy. (Chapter 13)

Radical quality

A concept originating from Sadao Nomura's book *The Toyota Way of Dantotsu Radical Quality Improvement*, requiring commitment from the entire organization for significant quality enhancements. (Chapters 8.2 & 15.4)

Scientific problem solving

Chief Product Engineers use scientific problem solving to address challenges and innovate with their team of specialists. This approach involves systematic investigation, data collection, hypothesis testing, and analysis to develop effective solutions and drive continuous improvement. (Introduction)

Set-based design

This approach explores multiple solutions concurrently, swiftly eliminating weaker options to converge on technically feasible and market-viable designs. Compared to point-based design, set-based design is less risky because it ensures informed decision-making, essential for successful product development. At Toyota, Chief Engineers examine numerous prototypes to quantify and resolve trade-offs, leveraging this knowledge in the form of trade-off curves to inform future projects. (Chapters 13 & 14.4)

Storyboard

A versatile tool utilized to portray emotional product experiences and communicate visionary concepts. It illustrates all stages of the customer's interaction with the product, from their preexisting problem through discovery, value creation, and integration. The storyboard is a visual narrative that aids in conveying ideas and fostering a deeper understanding of the product concept among team members and stakeholders. (Chapter 14.2)

Target cost

The variable in the equation "Profit = Price – Cost", representing the maximum allowable cost to ensure profitability. It is the focal point for improvement, as price is dictated by market conditions and profit margins are influenced by industry benchmarks and company goals. (Chapters 14.3 & 14.5)

Target costing

An approach aimed at achieving the product's target cost by enhancing overall value. This ongoing process emphasizes adding value throughout the entire product flow, ensuring alignment with key client preferences while focusing on continuous improvement. It is not about cutting costs to increase profit, but rather about optimizing costs without compromising on quality. Led by the Chief Product Engineer, target costing involves collaborative work sessions with specialists to identify opportunities for value enhancement and waste elimination across the different product functions. (Chapter 14.5)

Technical trade-off

Imagine developing a website search feature that balances speed and complexity. Users expect fast results, but also desire accurate matches, even when sifting through vast amounts of data. Enhancing accuracy may involve sophisticated algorithms that slow down response times. This dilemma epitomizes the trade-offs inherent in product design: improving one aspect often sacrifices another. Engineers must delicately navigate these trade-offs, exploring diverse solutions to strike an optimal balance. This iterative process fuels innovation, allowing products to adapt to user demands and technological limitations. (Chapter 14.4)

Trade-off curve

A crucial tool in product development, a trade-off curve quantifies the effects of a design change on critical performances and sets boundaries for feasible solutions. For instance, when creating a chatbot-based question-answering system, a team needs to balance flexibility and knowledge against sustainability and cost. They can experiment with various technologies for the tool, plotting the performances on a curve. This sparks innovative discussions, shifting the conversation towards strategic performance enhancements. (Chapter 14.4)

Thinking People System (TPS)

The Thinking People System, developed at Toyota, is the foundation of lean thinking. It focuses on creating value, continuous improvement, people development, and customer satisfaction. This system emphasizes efficiency, quality, and the growth of employees to achieve business success and the best outcomes. TPS is sometimes also read as the Toyota Production System. (Chapter 8)

Value

In product development, a clear understanding of value is paramount for success. This principle, central to lean, underpins both product and process improvement efforts. It involves discerning what customers truly find valuable and delivering it efficiently. By prioritizing value, teams can simplify their tasks, enhance customer satisfaction, and drive innovation. (Chapter 5.3)

Value analysis

Value analysis is the process of analyzing changing customer preferences, their Jobs To Be Done, the strengths and weaknesses of alternative solutions, and the value created (or destroyed) in a previous version of the product. We conduct value analysis all along the product flow before attempting to design a solution, to ensure that we clearly understand the technical trade-offs that will constrain our decisions. Value analysis is performed at the start of every takt cycle. (Chapters 5.3 & 8.1)

Value-based pricing

In lean product development, we find the right price by understanding customers and their context. We set a price based on what customers are willing to pay for our product, ensuring profitability by keeping costs under control. (Chapter 14.3)

Variable costs

These are expenses that fluctuate with changes in production or sales volume, such as raw materials, third-party services, and licenses. (Chapter 14.3)

VA/VE

VA/VE stands for Value Analysis and Value Engineering, a continuous innovation cycle dedicated to enhancing product value through customer feedback and competitive analysis. It involves scrutinizing product components and processes, on the gemba, to identify opportunities for improvement without compromising quality or customer satisfaction. This iterative approach aims to optimize value and maintain competitiveness in the market. (Chapters 5.3 & 8.1)

Vertical innovation

Vertical innovation is a suggested method for product changes, focusing on releasing upgraded versions of existing products to maintain customer interest in the brand. It's one of the two main takt times, prioritizing significant product improvements to meet evolving market demands. (Chapter 5.2)

Value engineering

Value engineering implements the changes identified in value analysis to enhance product performance without compromising customer experience. Unlike traditional approaches, which may focus solely on cost reduction and technical changes, Value engineering seeks to optimize value by improving product quality and functionality while maintaining or enhancing customer satisfaction. (Chapter 5.3)

Visual management

Visual management involves placing tools, parts, production activities, and indicators of production performance in plain view, enabling everyone involved to understand the system's status at a glance. It facilitates quick decision-making and fosters a culture of transparency and accountability within the organization. (Chapter 7.3)

Waste

In lean thinking, the emphasis is on making waste visible and eliminating it to optimize efficiency. This principle is crucial in design and development processes, where identifying and eliminating waste can lead to significant improvements. Lean distinguishes three main types of waste: labor-related, material-related, and equipment-related. These wastes are often categorized according to the seven-waste model: overproduction, waiting, transportation, inappropriate processing, excess inventory, unnecessary motion, and defects. Identifying and addressing these wastes is essential for streamlining operations and maximizing value delivery. (Chapter 8)

Whole product

The whole product concept, introduced by Theodore Levitt, ensures a comprehensive consideration of all aspects of the product experience. It encompasses various customer touchpoints beyond just the digital realm, comprising the complete set of experiences and attributes that define the customer's interaction with the product and the company. This includes features, user experience, and other physical, digital, and service elements, advocating for a holistic approach to product development and delivery. (Chapter 6)

ACKNOWLEDGEMENTS

SANDRINE

First and foremost, my deepest gratitude goes to Michael Ballé. Your teachings, challenges, and friendship have been the cornerstone of this book. You have guided me on a path of introspection, growth, and brilliance, forever changing my perspective on business and life. You have truly helped me break free from the "Matrix", and for that, I can never be grateful enough.

I am especially thankful to my *Build to Sell* co-authors and partners at Taktique, Flavian Hautbois and Caroline Besnard. Your immense dedication to our cause has been inspiring, and I am so proud to share this adventure with both of you.

To my colleagues at Lean Sensei Partners (LSP): Jacques Chaize, Anne-Lise Seltzer, Cécile Roche, Charles Bourinet, Julie Chevalier, Frédéric Fiancette, Catherine Chabiron, Siham Bentalab, Sophie Lasserre, Christophe Richard, Pierre Masai, Camille Flex, Bérénice Duthuillé, Richard Kaminski, and Margaux Mercier. Our fascinating discussions and learning sessions have made us stronger together. It's tough to be a consultant without being one, and I cherish our shared journey.

To my dear friends at Keenly, especially Regis Medina and Christophe Ordano. Your support and friendship have been invaluable.

To the participants of our *Build to Sell* training program, and all the entrepreneurs and avid lean practitioners mentioned in the book: Jonathan Vidor, Meredith Bell, Andrew Davis and everyone at AutoRABIT, Tom Parling and the Ocere team, Alex Depledge and the Resi team, JB Limare, Khuloud Odeh and the team at CGIAR, Julien Jacob, Thibaud Lemonnier and the Ocus team, Lucie Notaro, Nicolas Silberman and the Bpifrance Digital Factory team, Caroline Pailloux, Violette Le Buhan, Lucas Servant and all at Ignition Program, Roxanne Varza at Station F, Lexi Allen, Alice Robelin, Alexandre Brun, Claire Van de Voorde, and all the people at Theodo group I've worked with over several years, particularly Benoit Charles-Lavauzelle, Fabrice Bernhard, Caroline Sauvegrain, Pierre-Henri Cumenge, Emmanuel Vignon, Noémie Parker, Nicolas Taborisky, JR Beaudoin, Rodolphe Darves-Bornoz, Woody Rousseau, Marek Kalnik, Baptiste Michel, Aurore Malherbes, and Clément David. Your contributions have enriched this book tremendously.

To the Institut Lean France and Lean Enterprise Institute, it's exciting to work with you on developing lean thinking in the tech and startup world. Special thanks to Lara Anderson and Jenni Hurner.

To all my agile colleagues around the world who have been studying and practicing lean and lean engineering for years, including Denis Barthélemy, Dimitri Baeli, and Laurent Bossavit. I wouldn't be where I am today without our agile shared experiences and fascinating discussions over the past two decades.

To the team that made the book possible, it has been an honor working with such talented individuals: Diane Rochet, Giulia Sciota, Chris Brandt, Ian Koviak, Alizée Vallade, and Alizé Rivière.

To all who endorsed *Build to Sell*: your support is deeply valued. Knowing the book has inspired you is incredibly rewarding. Thank you for believing in our work.

To my friends and family: many of the people mentioned above are counted among my friends. My heartfelt thanks to my husband, Benjamin Mathiesen, who meticulously edited this book, and to my daughter, Emma Mathiesen, who provided expert opinions on graphics and logos. To my mother, Nadine Moreno, your patience and admiration have been a constant source of inspiration. Thank you all for your continued support, patience, and love.

FLAVIAN

What an incredible journey it's been co-authoring this book! I'll be forever grateful to my friend and mentor Sandrine for making me part of her crew, alongside my friend Caroline. Writing this book has been fun, tough, and a source of great personal growth, as all such endeavors should. To my former partners, colleagues, and mentors (some of whom are mentioned above) at TraxAir, Theodo, Sicara, Apricity, and Ocus, I owe my experience to you. To a great sensei Michael Ballé, your teachings on lean engineering have been a major contribution to my understanding and approach.

My heartfelt thanks go out to my friends who provided unwavering support along the way: Camille Croste-Montaner, Camille Poulain-Ferarios, Théophane Bahu, Laura Danet, Pierre Alvarez, Claire Rénier, Olivier Hamon, Arthur Frin, Laura Menge, Élise Pirlot, Carlotta Apel, Anna Halliday, Charles Bochet, Laurent Ros, Emilie Doan, Ivann Morice, Rémy Luciani, Emile Breton, Marie Moulinié, Domitille Elyn, Maxime Sraïki, Pénélope Vorilhon, Claire Servant, Solène Pons-Burtin, Damien Saby, Emna Kamoun, Thierry Colsenet, Xavier Lefevre, Jelena Weinstein, Madison Vander Ark, Charlotte Pascal, Louise Bouguet, Lisa Welmarz, Sophie Aguado, Stéphane Rodriguez, Sandra Donier, and Antoine Grenapin.

To my family of builders and explorers, thank you for your continued love, and for nurturing my curiosity and determination to pursue my dreams: Yvon & Isabelle Hautbois, Jean-Michel Hautbois and Claire Hautbois-Garault, Guillaume Hautbois & Anne Méro, Chantal & Jean-Marie Vulcain, as well as my beloved nieces and nephews Baptiste, Léandre, Albane, Armand, and Élise. May we build a better world together, each in our own special way.

CAROLINE

First and foremost, my deepest gratitude to Baptiste Michel and Marek Kalnik, the founders of BAM, for introducing me to the world of lean during my eight years with the company. This journey has been transformative. Along this path, I had the fortune of meeting Michael Ballé and Sandrine Olivencia, without whom I wouldn't be where I am today.

A special thanks to Sandrine for her invaluable teachings over the years, which have been a cornerstone of my professional development. Thank you for the incredible opportunity to bring all these learnings and experiences to life in this book.

To Flavian, thank you for instilling in me the courage to believe in myself and for being a steadfast partner in this endeavor.

To my design and product teams, thank you for continuously challenging me to test, learn, and grow in my lean product management practices. A special thanks to Héloïse Bonan, Clothilde Thouvenin, France Wang, Charlotte Fernel, Chantal Khin, Justine Storelli, Maïa Delcourt, and all the other incredible designers and Product Managers for your exceptional support and collaboration.

To my family, your unwavering support has been my foundation. To my parents, my sisters, and my husband Maxime Sraïki, I am profoundly grateful for your constant encouragement and love.

Lastly, heartfelt thanks to Rémi Guyot for his invaluable advice on the book's launch and to Hugues de Mezerac for facilitating this connection.